1.50

The House on the Chine
Robert Louis Stevenson at Skerryvore

SIAN MACKAY

SANCHO PRESS

First published by SANCHO PRESS 2013
www.sanchopress.co.uk
Copyright © Sian Mackay 2013
www.sianmackay.com

The right of Sian Mackay to be identified as the author of this work has been asserted by her in accordance with the Copyright, Designs and Patents Act 1988.

ISBN-13: 978-0952883715

All rights reserved. No part of this publication may be reproduced, stored in or introduced into a retrieval system, or transmitted, in any form, or by any means (electronic, mechanical, photocopying, recording or otherwise) without the prior written permission of the publisher. Any person who does any unauthorized act in relation to this publication may be liable to criminal prosecution and civil claims for damages.

This book is sold subject to the condition that it shall not, by way of trade or otherwise, be lent, re-sold, hired out, or otherwise circulated without the publisher's prior consent in any form of binding or cover other than that in which it is published and without a similar condition including this condition being imposed on the subsequent publisher.

A CIP catalogue record for this book is available from the British Library.

The cover drawing is reproduced by kind permission of Harvard Art Museums/Fogg Museum. Gift of Mrs. Francis Ormond, 1937.7.21.7
Photo: Imaging Department © President and Fellows of Harvard College
The cover map detail from the OS map (1898) is reproduced by courtesy of the Ordnance Survey.

Cover design: Adrian Hallam at Almond Design, Edinburgh
Production assistance: Diane A. Smith

Printed and bound in Charleston, USA

For Geoff MacEwan

Also by Sian Mackay

FICTION
Rafael's Wings
The Verdict of the Double-Six

NON-FICTION (as Sheila Mackay)
Early Scottish Gardens: A Writer's Odyssey
Behind the Façade: Four Centuries of Scottish Interiors
Mountain Music: Mallorca
Lindisfarne Landscapes
The Forth Bridge: A Picture History

The House on the Chine
is supported by a Creative Scotland award
and a residency at Yaddo, USA

CONTENTS

Introduction   9

I
All About Chines   25
Kidnapped   47
A Flash of Silken Wings   60
No Man's Land   75
Grit in the Oyster   98

II
The Mysterious Valentine   127
News from Edinburgh   140
The Summer Visitors   169
Art and Life   188
No Mere Comma   213

III
Interlude with Sam   233
A Weevil in a Biscuit   256
A Fine Bogey Tale   279
A Subjective Affection   301

Afterword   315
Acknowledgements   318

Introduction
Travels with a Pen: From Canonmills to Skerryvore

As Robert Louis Stevenson records in *Edinburgh: Picturesque Notes*, towards the end of the eighteenth century the Georgian New Town *began to spread abroad its draughty parallelograms . . . there was such a flitting, such a change of domicile and dweller, as was never excelled in the history of cities.*

Less than a mile north of Princes Street, 'comely terraces' sprang up beside the marshy meadows of the Water of Leith and Canonmills, a rural hamlet of cornfields, orchards and strawberry gardens. The ancient bridge over the river was replaced by a three-arched structure where hansom cabs waited to transport the new inhabitants uptown. By 1830, newly built two-storey residences with basements and gardens at Howard Place and the adjacent Warriston Crescent had become the homes of well-to-do refugees from the squalid Old Town. At 8 Howard Place, in 'a comfortable ground floor bedroom overlooking the back garden,' Robert Louis Stevenson was born on the thirteenth of November 1850.

The child had inherited a 'weakness of the chest' from his mother. When the low lying area of Canonmills proved too damp for their son's health, Thomas and Margaret Stevenson moved uphill to a prestigious

Georgian townhouse at 17 Heriot Row. Before they left Canonmills in 1857 the boy would have explored the nearby Royal Botanical Garden's Old Palm House with its splendid cast-iron spiral staircases set into stone buttresses. After several palm trees burst out through the roof, a new Temperate Palm House (1858) was put up beside it. The magical 'Botanics', the child's-eye-view of the river from Canonmills bridge, the minnows and tadpoles of the Water of Leith - these are among the never-to-be forgotten delights of the 'child's garden' of Canonmills.

Stevenson often returned to his geographical cradle: *there are other sights and exploits which crowd back upon my mind under a very strong illumination of remembered pleasure. But the effect of not one of them will compare with the discoverer's joy, and the sense of old Time and his slow changes on the face of this earth, with which I explored such corners as Canonmills . . .*

Twelve years after Stevenson's death in 1894, my father was born in a tenement flat overlooking the Water of Leith and, briefly, attended the same Canonmills nursery school as Stevenson had done. When I came into that world around the middle of the twentieth century, apart from the tramcars and a few post-war cars, the backwater peace of our district remained undisturbed. The front steps of my childhood house at 10 Warriston Crescent, where we played on sunny days, overlooked the back garden of Stevenson's birthplace. Poems from *A Child's Garden of Verses* made vivid the streets of Canonmills, where Leerie the Lamplighter illuminated the lamp posts (electrified in my day) and the clatter of grown-ups' feet disturbed children unwillingly 'put to bed by day', the Scottish summer evenings being so light.

Frederick Chopin was another 'discoverer' of Canonmills who lodged at 10 Warriston Crescent during his Scottish tour in 1848. Chopin died in Paris the following year, one year before Robert Louis Stevenson was born. When I was very young, my father and friends from Edinburgh's Polish community commemorated the centenary of Chopin's visit with a plaque on the front of our house. In Chopin's day, the property belonged to Dr Lyszczynski, a Polish émigré and homeopathic doctor whom Chopin consulted. The doctor's wife remembered the tubercular composer sitting for hours very close to the fire, and sleeping in the upstairs box room that would become my brother's bedroom

Thus was my childhood infused with the romance of the historical figures of Frederick Chopin and Robert Louis Stevenson. Chopin's music and his 'foreignness' enthralled me, but Stevenson was the greater hero of my imagination. Like many Scots, I came to regard him as kin.

Many years later, in the spring of 2005, I travelled to the island of Erraid off Mull. The craggy island with its row of staunch houses dominated the horizon soon after we left Fionnphort. I asked the driver about Erraid's curious houses, so unlike any west coast cottages I had seen before, but he was concentrating on the rough track, swerving now and then to avoid wayward lambs. Eventually he said, 'they were built in the nineteenth century for lighthouse keepers and their families.' I fixed my eyes on those distant granite houses enclosed within a high-walled garden, where I planned to stay awhile in a cottage rented from the community that lives on the island nowadays.

What awaited me there, apart from brightly painted doors, watching windows and long gardens? Had I been wise to come to such a remote place?

At the seaweed-strewn jetty, the driver took on the role of boatman, warned me not to slip, and handed me a life jacket.

'Safety first,' he said, though the sea was calm and the island less than a mile distant. Halfway across Fidden Sound, he shouted over the noise of the boat's engine, 'the writer, Robert Louis Stevenson, stayed on Erraid as an apprentice engineer to his family's firm, Stevenson & Sons. They put up the Dubh Artach and Skerryvore lighthouses in the Hebridean Sea. You'll get to see them through binoculars.'

In that moment, the lingering heartbreak I had taken this journey to recover from dissipated. Instead, I felt elated by this unexpected, otherworldly encounter with R.L.S. I had forgotten his association with Erraid, but it came to me then in a flash: Erraid was the island where David Balfour, hero of *Kidnapped,* swam ashore after his shipwreck. On this very island R.L.S. had thrown off the chains that bound him to engineering. Here, on Erraid, he resolved to tell his father that he was quitting engineering to become a writer.

When I stood, at last, on Erraid pier, it was as if a lark had ascended in the clear air of my own spirit. In one glance, I took in a lifetime of blues: blues of sea, sky, speedwell, harebell and scabious. I had arrived on a treasure island, to be sure. All I had to do was track R.L.S.'s footprints, find a sward of primrose gold, make a map, and mark it with an 'x'.

Everywhere I went, exploring Erraid's fabulous wild reaches, searching the community's bookshelves for anything I could discover about the island and R.L.S., I was in thrall to his historical tenure. For a few weeks in 1870 he had lived here as a reluctant apprentice engineer to the family firm. I saw through binoculars the Stevenson lighthouses, Dubh Artach and Skerryvore, dark spectres far out in the wild sea. On a bookshelf in one of the community houses, I found a copy of *Kidnapped* and read in Chapter 14 R.L.S.'s faithful representation of Erraid's savage beauty. It seemed likely I would write about Stevenson's stay on Erraid, until I discovered an intriguing reference to a home he had in Bournemouth in 1885: a villa he renamed Skerryvore, after the mighty lighthouse.

What had led the Scottish author to settle in Bournemouth of all places, I wondered? Why was he working on *Kidnapped* that year, with Erraid on his mind?

In the absence of facts all was speculation. Only when I returned to Edinburgh and its libraries did I discover that 1885 had been a pivotal year in Robert Louis Stevenson's writing life. At Skerryvore, despite the fact that he fell so ill he almost died, Stevenson not only worked on *Kidnapped* and received his first published copy of *A Child's Garden of Verses*, he also wrote essays including 'The Art of Writing' and finished work in progress - 'Olalla' and *Prince Otto*. Most fascinating of all, before the year was out Stevenson had signed the contract for the publication of a radically new genre of work, *Strange Case of Dr Jekyll and Mr Hyde*.

At Skerryvore Stevenson had close contact with several Americans: his wife, Fanny Van de Grift Stevenson, her son, Sam Lloyd Osbourne, the novelist, Henry James, the artist, John Singer Sargent, and the illustrator, Edwin Austin Abbey; the millionaire, Charles Fairchild, hovers in the background. To what extent did they influence the author's decision to close up Skerryvore and emigrate to North America in 1887? And what did the house that fostered one of the most extraordinary transitions in literary history look like? I soon discovered that Skerryvore had been bombed to smithereens during World War Two. To write about Stevenson's life there I would have to reinvent the villa. Only then might it be possible to comprehend what went on behind its façade to inspire the author of 'boys' adventure stories' to create his powerful psychological thriller, *Jekyll and Hyde*.

In Bournemouth Library I found a photograph captioned 'Skerryvore After German Air Raid, November, 1940'. Skerryvore was the only building in Bournemouth to be hit in a random act of vandalism before the Luftwaffe bomber swerved high and away over the English Channel. The lower half of the photo shows a monumental pile of bricks, lumber and debris. Above it, peeling wallpaper droops forlornly on gable walls rooflessly exposed to the elements. *None who saw it can have forgotten the aspect of the gable: here it was plastered, there papered, according to the rooms; here the kettle still stood on the hob, high overhead; and there a cheap picture of the Queen was pasted over the chimney.* Stevenson's description of a demolished tenement he saw in the High Street of Edinburgh serves for the extinction of Skerryvore. Like the Edinburgh tenement, Skerryvore was *suddenly cut off from the revolving years* and would have been forgotten altogether if Robert Louis Stevenson had not written prodigiously there.

After the entire ruin had been cleared, the gap site was recreated as a memorial garden in the 1950s by Bournemouth Corporation. To find it, I took a bus from the city centre to the suburb of Westbourne, walked down Robert Louis Stevenson Avenue (called Middle Road in Stevenson's day) and found myself on Alum Chine Road beside a signpost marked 'Skerryvore'. Nowadays, the original low wall and sturdy stone gateposts are all that remain of the built landscape Stevenson knew between April 1885 and October 1887, yet, to all who love the work of Robert Louis Stevenson this is sacred ground.

Venturing through the gateposts as Stevenson so often did, I noticed bricks set into the ground to delineate part of the original villa. Where the line of bricks wandered off its oblong course, there must have been bay windows giving wide views of the garden and, not far from the gateposts, an entrance porch. Wandering within the space outlined by the bricks, I imagined the dining room here, the living room next to it, the bedrooms upstairs, the kitchen with a door to the stable yard, the rubbish bins and the coal hole. And was there a bathroom?

The only other features on site were a wooden bench beside a bin for visitors' rubbish and a thee-feet high stone replica of the Skerryvore light. In truth, there wasn't much of a garden, and I blessed the fact that blustery November day when I first set foot in Stevenson's domain. No blowsy flowerbeds or posthumous paths impinged upon my intention to recreate, as nearly as possible, the Skerryvore he knew. A thick carpet of copper beech leaves obliterated distractions that might lurk underfoot as I wandered to the edge of the long garden and stood above the chalky ravine of Alum Chine ('chine' rhymes with 'dine'). Here Stevenson liked to sunbathe while Fanny created 'labyrinthine paths' on the slopes below.

On my next visit to Bournemouth Library, the archivist showed me a photograph of Skerryvore taken three years before the bombing. It was a sweet moment, staring at an image of the very house where *Kidnapped* and *Strange Case of Dr Jekyll and Mr Hyde* had been written.

The villa was one of many put up in Westbourne in the 1860s by entrepreneurial builders with an eye to giving value for money: homes of English bricks, with tall chimney stalks proclaiming abundant fireplaces within. On the sunny day in 1937, when the photograph of Skerryvore was taken (by 'S. J. White'), it was summertime. The windows and their louvred shutters had been flung wide open and a game of croquet set out on the lawn. Another photograph showed the white-painted entrance porch, unusually situated at the side of the house. A play of light and dense shadows on the ivy-covered walls suggested the photograph was taken in the late afternoon. Swerving wheel marks in the gravel hinted at comings and goings by bicycle or with wheelbarrow, a scene unaltered since the Stevenson family and their visitors entered Skerryvore fifty years before S. J. White.

My morning research continued in Bournemouth library and the bench in the memorial garden became my afternoon sanctuary. Unhindered by the overbearing presence of an actual house, I was free to reinvent the villa, outside and inside. I explored Alum Chine from source to sea and, from a bronze plaque set into a bridge over the rivulet of the chine, Stevenson's haunting likeness stared back at me above these evocative lines:

The House on the Chine

Robert Louis Stevenson
Lived at Skerryvore
Overlooking This Chine
From 1884 to 1887

In my nighttime lodgings, I sent myself to sleep listening to audio recordings of Stevenson's work including 'Olalla', 'Thrawn Janet', 'Markheim', *Kidnapped* and *Travels with a Donkey in the Cévennes*. Wandering down Alum Chine Road and its neighbouring streets, I photographed villas built around the same time as Skerryvore. Mr White's 1937 photographs helped me to identify an identical bay window here, louvred shutters there, similar gateposts, an entrance porch, until the principal architectural elements of Skerryvore were secure in my mind. One of the nearby villas resembled the Skerryvore of White's photograph. A pressed flower in a Victorian scrapbook, its paintwork peeling, its dusty windows closed to the passing decades. Order once reigned there. Nothing, I imagined, had disturbed the tranquillity of its owners whose nourishing meals were served three times a day, precisely on the hour. Fanny Stevenson was known to run her household like clockwork, partly to impress her in-laws and partly because a rigorous regime favoured her husband's return to health

In 1912, *The Bookman* sent a well-known caricaturist for magazines including *Vanity Fair* to Westbourne to make a drawing of Skerryvore. 'A good memory, an eye for detail, and a mind to appreciate and grasp the whole atmosphere and peculiarity of the 'subject' are of course essentials,' Leslie Ward wrote of his caricaturist's art. In 1912, 'everyone' had read Robert Louis Stevenson's tale of terror and it must have influenced Ward's perception of the place where the story was incubated. The drawing he made twenty-six years after the publication of *Strange Case of Dr Jekyll and Mr Hyde* (and eighteen years after Stevenson's death) contrasts starkly with the amiable, extant dwellings near Alum Chine Road.

Ward's Skerryvore is a house of secrets, its brooding 'atmosphere and peculiarity' palpable in his Arthur Rackham-like rendering of the elevation facing the garden and the chine. He depicted Robert Louis and Fanny Van de Grift Stevenson standing tête-à-tête under a cypress. Fanny wears a crinoline, Stevenson leans on his walking stick; Bogue, their Skye terrier, lurks nearby. Three long shadows edge across the grass:

All the wicked shadows
Coming tramp, tramp, tramp,
With the black night overhead

Perhaps Ward went to Bournemouth in cold November as I did. The louvred shutters of the Skerryvore he captured with his pencil are firmly closed over an upstairs window. A belching chimney sends curlicues of smoke into threatening clouds. A flight of birds caws above the sharply delineated cypress. The cypress casts its shadow over the façade. The façade wavers, half in sunshine, half in shadow.

In April 1885, the Stevensons were settling down; the black night has not yet come when the author will waken, startled by nightmarish inspiration for *Jekyll and Hyde*. The atmosphere was cheerful, as their friend, Adelaide Boodle, recorded. Another eyewitness, John Singer Sargent, painted a corner of the drawing room with the door open to reveal the hall and the staircase rising to the second floor in his 1885 portrait *Robert Louis Stevenson and his Wife*.

When I felt ready to take the artist's cue, cautiously I entered Skerryvore by way of the porch and stood in the dark hall. On my imagined way through its rooms, I evoked Stevenson working at his desk, felt the sleeve of his velvet jacket, smelled his lunch roasting in the oven, heard the tick of the grandfather clock and Fanny slamming a door in one of her moods. In time I hoped to comprehend, at least a little, Stevenson's complex relationship with his eccentric wife - and with Fanny's son, Sam, whose over-identification with his stepfather verged on the pathological. I prepared to become a 'fly on the wall' listening in to conversations between Stevenson and Henry James, John Singer Sargent and all the other visitors to Skerryvore that year.

Eventually, the Robert Louis Stevenson of my imagination blurred the edges of fact and fiction and came to sit beside me on the bench in the memorial garden. It was the thirteenth of November 1885, his thirty-fifth birthday, and he had just signed the publishing contract for *Strange Case of Dr Jekyll and Mr*

Hyde. Well-wrapped against a chilly breeze and threatening rain, he hummed the tune he intended to play on the piano during his birthday celebration: *Träumerei* - 'Dreaming' from *Scenes from Childhood*. Stevenson was fond of Schumann.

His otherworldly song transported me back to our childhood roots at Canonmills - and on, and on, through all our journeys - until I dreamed a dream of once upon a time, when the 'doomed and dazzling' writer took possession of the house on the chine.

Edinburgh 2013

I

Every defect in a man's character must out in his works,
as a flaw in a window must make a mark on the wall.
Robert Louis Stevenson to W.E. Henley, May 1885

All about Chines

With measured step he follows the edge of the lawn where it meets the gravel path. Like a landlocked mariner, he thinks, recalling the deck of the last ship he sailed. These days, when he hasn't the strength to venture far beyond the gateposts of the villa, pacing is his only exercise. Pacing calms his nerves and has been known to foster inspiration. He paces. One arm juts out at right angles from his thin body, the wrist limp, the long fingers grasping a cigarette. Occasionally, he pauses to watch the family pantomime in full swing at the side of the house. Then back and forth he goes again, longing for his family to leave him in peace to get on with his writing.

Alarmed by the Skye terrier's barking, the carriage horses waiting on Alum Chine Road stamp and whinny. Above the din, his crinolined wife shouts instructions to servants speeding with trunks and boxes from the villa to the coach. Everything left to the last minute as usual; typical Fanny Van de Grift Stevenson, he frowns. It is mayhem: *la vie bourgeoise*; too much for any man's sanity. Will they ever get away?

He catches sight of his mother, Margaret, statuesque beside the gateposts; patient as a saint in the long dark dress and starched cap of an Edinburgh matron. Even from this distance, he can hear his father arguing with the coachman about the correct way to place the luggage. Typical Thomas. Wrapping his red shawl tight against the skittish wind, he paces again, then stops when he sees his father yanking his watch from his waistcoat pocket.

'What's keeping ye?' Thomas thunders at no one in particular and leans against his wife like a monstrous child. 'We'll miss the London train.'

'Its all right, Mr Tommy!' Fanny cries. 'We are ready now.'

Thank God for that. He loves them, his nearest and dearest, but he wants them away. Writing alone has the power to rescue him from the rough family seas in which he swims. Writing is his lifeline, and, at last, the moment to grasp it draws near. A little stooped and unsteady, he weaves his way up the gravel path, kisses Margaret and Fanny and falls into Thomas' hoary embrace.

'Take care o' yerself, my dearie. We'll be back afore ye know it,' the old man mutters, then tears himself away and staggers into the carriage.

When the coach and pair pulls out with a crack of the driver's whip and thunders off towards Central Station, Louis stands at the kerb waving a large white handkerchief. He uses it to blow his nose and wipe his tears until, into the silence, the distant gong sounds for lunch.

He reflected as he opened the porch door that Fanny had been reluctant to go up to London. It had been touch and go. They had so recently moved in, she said. There was so much to do in the house, the garden and the chine. For one thing, she intended to investigate with Mr Beaucox the possibility of damming up the stream at the head of the chine to make a pond for ducks. It was a project dear to her heart and Louis had to work hard to deflect her.

The other night in the drawing room, he had rolled two cigarettes and handed one to Fanny. 'I will consult Beaucox about the dam,' he said, lighting them with a taper. 'It'll do you good to cast off your responsibilities and enjoy a few days in the capital.'

Fanny shifted uneasily in the blue bergère. 'Bluidy Jack might strike while I'm away.'

Why, he wondered, did she have to harp on about BJ? He closed his eyes and Fanny fell silent. A faint peal of bells from Saint Michael's, Westbourne, and the joy song of a blackbird bedding down her brood in the treetops of the chine calmed him a little.

'Lou,' Fanny said at last, 'are you all right?'

'Aye.' He saw her through the slits of his eyelids. 'I'm fine, but there's no need to bring up BJ - we must not expect me to fall ill. If I am to get better then we must go along the route that I am already better - and I am a good deal better these days.'

'Still, I don't like to leave you, just in case.'

'There's no case to answer, Dutch. I am well enough.' He opened his eyes and studied Fanny.

'About me going to London, I do have an idea,' she

said. 'Valentine helped me to nurse you in Hyères. Remember how she slept in your room when I took that trip to Nice? You could have her in your room if I go to London?'

At the thought, Eros' sweet arrows pricked his inner thighs and he almost suggested, for decorum's sake, that Valentine could sleep on the landing outside his room. Every day when work was done, the servants returned to their own homes in town. Valentine was the exception whose domain was a box room near the kitchen. He considered saying to Fanny that the lass could bide where she was, that he'd summon her to his room by the bell if necessary. After all, every room in the house had a bell-pull wired to the call box in the kitchen. Yet, here was his wife proposing the lass should sleep *inside* his room and - decorum take the hindmost - he'd be a fool to protest against it.

'Very well,' he said. 'But you must outline the scheme to Valentine before you go.'

Fanny spent the next day packing in a flurry of concern for Bogue. The dog was acting strange, she said, and Louis convinced her to consult a London veterinarian. Now, at last, they had all gone: Margaret, Thomas, Fanny and the bellicose Bogue. What a relief! For the first time since they moved into the villa at Easter, there was no one to prevent him from doing as he pleased.

*

How they came to be living in a villa on the edge of a Bournemouth chine became a source of wonder to Robert Louis Stevenson. Often he relived the story in his mind: how he and Fanny had sailed over from France to London a few months earlier with Valentine Roch and Bogue. They were in flight from the cholera epidemic sweeping southern France where they had set up home. The timing of the epidemic had been terrifying since it hit the area at the same time as Louis was recovering from an illness so severe it almost killed him. His main symptom was 'blood-spitting' from his lungs, a malignant condition he named as he might a pirate in a story, 'Bluidy Jack', or 'BJ' for short. He was still far from well when they lingered in London, visiting friends and consulting doctors who advised months of rest in a temperate climate. Mercifully, apart from the usual complaints of Victorian women, Fanny Stevenson was sufficiently robust to care for her husband. Sore throats, 'brain fevers', stomach aches and heart troubles were among her specialities, but, increasingly, hypochondria took her to her room after trying episodes with Louis.

Towards the end of 1884, they left London for Bournemouth where Fanny's teenage son, Sam, was at a boarding school. They took lodgings on the West Cliff and Louis embraced the temperate sea breezes, wrapped in his red shawl, his hair unkempt and blowing in the wind or tamed under a wide-brimmed hat. The very model of a Romantic poet, or 'an animated bundle of shawls and wraps' as a neighbour described the arresting newcomer. It was a miracle he could walk at all. Indeed, he was often confined to a wheelchair pushed by Fanny, Valentine, or his seventeen-year-old stepson, who called him 'Squire'.

I doubt I'll ever be in a boat again, or a theatre, he wrote to a friend; *I was last in a theatre ten years ago to hear a Gilbert and Sullivan operetta . . . These days, a short walk and a long talk are all that's left to me, and very good things they are too, at least the talk. Since my last illness I've discovered a short walk with definite limits is against the very genius of walking. The true walker either rambles or travels, seeking new views, another hilltop, different ways to go. He makes for a dingle, gets distracted by a wood, goes further than he intends. That is the spirit of the walker. I have had to accept a dismal truth; I'm not able to have adventurous rambles in the square half mile around this house where much of the terrain to be conquered is visible from my windows.*

Before they arrived in Bournemouth, the Stevensons had never heard of such a thing as a chine. Fortunately, the *Guide to Bournemouth,* published annually, and the local section of Sydenham's Library and Reading Room on the Pier Approach made information about the town and its environs readily available to newcomers. Keen to understand the world they found themselves in, Sydenham's was a magnet to the Stevensons and the *Guide to Bournemouth* essential reading.

Vividly, a balmy autumn morning came back to Louis when Sam had driven him in the wheelchair from their lodgings to Sydenham's. They took the route via the

Pleasure Gardens, exotically planted with palm trees and rose beds, where a crowd had gathered to hear the Italian Band's rendition of tunes from 'The Pirates of Penzance'. Stop a minute, Sam, he pleaded, and they heard out 'I am the Very Model of a Modern Major-General' before hurtling on at exhilarating speed towards the sea. Sam hollered a greeting to blazered chums loitering at the ice cream stall, and, when the Pier heaved into view, Louis rose a little in his seat. The ornate cupola and white painted promenade soaring high above the English Channel promised adventure, on however small a scale. Although his body was gaunt after his recent critical illness in France, mentally he was in fine fettle and impatient to reach Sydenham's. He had heard the library was a comfortably appointed oasis with uninterrupted views over the sea, eastwards to the Isle of Wight and westwards to Purbeck. Best of all, he had a borrower's card and was at liberty to take home any books he pleased. What a keen pleasure to get Whitman's *Leaves of Grass*, Hardy's *Far from the Madding Crowd* and Dostoievsky's *Crime and Punishment*, treasures he had been forced to abandon in France. *I've read the Dostoievsky in a French translation, aye, but it stands rereading in any language*, he remembered saying to Sam, whose education was a serious matter. *To read Dostoievsky is like having a brain fever.*

Sam offered to carry the books in his satchel and, after that, they spotted Fanny. She had made her own way to Sydenham's and was comfortably settled in a leather armchair at the quiet end of the room. 'I'll be off then, Squire, Ma,' Sam said, securing the brakes of the wheelchair with his sturdy foot. 'I'll be waiting at the entrance should you need me,' and he loped away with a cheery wave.

Louis was accustomed to finding his wife one day in heaven and the next in hell, but that day Fanny had been happily engrossed.

'I'm reading a book about Bournemouth, and I'll go back to the beginning now you've come, for the detail is captivating . . . "The beauty of the coast scenery can scarcely be imagined by those unacquainted with it,"' she began, whereupon Louis interrupted, 'Nowhere in the world matches the Scottish west coast for beauty.' It was a safe enough statement since Fanny had never set foot in the west on her Scottish sojourns and could scarcely disagree. She gave a deep sigh and read on: '"A great source of interest along the coast is the number and beauty of the chines or ravines which penetrate the land to a considerable distance."' 'Read more about these chines,' Louis said and Fanny frowned, 'Lordy, must you interrupt so? Chines come further down the page.' She continued in her steady drawl: '"The conchologist may derive much amusement from a ramble on the beach where a variety of shells and specimens of the Sea Anemone and other Zoophytes are frequently found with large quantities of pyrites."'

Sydenham's had about it a sacred hush that mirrored the tranquil sea beyond its windows. Two couples stood looking out, the women stiff in pale crinolines and elaborate bonnets, their men in grey frock coats and top hats. Louis observed them while he listened to Fanny and offered up thanks that they had left behind *conscious moral rectitude* in favour of *la vie bohème*. If those toffs didn't have their fleets of servants they'd be got up like us, he thought of saying to Fanny, but decided not to interrupt her again. The promenaders glanced furtively at the odd couple: Louis deathly pale, ungroomed and cocooned in a tartan rug; Fanny, hatless and wearing a strange loose dress of brown linen embroidered at the yoke. An odd couple, inextricably linked. A more quixotic couple would be hard to imagine.

Robert Louis Stevenson was thirty-four years old, five feet ten inches tall, and weighed not much more than eight stones when they first arrived in Bournemouth. Fanny Stevenson was barely five feet tall, a plump matron, ten years older than her husband. Louis' hair was light brown, lanky and shoulder length. Fanny's was dark and greying, thick and curly. His face was rather beautiful and aquiline, his brown eyes expressive and wide set, his full mouth emphasised by a modest moustache. Fanny had Dutch-American and Navajo Indian blood, 'dusky' skin, a well-proportioned face with high cheekbones, dark, penetrating eyes under thick brows and a markedly down-turned mouth. Louis' delicate health often forced him to wear an old red shawl over his 'poet's' black velvet jacket, flannel shirt, red tie and corduroys. When he made the effort to smarten up, he wore clothes with casual elegance, and moved, when he was well, with swift grace. Fanny lumbered beside him. In California she had picked up the habit of wearing figure-disguising pinafores and loose smocks called Mother Hubbards. During the Bournemouth years when she became desperate to fit in, she wore corsets under fashionable high-necked blouses, ankle length skirts and fitted dresses. Louis was in many respects the eternal boy, and Fanny, whom anxiety and 'a woman's time of life' had aged since their marriage, could easily be mistaken for his mother.

When Louis turned his head he could see Sydenham's central shelves where borrowers searched for books, eager as squirrels after nuts. Then he spied a woman slumped in a bath chair being pushed around the room. His heart went out to her. A *sickist*, a hostage to fortune like himself. Later, when Henry James became his friend, he realized that the invalid had been Alice James, the American novelist's sister.

Fanny stopped reading and Louis met her puzzled gaze. 'Oh dear, pyrites and zoophytes, this is becoming very technical, Lou.'

'Go on; continue please. Technical it may be, but the text has captured my imagination.'

'It says: "The layers of rock under Bournemouth Bay contain beds of alum shale . . . "'

'Alum is to be found here, of all things.'

'I guess so, for dyeing and tanning in the old days; I don't suppose they do it now. When I was but a chit of a girl, squatting at a mining camp in Nevada and newly married to Sam Osbourne Senior, I concocted a honey for griddle cakes by boiling sugar with a lump of alum.'

'Do not be distracted by mock honey, wife,' Louis urged, and Fanny's intelligent brambly eyes returned to the book. Provoke as he might, it was well nigh impossible to get the better of a wife with an American drawl.

She cast him a meaningful look. '*Now* we are coming to the chines . . . "Naturalists have long been impressed by the number and beauty of the chines which neglect has left in their natural desolation. Alum Chine is the largest. It takes a winding course and presents a considerable variety of shrubs and scattered pine trees along its banks. About half-a-mile from the sea the chine divides. To the left, a very picturesque ravine branches off until it reaches the boundary of Hants and Dorset; to the right through a deep, dank, dell, a rivulet flows in rainy seasons from its exceedingly abrupt termination."'

Her voice tailed off when Louis suddenly rose from the wheelchair and tottered towards the windows saying he must see these chines. Fanny signalled urgently for Sam. The boy rushed to support Louis with strong young arms and Fanny assisted as best she could. She barely reached her husband's shoulders. They peered out westwards over the shining sea and Louis was the first to point out with a nicotine-stained index finger the distant Alum Chine. 'Over there! It has a gaping entrance to the sea. I must explore it.'

'When you're well, we will make an expedition to Alum Chine,' Fanny soothed. But she realized it was a vain hope; it would be a long time before her husband was up to such an adventure.

Impatient to explore Alum Chine herself, a few days later Fanny walked along the corniche until she found the entrance between the high banks of the chalky ravine. Gradually the way narrowed and darkened under a canopy of trees and densely growing shrubs. Trees, thin and tall from lack of sunlight, dwarfed her tiny figure as she passed. Alum Chine was an eerie place where fairy tales might be set, or even one of the shilling shockers so popular with Victorian readers. Shortly before the chine petered out, Fanny followed a steep path that transported her beyond desolation, into the suburb of Westbourne at Alum Chine Road. In this tranquil, pastel world she admired new villas of great variety and size. One or two were for sale, others for rent. She sensed at once, here was the perfect place to make a home. Here Louis could write and get well. Here she, too, might write a little, though her main preoccupation would be to create a garden.

Bournemouth's remarkable expansion dates from 1810 when the entrepreneurial Lewis Tregonwell and his wife drove their carriage through the heathland by the sea. They were so taken with the health-giving atmosphere of the area they built a holiday home, cottages to house their servants and others for holiday lettings. Slowly but surely, the temperate climate and the healing sea air began to attract invalids - and prospecting doctors - from all over Europe. The seaside hamlet expanded into a town. By the 1870s, Bournemouth's population numbered 17,000.

One writer commented, 'It would be impossible to find anywhere such a vast array of houses of all sorts and sizes in which there is less architectural merit.'

William Morris judged the villas 'simply blackguardly', the homes of 'ignorant, purse-proud digesting machines.'

Any town dedicated to the ageing and the sick was bound to need churches, hotels and boarding houses. These sprang up, too, with ancillary businesses such as Sydenham's Library and Reading Room, removal firms, funeral parlours and chemist shops. The Theatre Royal opened in 1882; Central Station and a new pier were operating by 1885. That year, King Oscar of Sweden and Norway arrived to lay the foundation stone of the Mount Dore Spa, built to resemble a French chateau. The Mount Dore, a first class hotel and hydropathic spa offering a variety of mineral and vapour baths, mirrored Bournemouth's aspiration to become an internationally renowned health resort. The mineral water was imported from its sister Mount Dore Spa in the Auvergne whose chief physician travelled to Bournemouth during the winter months. There he supervised treatments for illnesses including rheumatism, tuberculosis, syphilis and gout. One observer noted that 'the luxurious sitting rooms, ballroom, billiard and smoking rooms, not to mention Turkish baths, enabled patients to malinger in the lap of luxury.'

The Stevensons were broke. Venues like the Mount Dore Spa were well beyond their means. Louis' earnings from writing had been sporadic, chiefly as a result of his poor health. *My finances are strangely at sea,* he wrote to Charles Baxter, his Edinburgh lawyer friend, *but there's a good time coming.* Thomas Stevenson (whom Fanny called 'Mr Tommy') frequently had to bail them out. How could they possibly afford a home in desirable Westbourne? If anyone could manifest the impossible it was the resourceful Fanny. She guided her in-laws, down from Edinburgh on 'a wee holiday', to Alum Chine Road to see the head of the chine. Thomas Stevenson declared it a picturesque wonder whose steep shady banks reminded him of Colinton Dell near Edinburgh.

The elder Stevensons were impressed by Fanny's devotion to Louis and Sam, but Thomas worried about Sam's education. His boarding school promised to prepare pupils for 'Public Schools, Army, Navy, Medical and all Public Examinations'. Yet, 'for all its good intentions, a school in Bournemouth is a hiding to nothing by way of prosperity in a decent profession,' he said, and made arrangements to accompany his surrogate grandson north on the train. He installed the boy in Louis' former room at his house in Heriot Row and enrolled him at Edinburgh University.

Everyone agreed Thomas Stevenson was living out his last years, and Robert Louis Stevenson often said a coin might be tossed as to whether the father or the son would die first. Thomas occasionally had business to attend to in London relating to the firm of Stevenson & Sons' peerless reputation for the construction of lighthouses off the coast of Scotland. Bournemouth was no distance by train from London, a bonny place to escape the chill winds of Edinburgh and cast off Northern dourness. The old man relished strolling, arm-in-arm with Margaret, through the Pleasure Gardens and Invalids' Walk. Another odd couple, they stood out among Bournemouth's great and good like Jack Spratt and his wife: Margaret thin and stiff in her old-fashioned Edinburgh dress; Thomas overweight, his beefy paunch corseted under the waistcoat of a Harris Tweed suit. His gait rolled from too many sea voyages inspecting the Stevenson lighthouses, his moleskin hat was a size too small and his sideburns extended unfashionably from ears to chin. George Reid's oil painting of Thomas Stevenson in the Scottish Portrait Gallery shows a handsome elderly man, with a dissatisfied, almost quivering mouth and earnest eyes that seem to lament, 'I have tried all my life to understand life, yet I have not succeeded.'

On frequent visits to Bournemouth, they took afternoon tea at the Imperial Hotel, sampled various baths and treatments on offer at the Hydropathic Clinic and consulted one or other of the medical specialists who had settled in Bournemouth like bees in a honey hive. Doctor Dobell, the elder Stevenson's physician of choice had gained a devoted following after the publication of his book, *Medical Aspects of Bournemouth*. (Louis had already consulted him, but intended to transfer his custom to a Dr Thomas Bodley Scott.) Margaret and Thomas fell for the soothing suburb of Westbourne and Fanny's notion soon infected them: given the right encouragement, she and Louis might consider settling down here for the sake of Louis' health.

After that things moved swiftly. Before Louis had a chance to hang up the calendar for New Year 1885, Thomas had offered to buy Fanny a villa as a belated wedding present. By chance, Sea View, at number sixty-one Alum Chine Road in Westbourne, came onto the market and Thomas Stevenson purchased it from a Captain Best and signed it over to Fanny.

Not Robert Louis' name, not both their names, but Fanny's name alone appeared on the Title Deeds. Thomas had effectively given his daughter-in-law dominion over his impecunious and sickly son. This act would put a stop to Louis' bohemian wanderings of the past few years that had all-but killed the son and broken the father's heart. Enough was enough, and, with Fanny's connivance, Thomas had Louis pinned down at last. His son had no choice but to accept with good grace his kidnapping.

The two-storey house was built of yellow bricks with a blue slate roof. Graham Balfour, Louis' cousin, described its setting in 'half an acre of ground very charmingly arranged, running down from the lawn at the back, past a bank of heather into a chine . . . full of rhododendrons, and at the bottom a tiny stream.'

The sea was less than a mile away, the air briny and pine laden, yet only a sliver of the English Channel could be viewed over the trees of the chine from a south-east facing bedroom window on the second floor. The villa's name would have to be changed, everyone agreed on that. 'You cannot expect me to live in a house called Sea View when you cannot even see the sea,' said Fanny.

The garden's oblong lawn petered out high above the edge of Alum Chine, a precipitous feature Fanny planned to exploit with winding paths, arbours and charming resting places where Louis might be tempted to write. The villa was secluded, yet not isolated. It stood proud at the junction with Middle Road, and Middle Road led straight as an arrow to the new shops and flats of Westbourne, the Arcade and the branch line station. Here visitors eager to see Louis in his new domain would soon alight: his cousins Katherine and Bob with their children, his Aunt Alan, Henry James, John Singer Sargent, Sydney Colvin, Teddy Henley, and a procession of artists eager to capture for posterity the author of *Treasure Island*.

Shortly before they moved from their West Cliff lodgings to Alum Chine Road, Louis wrote to Edmund Gosse: *I am now a beastly householder, but have not yet entered on my domain . . . I shall call my house Skerryvore, when I get it: SKERRYVORE: c'est bon pour la poéshie. I will conclude with my favourite sentiment: The world is too much with me.* ROBERT LOUIS STEVENSON, *The Hermit of Skerryvore*. He referred to the villa as 'my house' or 'our house' but never as 'Fanny's house'. His London friends spoke wonderingly of 'Louis' revolt into respectability in some obscure suburb of Bournemouth.' The truth was that Robert Louis Stevenson's so-called 'revolt' had been a matter of survival, but he soon discovered a hermit's life well suited his life as a writer.

Since Valentine could not be expected to manage such a house on her own, staff was engaged from the town: Mrs Maryann Watts as cook-cum-housekeeper, her daughter, Agnes, as housemaid, and Mr Beaucox as handyman and gardener. The firm of Charles Coats was booked to convey by wagon the trunks and packing cases they had brought from France; and, as soon as they were in the door, Mr Tommy hatched a further seduction: Fanny was to have five-hundred pounds to furnish the villa. He would accompany her himself on a raid of London's auction houses and antique shops.

Finding himself with a wife, a stepson and a villa to maintain, Louis waved a reluctant farewell to *la vie bohème* he had cultivated these past years. When Fanny took Valentine on a quick trip to close up their previous home, La Solitude, on the French Riviera, the truth sank in: he would never again live in France. After Sam had left for Edinburgh with the parents, Louis got Beaucox to shut the wheelchair in the coach house. Although he couldn't walk far, on good days he explored the garden and, supported by Fanny or Valentine, the byways of Alum Chine Road. This achievement led him to believe that, one day, he would be strong enough to explore the abyss of the chine that lay tantalisingly beyond his reach.

They had a roof over their heads and cash for basic furnishings, courtesy of Mr Tommy, but the younger Stevensons could not afford to kit out the villa according to Victorian middle-class taste. Characteristically, Fanny Stevenson turned this lack to her advantage. 'Our styling is sparse and simple by comparison with the high ideals of our age,' she wrote to her parents-in-law, 'but I like it all the more because of that. Since we never thought to own a home of our own, every day our presence here appears miraculous. It is comforting to know we have a home we can count on. No more will we be forced to fly hither and thither like Noah's dove with an olive branch in its beak.'

Like the Bournemouth villa, their previous home had been situated in a popular health resort. There, in 1883, the Stevensons had rented 'an eccentric Swiss-style chalet' called La Solitude above the entrance to the ancient town of Hyères-les-Palmiers. Louis had always been fascinated by distant views from high places from which the landscape below resembled a map. Skerryvore looked over Alum Chine and La Solitude *clung conspicuously to a low cliff whose summit was romantically crowned by the ruins of a Saracen castle*. Fanny described La Solitude as 'a doll's house, with rooms so small that we could hardly turn round in them; but the view from the verandas was extensive, the garden was large and wild, with winding paths and old grey olive trees where nightingales nested and sang.'

It was here they had hired Valentine Roch, the French-Swiss daughter of a local farmer, as Fanny's maid and assistant to the cook. Louis delighted in the surroundings - *Eden and Beulah and the Delectable Mountains and Eldorado all rolled into one* - but the house itself was claustrophobic: *I have to tinker at my things in little settings.*

He had been overjoyed when Charles Baxter and Teddy Henley visited them at New Year 1884. Henley had become editor of *Cassell's Magazine of Art* and was living with his wife in London. Since their Hyères 'doll's house' could not accommodate visitors - the dining room was so small dinner plates had to be served onto the table over the heads of guests - Louis' friends had to stay at a nearby hotel. It was Louis who suggested a 'boys only' trip to Menton and Nice, far from the gaze of 'Cassandra', as the group dubbed Fanny. The mythological Cassandra foresaw the destruction of Troy, and Fanny feared the proposed trip might destroy Louis. She had already lost her youngest child, Hervey, to an early death and was not about to lose her husband. Like Cassandra, Fanny's intuition turned to helplessness when the group dismissed her warning and set off, leaving her inarticulate with rage. It was high jinx all the way until Louis collapsed on the Promenade des Anglais in Nice and his subsequent serious illness forced Fanny to rush down from Hyères to rescue him while everyone else went home.

After the melodramas and constrictions of La Solitude, the Stevensons 'in happy security' expanded into Skerryvore's generous spaces. They each had a room of their own, there was a dining room and a drawing room for entertaining, a guest bedroom, a bathroom, an ample kitchen and ancillary buildings in the grounds.

Despite the fact that Skerryvore was a mere cottage beside Thomas and Margaret Stevenson's generously proportioned Georgian townhouse on three floors plus the basement, 17 Heriot Row became one of Fanny's models for the smooth running of her new home.

When Louis had taken her to Edinburgh to meet his parents for the first time in 1880, there had been, in Fanny's opinion, one lamentable lack in their otherwise impressive home. The engineering advances of the times allowed travellers to catch a train from Edinburgh to London, but a plumbed-in bath or water closet was hard to find in the Athens of the North. Obliged to wash at a stand equipped with a porcelain toilet set and chamber pot and to bathe in a hipbath filled from a bucket, Fanny lamented the absence of comforts taken for granted in America. She soon discovered that Margaret and Thomas could afford the best bathroom suite money could buy, and that their hesitancy to install one stemmed from the city's unreliable water supply. They were waiting for the Edinburgh and District Water Trust to announce itself capable of supplying the whole city. Besides, what was the hurry to introduce improvements when reliable servants were readily available for carrying buckets of clean water upstairs and bedpans downstairs? Added to that, there was money to be made from the vast quantities of night soil produced in the growing city. Every morning the ordure was collected by a carter at the back of the houses and sold to market gardens on the outskirts of the city.

A few years after Fanny's visit, Edinburgh's 'sanitary trade' had prospered and a bathroom was installed in the dressing room next to the master bedroom at Heriot Row. It was equipped with a flushing water closet, a full-sized bath with shining brass taps, and a shower fitted into the cupboard containing the water tank.

Skerryvore's more modest bathroom contained basic sanitary ware: sink and bath, all fitted with brass taps, and a flushing toilet. Louis usually preferred to bathe in a hipbath in his room rather than risk the draughts of the bathroom. Besides, he liked the traditional ritual when, after stirring up the fire, Agnes would fill his bath with hot water, just as the servants at Heriot Row had done in the old days. When the Squire of Skerryvore was happily immersed near a blazing fire, Fanny would arrive, her sponge foaming with Pears soap, to wash her husband's back.

Kidnapped

According to the state of his health, Robert Louis Stevenson worked at the desk in his room, the desk in the drawing room, or at an invalid table erected above his knees when confined to bed. He fell ill shortly after the move to Skerryvore and sent notes to Charles Baxter: *Been ill. Shall write soon perhaps today*; to Henley: *I cannot write: That's All. Even a boy's story beats me flat*; and to his parents: *Fairly well; but once more dry rotten.* He adds: *The house is enchanting.*

His bedroom and the drawing room windows overlooked Skerryvore's long garden and offered glimpses of nature's slight alterations from one moment to the next: the sun casting shadows of tree and branch upon the lawn; motionless shadows on bright sunny days, dancing shadows when the wind got up, and shadows that disappeared altogether on cloudy days. From his window, he could keep an eye on his favourite sunbathing spot at the foot of the garden above the abyss of the chine.

With Fanny away in London, Louis' first day of freedom begins with footsteps on the stairs. Valentine enters the master bedroom, opens the curtains, encourages him to sit up against his pillows and puts down the breakfast tray. 'Only Henry James is to be admitted, if he calls,' he says. 'I'll be slinging ink at *Kidnapped* all morning.'

From the vantage point of his iron bedstead he looks about the increasingly familiar room; his Georgian writing desk set centre stage between the end of the bed and the fireplace; the cream-painted fireplace embellished with tiles depicting floral subjects; two lug chairs standing on either side of the fireplace as if in conversation - green upholstery for him and gold for Fanny. To their delight, old Captain Best had donated objects too large to fit into his retirement home on the Poole Road. Best's cheval glass, a marble-topped washstand with decorative jugs and bowls, and a shaving mirror above crisp white towels, now formed Louis' toilet area near the door. There had been no need to redecorate the room; the pale green wallpaper with its Oriental bamboo design was pleasing to the eye and echoed the garden beyond the window, though the burgundy velvet curtains fought against this idea and would have to be changed.

Apart from his desk, his favourite object was the three-panelled scrap screen standing in the corner near the bay window. There, fanciful cupids romped upon the clouds of Raphael. Ornate bouquets of exotic flowers burst beyond the confines of gauzy wrappers and boxes of chocolates rejoiced in fancy ribbons. He considered the artists who produced these images - so lifelike, yet larger than life - to be geniuses in their way. There were seaside scenes and country scenes, roaring seas and striped parasols, farms and animals, hills and glens, exotic birds from faraway lands he was unlikely ever to be well enough to visit. Parrots, parakeets and hummingbirds, set against distant views of beaches fringed with palm trees, recalled his own fictional Treasure Island. There were children at play with dolls and trains and hoops and soap bubbles, their ringlets escaping from bonnets and caps. Golden haired children clad in frilly dresses with petticoats showing under navy-blue coats, or sailor suits such as he himself had worn as a child.

Nowhere did the screen reveal the struggles and hypocrisies of his age; an age of unrest and riot in Europe, of dynamite and assassination, of sexual repression and exploitation of the masses - considerations that often perplexed Louis. And it didn't surprise him that not one scrap on the entire screen suggested the darker side of life; no invalid on his sickbed had been pasted up there, no tottering, humpbacked old folk, no huddled masses in dark city streets or gloomy factories, not even a Tiny Tim on his crutches nor a bandaged soldier limping back from the Crimean War. But this morning he felt well and would not sink into gloom over the vicissitudes of the late nineteenth century.

Cautious with wonder, he peeled back the floral sprigged counterpane and sat on the edge of the bed recalling his nocturnal adventures. They never ceased to amaze him. Last night there had been at least one bogey dream. *Somnia quae mentes ludunt volitantibus umbris*, he muttered under his breath, mimicking the Shorter Catechism he had learned by rote in childhood . . . *dreams that mock us with their fleeting shadows* . . . He had been staring into sea calm as glass, mesmerized by dark green and rose madder weeds dancing against a white sea bed, when suddenly a monstrous fish swam into the scene and, the moment he lifted his spear to spike it, the piscine maw had become the glaring face of his father.

For comfort's sake, he spread a slice of toast with Gentleman's Relish and his hand trembled at the thought of the unfathomable depths a man could sink to in his sleep.

A monster fish with father's face?

Take care o' yerself, my dearie!

From what uncharted regions did they spring, these Africas of the mind, these nocturnal games that wrecked a man's peace? Almost every night, he was plagued with their fleeting shadows. In an attempt to throw off this one, he put on his dressing gown, green as the leaves of summer, groped under the bed for his Turkish slippers and went to look out at the day.

Pigeons cooed in the dovecot near the stables. 'Piejohns', Fanny called them; anything that moved was fair game for her culinary imagination. Swarthy Beaucox, engaged in a horticultural rite in the garden below, took off his cap and wiped his brow with a red pocket-handkerchief. Louis noted the unbuttoned collarless shirt, the hairy chest, the rolled up sleeves and the muscular arms, before he came away from the window lest the gardener suddenly look up and see a voyeur. It promised to be another fine day, but he had more than sunbathing on his mind.

Cradling his teacup, he paced from screen to fireplace reviewing the architecture of the night. When he examined the archipelago of tealeaf islands clinging to his porcelain cup, it occurred to him that each island represented a book still to be written. The thought of the paper-and-ink engineering works he had still to write made his eyes dance. *Treasure Island* had brought him a modicum of success. Surely further books in the same vein would make his fortune and free him once and for all from dependence on Mr Tommy. The future beckoned bright. The first chapters of *Kidnapped* lay on his desk. No time to lose. High time to get shaved and dressed. He threw off his robe, admired in the cheval glass his still youthful, though emaciated, body with its splendid male member, and he spared a thought for one of his heroes: *As you see, Mr Whitman, I, too, contain multitudes.*

Robert Louis Stevenson dug deeply into his memories of Scotland to uncover the inspiration for *Kidnapped*. *There is an isle, the memory of which besieges me, and memories are fairy gifts that cannot be worn out in the using.* The isle he refers to is Erraid off the southern corner of the Ross of Mull, which had also partly inspired *Treasure Island* (1883). Credited as the inventor of pirate stories, Louis had captured the public imagination with that book. By 1885 it had earned him 300 pounds, as he confided in a letter to Edmund Gosse. When he settles down to write *Kidnapped*, his second adventure story for boys, Erraid is so vivid in his mind he strands its hero on the island. Louis had been sent there as an apprentice engineer and knew the terrain well. Early editions of *Treasure Island* and *Kidnapped* were prefaced with Louis' maps, redrawn by draughtsmen at Stevenson & Sons in Edinburgh.

The author must know his countryside, whether real or imaginary, like his hand; the distances, the points of the compass, the place of the sun's rising, the behaviour of the moon, should all be beyond cavil . . . The tale has a root there; it grows in that soil; it has a spine of its own behind the words.

Despite his poor health, Louis had always been expected to join the family engineering firm. Once, on a tour of the Western Isles aboard the *Clansman* with his father and uncle, Alan Stevenson, they had been scouting for shore stations where the next lighthouses might be constructed. Edmund Gosse, a young tourist bound for Glasgow, was aboard the *Clansman*, too, and he noticed Louis 'for some mysterious reason . . . the advance with hand on hip, the sidewise bending of the head to listen.' On that voyage, the *Clansman* anchored in a remote sea loch to bring on board Highland exiles to work in industrial Glasgow. These crofters had been cleared from their homes by landlords intent on creating a deer forest with no thought for the human cost. Louis, Gosse and the other passengers on the upper decks watched silently while *the hopeless black mass of humanity entered the vessel.* Now, Louis planned to revive the scene in a chapter of *Kidnapped* when the novel's hero sees an emigrant ship setting off from Loch Aline: *the exiles leaned over the bulwarks, weeping and reaching out their hands to my fellow-passengers, among whom they counted some near friends . . . the chief singer in our boat struck into a melancholy air, which was presently taken up both by the emigrants and their friends upon the beach, so that it sounded on all sides, like a lament for the dying. I saw the tears run down the cheeks of the men and women in the boat, even as they bent at the oars.*

Tiree had been the onshore site for Stevenson & Sons' Skerryvore lighthouse, completed in 1844, six years before Louis was born. Erraid would become the shore station for Dubh Artach, 'the Black Rock'. There, *stones might be quarried and dressed, men might live, and the tender lie at anchor with a degree of safety from storms.* In his capacity as apprentice engineer, Louis had returned to Erraid in 1870 to inspect the progress of Dubh Artach. He had reached a critical juncture in his life when, despite his father's fierce opposition, he was planning to quit engineering and devote himself to writing.

Louis' cousin, Bob Stevenson, visited him on Erraid. Bob had been Louis' hero in childhood. Tall and handsome, Bob's ready wit and kindness charmed everyone, and he had overshadowed his sickly younger cousin. Bob's sister, Katherine, often joined them in boisterous games of cowboys and Indians, pirates and tug-o'-war in the garden of their grandfather's manse at Colinton near Edinburgh. Together they roamed the Pentland Hills and rode their ponies on the sands at North Berwick. Bob's father, Alan, had died by the time he visited Louis on Erraid and, having resisted family pressure to join Stevenson & Sons, he was already up at Cambridge preparing to be an artist.

Louis' memory served him so well that, fifteen years later at Skerryvore, he could picture himself and Bob, their trousers rolled, paddling in the Inner Hebridean Sea. *Beyond the shore station for the construction of the lighthouse there was no living presence but the limpets on the rocks, the crying gulls and a few gray old rain-beaten rams that we'd rounce out of their ferny dens between the boulders.* Now and then they kicked up glistening sprays of sea, as if to stress important moments in their discussion. *We roamed the island speaking of the great uncharted desert of our futures and wondering what might befall us on our journeys through life.* A pair of buzzards shrieked on the cliffs above the bay, sheep bleated on the pasture behind the dunes.

'The engineering wrecks me,' Louis confided. 'I'm born to be a writer, yet father's so set on me being an engineer, he refuses to see I'm not cut out for it.'

Their wellington boots sank into muddy ground scented with bog myrtle, their bare feet left imprints in the white sand of Balfour Bay. Bob put an arm round Louis' shoulder. 'There's nothing to be gained by prolonging your torment,' he said. 'Take on Uncle Tom as soon as you get back to Edinburgh.' As they negotiated the rugged land to the north of the island, Bob made Louis repeat, over and over again: *I can, I will, I ought, I must tell the old tyrant to stick his lighthouses up his arse!* It became such a joke they collapsed onto the heather, clutching their bellies with the pain of their laughter.

Then they stood on a bluff overlooking a long sandy inlet. The sand was blindingly white. The sea had retreated so far it was a thin blue line on the horizon, and it had left fearsome jagged outcrops in its wake. 'These black islets become treacherous reefs when the tide's full in,' Louis explained to Bob. 'They're part of the Torrens archipelago that menaces shipping in these parts, the reason for the Stevenson lighthouses.' The inlet and the rocky outcrops were an impressive sight, a landscape of imaginary treasure islands. But the real reason Louis brought Bob here was to show him how, twice every twenty-four hours, when the tide goes out, Erraid becomes part of the mainland.

The tide was out. Louis led the way down to the narrowest point of the inlet, and they walked across the wet sand to the mainland at the Ross of Mull. Bob was quick to seize upon this uncommon feature of the landscape as a metaphor for Louis' untenable position. 'There you have it,' he said, clapping Louis so heartily on the shoulder he almost fell over. 'Choose your time carefully, tell Uncle Tom where to stick his engineering, then walk to freedom on your metaphorical mainland.'

Louis later recalled in 'Memories of An Islet' (1887),

the fine rabbit stew waiting in the pot when they returned from their adventure. Afterwards Mr Brebner, the chief engineer, rehearsed the Sabbath sermon he planned to deliver to the Stevenson employees, a ragtaggle encampment of navvies living in hastily constructed hovels on the hill behind the cottages. With the exception of the Sabbath, the men laboured daily between the quarry and the onshore construction site for the lighthouse. Like all the Stevenson lighthouses, every element that made up Dubh Artach was manufactured onshore, then shipped by tender to the forbidding rock.

Fanny also fostered Louis' desire to create another 'boys' adventure'. In 1884 she had announced her intention to write a historical thriller and Louis gave her his abandoned play *The Hanging Judge* to plunder as she wished. Fanny planned to set a trial scene at the Old Bailey and, never one to do things by half measures, she commissioned a London bookseller to send everything he could lay his hands on concerning trials at the Old Bailey around 1750. Package after package arrived at their West Cliff lodgings, and one of them happened to include an account of the trial concerning a notorious murder in Appin. Louis had always wanted to write a story set in the Scottish Highlands with echoes of this incident, so he seized Fanny's package as a 'fairy gift': *and the man accused of the murder, Alan Breck Stewart, can jump more or less fully formed, down to his silver buttons, blue coat and tartan breeches, into my novel . . . Whether or not he was guilty is not my point; I'm not after historical accuracy. Kidnapped, as I'm calling my story, will not be a slavish account of the Appin trial, not by any means. After all, my book's not intended to furnish a scholar's library; it'll be a book for boys to read when the schoolroom tasks are over and bedtime draws near; a book to send the young reader to sleep with feisty images to mingle with his dreams.*

With his newfound energy and in Fanny's absence, Louis keeps to his upstairs room preparing to write about a shipwreck in 1751. A shipwreck that would have been prevented a century later, when the Stevenson lighthouse had been put up to cast *its guiding beams into the terrible darkness of terrifying storms*. The first chapters were already written, in which the narrator, a Lowlander Whig named David Balfour (after his own maternal ancestors), seeks out his Uncle Ebeneezer at the House of Shaws. Unbeknown to the boy at the beginning of the story, this derelict mansion outside Edinburgh is rightfully his. To get Davie out of the way, the cunning Ebeneezer has him kidnapped by the dastardly Captain Hoseason aboard a vessel called the *Covenant*, bound for the Carolinas. A fiery Jacobite rebel called Alan Breck Stewart comes aboard, and the *Covenant* takes a detour to Glasgow via the treacherous Inner Hebridean Sea to set him ashore. That was it in a nutshell, and this morning Louis aims to write chapter thirteen, narrated by David Balfour.

He takes up his pen and the *Covenant* tears through the sea, pitching, straining, and pursued by a westerly swell:

As we got nearer to the turn of the land the reefs began to be sown here and there on our very path . . . and the sea breaks in fountains on the merciless reefs and falls like rain upon the deck. The brightness of the night showed us these perils as clearly as by day. By this time, now and then sheering to one side or the other to avoid a reef, but still hugging the wind and the land, we had got round Iona and begun to come alongside Mull.

The tide runs very strong and throws the brig about, then catches her and she comes into the wind like a spinning top. The next moment she strikes the reef with such a dunt, all the hands are thrown flat on the deck. The reef, lying low and dark upon the larboard, is off Erraid.

Alan Breck confides in Davie, this is the worst possible place for him to try to get ashore, for it is the land of his sworn enemies, the Campbells. Louis smiles - *that* should send a shudder through the readers.

There followed a sea so huge that it lifted the brig right up and canted her over on her beam . . . Whether the cry came too late or my hold was too weak, I know not; but at the sudden tilting of the ship I was cast clean over the bulwarks into the sea.

When Louis dips his pen again he finds the inkwell almost dry and writes on a scrap of paper: *B'cox, please get six bottles Stephens' Ink.* From the bowels of Skerryvore rise the teasing smells of a roasting lunch - lamb, he hopes, with potatoes and carrots - the laughter of women, interspersed with 'sshhhs' and 'wheeshts', the slamming of a door. Agnes and Valentine up to some prank, no doubt. He would see to them after he got the Balfour boy stranded on Erraid.

I went down, and drank my fill; and then came up, and got a blink of the moon; and then down again. They say a man sinks the third time for good. I cannot be made like other folk, then; for I would not like to write how often I went down or how often I came up again. All the while, I was being hurled along, and beaten upon and choked, and then swallowed whole; and the thing was so distracting to my wits, that I was neither sorry nor afraid . . . Presently, I found I was holding to a spar. The shores of Erraid were close in; I could see in the moonlight the dots of heather and the sparkling of the mica in the rocks.

A Flash of Silken Wings

In letters and memoirs, Robert Louis Stevenson's wide circle of admirers attested to his 'multitudes': courage, tenacity, wit, intellectual range, warmth and generosity. He was ambitious and passionately driven to write, though modest about his achievements: *I am a person with a poetic character and no great poetic talent*, he wrote. Everything he published was hard won: *I may say plainly, much as I have lost the power of bearing pain, I had still rather suffer much than die*. His flamboyant theatricality and graceful sensuality attracted both men and women. Edmund Gosse's Louis is 'restless and questing as a spaniel.' John Singer Sargent's Louis is 'the most intense creature I have ever met.' Teddy Henley's intimate poetic tribute acknowledges Louis' charisma as well as his divided self:

An Ariel quick through all his veins
With sex and temperament and style;
All eloquence and balls and brains;
Heroic and also infantile.

The heroic yet infantile author was a popular member of London's all-male Savile Club at 107 Piccadilly where Sydney Colvin had introduced him in 1874. Stevenson 'pervaded the club,' wrote Edmund Gosse; 'he was its most affable and chatty member; and he lifted it, by the ingenuity of his incessant dialectic, to the level of a sort of humorous Academe.' The club's impressive membership included Henry James, W.B.Yeats, Leslie Stephen and Thomas Hardy. Louis revelled in its literary atmosphere. During the Bournemouth years when he was seldom well enough to travel up to London, he missed the club, and, years later in Samoa he wrote in his diary: *It is Friday today. I wish I were in the Savile.* He made significant contacts at the Savile where the main requirement of membership was an ability to hold interesting conversations. The club's motto *Sodalitas Convivium* expressed the equality and camaraderie it aimed to foster among its artists and scientists. But, no matter how prominent members were in their professional lives, they were expected to 'leave their halos in the hall'. Savilians, as they were called, played snooker and cards, drank and ate good food at two long tables, a friendly arrangement designed to oil the wheels of social contact. No one, it was said, need ever feel alone at the Savile. And it was there, in 1879, Louis met Henry James whose first impression was of 'a shirt-collarless bohemian and a great deal (in an inoffensive way) of a *poseur*.' After he became one of Louis' closest friends, James altered his opinion and declared him 'a genius indeed'.

Henry James arrived in Bournemouth on the eighteenth of April 1885, and made straight for Skerryvore. He had left behind the distractions of

London to concentrate on writing a novel and to devote time to his invalid sister. After the death of their parents in New England, Alice James had crossed the Atlantic with her companion, Miss Loring. They had been attracted by Bournemouth's reputation as a health resort, and James had followed them, taking up lodgings not far from Alice's townhouse. His sister's arrival in England had 'the effect of laying the past like a heavy parcel' in James' lap, but he was fond of Alice and aware of his brotherly responsibilities.

Another American, John Singer Sargent, had paid a visit to Bournemouth before Henry James came down. At Louis' West Cliff lodgings in 1884, the artist painted his first portrait of the author. No one, 'least of all Sargent,' liked the result. Fanny said the portrait showed her husband as 'a weird, very pretty, chuckle-headed, slightly contorted poet,' and she hid the painting so skillfully it was never seen again.

Coincidentally, Sargent and the Stevensons all sailed from France to England in 1884. Louis was already acquainted with Sargent, having met him in Paris in the 1870s when he had been *on the run from the foul climate of Edinburgh* and the restrictions of his parental home at Heriot Row. His cousin Bob Stevenson and Sargent had been fellow students at the Paris studio of the celebrated Carlous-Duran and, after Louis arrived on the scene, Bob and Louis got up to *a deal of bohemian mischief.* They went down to Grez-sur-Loing near the forest of Fontainebleau, where Sargent impressed the laid-back colonists with his industrious devotion to painting. It was here Louis first met Fanny, an artist-in-residence, who had brought along her teenage daughter, Belle. Sargent painted Belle's lover of the time, the Irish artist Frank O'Meara.

With the help of Henry James, Sargent had rented a studio in London's Tite Street where Oscar Wilde and his wife, Constance, were neighbours. Sargent and James had become firm friends, after they met during the Paris Exhibition of 1884. That year, Sargent found himself at the centre of a *cause célèbre* over his exhibition portrait of Madame Gautreau, aka 'Madame X', wearing a low-cut dress with a fallen shoulder strap. It had scandalized the critics. Shunned by rich and famous patrons who had previously queued up to be immortalized with oil paint and canvas, Sargent had been sinking into poverty until Henry James persuaded him to move to London. There, James was convinced, Sargent would find willing sitters and Robert Louis Stevenson became one of his first. Louis was delighted when Sargent moved to London and Henry James came down to Bournemouth.

The novelist had been unable to find Skerryvore's front door when he paid his first call. Eventually he knocked on the tradesman's entrance and was let in by Valentine who took him to be a carpet layer wanting his bill paid. Fanny described James' visit in a letter to Louis' parents, but, eager to show herself in a good light as 'Lady Skerryvore', made no mention of the great man's arrival by way of the kitchen: *We have had a very pleasant visitor. One evening a card was handed in with 'Henry James' upon it. He spent that evening; asked to come again the next night, arriving almost before we had done with dinner, and staying as late as he thought he might, and again asking to come the next evening, which is tonight. I call that very flattering. I had always been told that he was the type of an Englishman, but except that he looks like the Prince of Wales I call him the type of an American. He is a gentle, amiable, soothing, sleepy sort, fat and dimpled. We find ourselves excessively fond of him.*

In a letter to Sydney Colvin, Fanny confided one of the simmering discords at Skerryvore. In the presence of visitors, whose one aim was to commune with Louis, she felt ignored, 'a mere comma in his life, and a superfluous one at that'. Colvin was in line to advise on her husband's future biography and must know something, at least, of the truth. *I think there is no question that he [Henry James] likes Louis; naturally I have hardly been allowed to speak to him, though I fain would. He seems very gentle and comfortable, and I worship in silence enforced by the elegant though brutal Mr Stevenson.* At first, Henry James disliked Fanny, but he warmed to her on closer acquaintance.

In the spring of 1885 James called at Skerryvore almost every day. 'My only social resource is Robert Louis Stevenson, who is more or less dying here,' James wrote to a friend. 'He is an interesting, charming creature, but I fear at the end of his tether; though indeed less apparently near death than he has been at other times.' The art of writing was central to their discussions. When they celebrated their reunion at

Skerryvore in April 1885, Louis had just published an essay, 'On Some Technical Elements of Style in Literature', in the *Contemporary Review*. 'Borrow it and read it, James,' he urged, 'and you'll come across my claim that the art of literature stands apart from its sisters, music and painting, for example, because the material in which the literary artist works is no less than the dialect of life.'

The day after Louis brought the shipwrecked David Balfour safely to shore at Erraid is warm and sunny at Skerryvore. Unable to resist sunbathing, he sets off across the dew-wet grass cradling Meredith's novel *Diana of the Crossways* and his tartan rug. He thinks he might write a letter to Henley or Colvin or cousin Bob, the new band of musketeers ever since his beloved friend Ferrier - one of the original Three Musketeers of his Edinburgh youth - had died while they were in France last year. Hearing that news had been one of the worst moments in his life. Impossible to remember Ferrier's death without tears, so he pauses for a few moments, supported by the lime tree until the emotion passes over. Thankfully, there was no sign of Beaucox. Gone into town for John Innes compost and my ink, Louis supposes, returning his damp handkerchief to his trousers pocket. Nothing to disturb the peace of the morning but the songs of bustling birds. He shakes out his rug and spreads it on the bank above the gully, still considering the letter. He would mention Skerryvore's pond and pigeon house, the stable and coach house, even although they had no horses or coaches to put in them. He would praise Fanny's kitchen garden and greenhouse where she had already planted salad leaves, tomatoes, corn and raspberries. These will not match the deliciousness of wild Scottish raspberries, he had told his wife, but they'll make a grand *cranachan* with the addition of cream and oatmeal. Contentedly, he lies on his back amused by that cheery notion.

It was true that the chine brooding darkly below brought to mind Colinton Dell, as his father had remarked, but this morning Louis sees something different in the configuration of trees and the steep drop down to the rivulet: a genteel version of the rustic platform at the Silverado mine in California where he and Fanny had gone on honeymoon in 1880. In that fantastical world of lumber and old iron, half-buried under the leaves of dwarf madronos, they had lain on hard beds of straw, listening to the cries of coyotes in the night. What bliss it had been to sunbathe naked on the shack's wooden balcony three thousand feet above sea level and to sit alone at sunrise eating his breakfast of coffee and porridge and reading out-of-date editions of *Cornhill's Magazine*. England had its compensations, though. It was far easier to get his hands on books.

He leans on his elbow and opens Meredith's novel, a melodramatic tale, hot off the press and recently borrowed from Sydenham's. An Irishwoman, famous for her beauty and wit, becomes the bride of a tyrannical

Englishman of Irish descent, Lord Larrian. They meet at a public ball held in the Assembly Rooms in Dublin to celebrate the return of Lord Larrian after a victorious Indian campaign. Diana, of course, catches his eye . . .

Louis is so immersed in the drama, he gives a start when a deep voice calls, 'Anyone at home?' and Henry James comes across the lawn saying 'don't disturb yourself, Stevenson, for I can't stay long.'

The realization that the friend he has christened 'the Prince of Men' could not be expected to loll on the tartan rug tempers Louis' buoyancy even as he clutches Henry James' comfortable hand. He must secure a chair, and, in the nick of time, Beaucox appears from behind the lime tree. When Louis ignores James' further protestation that his visit must be short and seduces him to the edge of the chine in search of kingfishers, James wonders that kingfishers might be seen hovering above such a trickle of water as glitters through the foliage far below. Louis suppresses a sudden fierce longing to take Henry's arm and laughingly admits he's unsure about the kingfishers but likes the idea. They make an odd pair, peering into the chasm for flashes of silken wings; James portly, bearded and balding, Stevenson stick-thin, with long straggling hair and moustache. James wears a suit of broadcloth with a silk cravat, white and speckled with lilac. Louis has on a collarless shirt and breeches in off-white linen. But the most remarkable feature of his garb is the striped knee-high stockings he put on that morning in a fit of nostalgia for high days and holidays at Grez-sur-Loing. A decade ago when they had stayed at the artists' colony, he and cousin Bob had owned several pairs of these fashionable bohemian stockings, as Louis explains to James.

'Ah, France, I give thanks daily that the Continent is not far away,' James says, turning his back on the chine as soon as Beaucox appears with two garden chairs. Valentine follows with a tray of cake and lemonade in glinting glasses set with straws. As soon as they are alone Louis confides, 'My wife has never recovered from her embarrassment over Valentine bringing you in through the tradesman's entrance.'

'There are times when I would rather be a carpet layer than an author,' James chuckles. '*The Bostonians* has led me a merry dance and, though I am almost done with it, my uncertain financial situation demands I press on with *The Princess Casamassima* without delay. It is to be serialised in *Atlantic Monthly*.'

'Good news, James. And is the Princess another model of your American heiress let loose in Europe?'

'Ah, there you might be in for a surprise.'

'I suppose you want to keep the genie in the bottle?'

'Quite so. It will leap out soon enough with the publication of the first episode in the autumn.' James samples his lemonade then pats Louis' arm, 'you look well this morning, Stevenson.'

'I am. My mind shows symptoms of reawakening - since my wife went up to London with the parents I'm back at work on an adventure story for boys, and I cannot ask for more . . . these days, a short walk and a long talk are all that's left to me. And, by the way, I have decided to name my house Skerryvore, though what Mrs Stevenson will say to it remains to be seen.'

'Skerryvore? It sounds guttural, rugged. Scottish, I suppose?'

'Gaelic. It means Great Skerry. It's the name of a Stevenson lighthouse put up in the Hebridean Sea over forty years ago. Its anglicized form is harsh, I admit. The Gaelic *An Sgeir Mhòr* is more poetic, but Bournemouth is so *English* we'd be hounded out of town if we put something as foreign as that up on a sign at the gate.'

They laugh, both at once, and sip their lemonade like happy schoolboys. Louis bends over to pick daisies growing at his feet. Spring is giving way to summer at Skerryvore.

'By the way,' James says. 'I banged into Sargent at the Savile. 'He wants to paint you again this summer.'

'Is he to paint you, too?'

'Oh, he has made one drawing and plans another but I am far from ready to sit for an oil. Sargent will have to wait until I deserve that sort of attention.'

'Surely some portrait of you exists?'

'Oh, yes, yes; my parents commissioned Le Farge to paint me when I came to manhood, and there are many photographs.'

'When I was an adolescent, apprenticed to be an engineer in the Stevenson family firm, my father took a fancy to a portrait at the Royal Scottish Academy of a boy posed with a microscope and went so far as to write to the artist - it was James Faed - to see if he might portray me as a budding engineer. Then, would you believe, father changed his mind and wrote again to say, all things considered, I was too stupid looking to make a picture like that.'

He cradles the daisies in his hand - *Take care o' yerself, my dearie!* - and summons a smile. 'Father's the kindliest and severest man in the world; a walking contradiction, in point of fact. Whenever I'm ill I find the bogeys of childhood rise up to haunt me - the Presbyterian duality of my father and the hellfire and damnation stories of my old nursemaid. But take some cake, man; on days like this when I am well I am wondrously able to fend off the spectres of the past. I wonder if your sister Alice finds the same - that illness encourages morbidity?'

'I find the same,' Henry says, biting into a slice of Dundee cake. 'I am not always well myself.'

A small silence fell. Henry James' forte lay in listening rather than talking, and he gave away little of a personal nature. In the lull, Robert Burns' poem to a mountain daisy crushed under the plough comes to Louis' mind. He considers reciting it aloud in Scots, but that might baffle James. How, he wonders, can he re-route their conversation away from illness, and away from pleasantries, to what really mattered to them both: the art of writing.

'By the way,' James suddenly says, 'I hear your *Treasure Island* has infiltrated the highest corridors of power and that Gladstone likes your book.'

'Gladstone would do better to attend to the imperial affairs of England - but tell me more about *The Bostonians*, are we to see it published soon?'

'That, I'm afraid, is in the lap of the Gods. Osgood, my American publisher, has gone bankrupt. And I have received not a penny of the five thousand dollars promised. In fact, I'm forced to re-negotiate the sale of the rights to Macmillan for both *The Bostonians* and *The Princess*. At least I'm due a cheque from *Atlantic Monthly* for the serialisation of *The Princess*.'

'One soldiers on. Writing is a hard mistress. Aye, but here's the rub,' Louis says. 'Are we engaged in craft or in art?'

'I incline to the latter, and, as I have said before, it is a luxury in this immoral age of ours to encounter someone like yourself who does write well, Stevenson, someone who really is acquainted with that lovely art.'

'Yes, the lovely art. Though for my own education as well as the readers' I want the whole business - literary craft or art? - ventilated in the press. The purpose of novel writing is not, in my view, to closely imitate life as you have claimed, James. There our opinions must continue to differ. Life is monstrous - it is infinite, illogical, abrupt and poignant, whereas a work of art is neat, finite, self-contained, rational, flowing and emasculate.'

'Emasculate, how so? You mean the art we authors pursue is feminine?'

'Yes, in the sense that the essential maleness of any artist of that gender shifts into poetic gear during the act of creation. We bring forth into the world something that did not exist before our imaginations invented it. In that sense, we engage our most creative selves. We give birth to the new.'

'And gaiety, Stevenson, surely that is important?'

Gaiety? Louis tugs a corner of his moustache. What had gaiety to do with anything? He was recalling Henry James' published essay, 'The Art of Fiction', parts of which he had considered dreadful nonsense. He had even published a repost in *Longman's Magazine* never dreaming he would one day meet the American face to face. Story was more important than form, he insisted, opposing James's penchant for form. He wonders if their conversation this glorious morning is in danger of straying into deep water.

'Yes gaiety, Stevenson. The opposite of the so-called conscious moral purpose that some fatheads - who, by the way, have never attempted to create novels themselves - claim to be the chief aim of novelists. Forget all that, I say. Let the novel compete with life; let it recreate reality as music and painting do. It's what you do best, Stevenson. You recreate life and add to it the native gaiety that weaves through everything you write.'

Louis felt flattered, but also a little flattened by his friend's assertion. In his view the challenge of an author was far more than to reflect gaiety, far more complex in purpose than to deliver perfectly formed work. As he had written in the *Contemporary Review*, the material the writer works from was no less than the dialect of life. In the weeks to come, he looked forward to serious discussions with James about the technical elements of style, about the painful suppressions involved in their art, and so on. For the time being, it was a relief to know he could depend on HJ's sponsorship of his growing credibility in the eyes of the London literati. Backed by HJ's gravitas, no one could judge him a simple romancer or pale *belletrist*.

'Whatever the nature of our art, it's damned hard to make a living at it,' Louis says. 'Whenever I think I would like to live a little, to steal time away from scribbling, I hear the butcher's cart resounding through the neighbourhood, or some other carter waving his bill, and I'm forced to plunge my pen in the ink once more. Here I am, a grown man with a wife and stepson to support - I've produced stories, poems, a play and a novel - yet still I'm forced to turn to Father Tom for dollars. Whatever past faults can be laid at his door, he's a generous parent now.'

Henry's palms merge as if in prayer. 'I depended upon my parents a good deal, too, at the beginning of my career. Now I must row the boat alone and come up with episode after episode of *The Princess Casamassima* for serialisation.' With a deep sigh he confesses, 'These days, as you know, my sister Alice ties me to England, though dearly I long for Italy.'

His friend's speech suggests to Louis profound pools

in a slow moving river . . . and now Henry is rising off his chair saying he really must get back to Alice who is rather poorly.

The week before, Henry James had sent a hansom to fetch the Stevensons for afternoon tea at his sister's townhouse. The minute Louis saw Alice James lying on her day bed, he recognized her as the invalid he had glimpsed in a bath chair the first time he visited Sydenham's. His heart went out to her once more when he discovered Alice's tubercular state hadn't dampened her acerbic wit. For Alice's sake, he quashes his disappointment that HJ must leave so soon. Nothing for it but to progress slowly towards the gates, inclining his head the better to hear Henry's pronouncements on his sister's health above the din of Beaucox's lawnmower.

Before they part, Louis proposes a brief detour to see the bronze bell hanging at the back of the house. 'Thomas and Margaret sent it down from Scotland. It came off an ancient ship wrecked at the Skerryvore rocks long before the Stevenson lighthouse went up.'

He loosens the bell's thick rope, gives it a yank, and its clangour takes flight beyond the confines of the Stevensons' modest estate, over the rooftops of the villas on Alum Chine Road and in through the open windows of Lilly Langtry's drawing room, where she awaits the arrival, at any moment, of the Prince of Wales.

No Man's Land

Louis sits in the sun writing to his mother: *Angel James continues to visit us balmily; we steadily like him better; he is a real fine gentleman* . . . Then he seeks out Beaucox, transplanting seedlings in the twiney warmth of the greenhouse. He keeps to the door and delivers Fanny's proposal for damming the rivulet in the chine. Beaucox hands him a box containing six bottles of ink. No need to linger with this man of few words who makes him feel uncomfortable about his new status of householder. By employing servants he feels he has betrayed the socialist ideals he nourished before this enforced detention at Skerryvore.

In Fanny's absence, mastery of the household must be demonstrated; he must not let the side down. He tucks stray strands of hair behind his ears and enters the kitchen, steeling himself for Mrs Watts' inevitable protests.

'It's time for a walk with Valentine,' he says.

She looks up from her task of rolling pastry. 'I need the girl to help with the dinner.'

Louis marvels at her floury arms, thick as hams. 'I won't keep her long. Please fetch her from her quarters.'

Rarely had he entered Fanny's domain. Pacing the red brick floor, he marvels at the order Fanny has achieved in such a short time: the cast-iron coal-burning range overhung with gleaming brass and copper utensils, the central deal table where meals are prepared and the servants eat, the open shelving filled with pots of jams and pickles, the pie-safe with wired windows to keep out flies. They had one at Heriot Row. He peers into the cool scullery where a large copper vessel set into a brick fireplace awaits the weekly wash. Gingerly he opens the servants' door leading to the stable yard and a tremor rises in his belly. What presence lurks here? He stifles a cry and comes face-to-face with a creature all in black with ghoulish eyes. He stares at the man offloading his sack, then closes the door with a trembling hand. He leans against it drawing breath, conquering sudden weakness in his joints and wondering why Watts was a long time coming. To calm his nerves he retreats to the dining room, pulls on the bell and dashes back to the kitchen for the distraction of seeing its motion transferred to the call-box above the kitchen door. When a creaking floorboard alerts him to Watts' imminent return he slips away down the hall to wait for Valentine in the security of the outer porch.

A tune in his head sets his foot tapping on the Minton tiles and helps to dispel his encounter with the coalman. Verse follows verse of 'Oh, whistle and I'll come to you my lad'. The bogeyman begins to fade, replaced by cheery memories of the first time he saw Valentine. They had hired her directly from her country folk at Hyères. She had been no more than seventeen, pitifully shy and monosyllabic even in her own language. Naturally, she spoke no English. Valentine was destined to become Fanny's 'lady's maid', the Vandegrifter's general factotum; (sometimes he called his wife Vandegrifter, Pig, Dutchwoman, or some other nickname. She accepted without protest his odd terms of endearment and clung to 'Lou', 'Papa' or 'The Squire' for his.) Most days, Fanny had given Valentine an English lesson in La Solitude's garden where orange bougainvillea and white jasmine rampaged up the ochre wall. The lessons concerned the essentials of daily life: *le pain* - bread, *le fromage* - cheese, *le jardin* - the garden, *la maison* - the house. A new list of words every day. Gradually mistress and maid developed a bond so comfortable Valentine began to show signs of enjoying life. She had been known to smile and even to giggle, but Louis had noticed a sadness in the lass since they arrived in England.

At last Valentine appears wearing a summer cape over her dark housedress and a fluted bonnet tied with blue ribbons. Ah, *Mademoiselle*, how pretty you look, he wants to say in French, but Valentine steals past him under the twinkling fanlights of the porch. That was a pity since he relishes speaking French with Valentine, keeping the language up to scratch, reminding them both of the land they love on the other side of the Channel. Nothing for it then but to fasten his shawl about his shoulders with a Scotch pin rescued off a kilt he had worn for a lark in his student days.

He follows Valentine through the gateposts onto Alum Chine Road. He wants to sing and dance in the warm summery air, only he must conserve the energy so lately returned to him. He hadn't so much as coughed for a week, let alone spat blood. If Valentine was disinclined to walk beside him, at least he could study the perfection of her form from behind: the neat head, the hair pulled severely back into a silky dark-blond plait tied with a tartan ribbon the parents had given the lass as a present; the well-turned ankles in their dainty pumps. Her waist, the hourglass waist, and the billowing skirt, suggested nothing so much as a cello. Her face, when she smiled, was that of an angel. Her skin resembled Hyères peaches, her eyes were dark blue as Mediterranean mussels. There is something deprived about the girl, though, that worries him.

Further down Alum Chine Road, the coal wagon and the blackamoor delivering sacks to a neighbouring villa crosses their path. A gross blot of darkness on the pastel-coloured world of Westbourne. This second sighting of the coalman carries Louis back to the cities he has left behind - Edinburgh, London and Paris - with their belching industries and huddled poor. He follows Valentine past the wagon, reliving his student days; days when he had founded the L.J.R. Society with cousin Bob and spirited Edinburgh friends. With revolutionary zeal, he had written to fellow members of The Liberty, Justice and Reverence Society: *We will be linked with the spirit of Walt Whitman: humanity, love of mankind, sense of inequality, justification of art and decline of religion will be chief topics for our deliberation.* He had discovered Whitman in the 1870s, declaimed him in the howffs of Advocate's Close, and loved him ever since. *Ah, Whitman! Sing me a song of the lad that is gone!* This Squire's life is but a charade, a disguise, a dream I'll wake up from one day and sign up to Mr Hyndman's Social Democratic Federation and join the reformers of the Fabian Society. These days, all he can do is read accounts of the Society's impassioned works on behalf of the downtrodden poor in *The Times* but he makes a vow to back the cause when his strength returns.

Valentine is off in the lead again, past honey-coloured villas that resemble his own Skerryvore. Properly speaking, a maid should walk behind a master; not that he or Fanny observed many rules of social propriety. Could it be that Valentine, properly dressed as a lady's maid, was ashamed to be seen beside her bohemian master with his flowing hair, red shawl and unironed flannels? Is that why she went ahead, as if disowning him? He wondered, since he knew that whenever he and Fanny were sighted in the neighbourhood, the natives grew restless. He had the information from Fanny who had it from Mrs Watts, who had it from the fishmonger in town.

'It started with you, Louis, stalking about in your shawl, your unkempt hair blowing in the wind on the West Cliff when we had lodgings there,' Fanny said.

'Oh? And you, what about you?'

'Isn't it obvious? Comments about me are sparked off by my Dutch-American, Van de Grift features. My skin's darker by far than any to be seen in the entire town. We stick out like sore thumbs. Added to that we don't observe the ridiculous social rituals of southern pork-puddens.'

'Pork-puddens, wife,' he had chuckled, 'where did you pick up that?'

'In a letter you wrote to one of your friends in the north.'

Fanny said the word hit the nail on the head to describe their hoity-toity neighbours who whispered behind their hands, 'the Stevensons cannot be classed as one of us.' As it was, they could never have tolerated visits from such tiresome folk. They were more than content with their growing circle in Bournemouth: Henry James in particular, the Boodles and the Shelleys. An elderly poet neighbour, Sir Henry Taylor, had introduced them to Lady Jane and Sir Percy Shelley at their Bournemouth home, Boscombe Manor. There, they guarded the death mask of Sir Percy's grandmother, Mary Wollstonecraft, and an urn containing the heart of his poet father, Percy Bysshe Shelley

Valentine turns into the leafy lane sloping down to the chine. Far older than her years, he thinks. The publication of his volume of poetry, *A Child's Garden of Verses,* had coincided with their flitting to the villa at Easter time and Valentine kept a signed copy on her bedside table. For her, it served as an English primer from which she learned to recite her favourite poems by heart. The book's dedication to his childhood nursemaid, Alison Cunningham, 'Cummy', would not have escaped her all-seeing eyes: *My second Mother, my first wife, The angel of my infant life.* During his terrible illness at Hyères, Valentine had watched over him when he wrote the last poems for *A Child's Garden*. There was intimacy in that. Propped on a hill of pillows, he wrote with his left hand on a board balanced over his legs. His right arm had been bandaged to his side to prevent haemorrhages. Cummy was an old woman now, attending to the needs of young Sam in Edinburgh. Louis gave thanks that he had his Valentine, a substitute Cummy, a youthful angel, at this midpoint of his life.

But there's something the matter with the girl, he thinks, cautiously descending the path behind her. It strikes him that, before young Sam had been abducted to Edinburgh by his parents, Fanny's attitude to Valentine had altered. He had overheard his wife lecturing Sam in long monologues about the importance of making a 'good marriage'. Valentine had been forbidden to enter Sam's room. Louis hadn't given it much thought, but now it struck him that Fanny feared her sexually maturing son might sow his first wild oats with a domestic. That would never do, he thought ironically, though upstairs-downstairs couplings were common enough. It gladdened his own heart to recall his youthful adventures in the back alleys of Edinburgh. A soot-blackened industrial section of the city rose up in

The House on the Chine

his imagination, hidden from the gaze of the posh Georgian street where his family lived. His own back alley conquest, Mary, resembled Valentine, he thinks, his eyes piercing the arboreal tangle of greening twigs whose roots lay deep in the chine. Fanny, he sighs, might be the matter with Valentine.

All of a sudden he feels dizzy and his ears buzz. He grabs hold of the iron railings edging the path and sinks to his knees. Valentine rushes to his side, 'I'll get Beaucox and the wheelchair,' she cries. He takes a few deep breaths, 'There's no need, lass. 'Twas a *petit mal*, that's all. Keep your arm in mine and I'll be all right.' He dreads the onset of illness, yet the notion that he has the Vandegrifter's permission to have the girl in his room raises his spirits. He wants to ask Valentine if Fanny mentioned the scheme, but has not the strength as they retrace their steps in silence. Valentine serves him hot sweet tea and shortbread in the drawing room. 'I'm fine now, lass.' He smiles up at her from the divan, 'I'm right as rain, though maybe it's time to get myself a walking stick.'

After a short rest, the sun has left the garden but still illuminates the porch. He fetches *Diana of the Crossways* and his writing case. He'll get a letter off to Fanny in the second post.

My dear fellow, he writes, *there's no place like home . . . discussed with le Beaucox about the dam . . . strolled in garden, flowers mighty pretty. Dined: Valentine and Agnes out on messages, your dear parent keeping house, sitting now in the porch, now out on the gravel, reading Meredith, looking at rhododendrons, and red hawthorn and hearing the piejohns, whirring about and saying damn . . .*

He adds an afterthought: *Valentine very pretty in her cap.*

The following day, heavy rain prevents Louis' return to the garden. Agnes arrives to remove the breakfast tray, her voice so gallous *La Bello* comes to mind for her nickname. He quizzes her about her work at Skerryvore - is she happy? And her mother, Mrs Watts, is she well? When she answers work was work but she'd rather be a lady's maid than a chambermaid, he stops himself from saying 'like Valentine?' Anyway the lass bolts away, like a hare, Louis thinks, pursued by uncomfortable presences in a stubble field. There is unrest below stairs and it saddens him - servants should be happy! – but Fanny, with her new found confidence gleaned from *The Book of Household Management*, would deal with it on her return.

Back at his desk he reviews 'The Loss of the Brig'. Chapter thirteen of *Kidnapped* is complete. He decants into his silver-topped inkwell one of the new bottles. He puts a fresh sheet of blotting paper into the leather holder that takes up half his desk and secures a new nib onto his pen. When the tools of his trade are ready, *Chapter XIV, The Islet*, he writes.

With my stepping ashore I began the most unhappy part of my adventures . . . It was half-past twelve in the morning, and though the wind was broken by the land, it was a cold night. I dared not sit down (for I thought I should have frozen), but took off my shoes and walked to and fro upon the sand, barefoot, and beating my breast, with infinite weariness . . . The time I spent upon the island is still so horrible a thought to me, that I must pass it lightly over . . . All day it streamed rain; the island ran like a sop; there was no dry spot to be found; and when I lay down that night, between two boulders that made a kind of roof, my feet were in a bog.

Louis smiles; heroes must suffer to gain their freedom.

Davie sees a red deer, finds a guinea-piece, then another, and another . . . hope rises in his young heart, then, at long last, the sun comes out. From the vantage point of a high rock he sees a cobble rounding the island of Iona with a pair of fishers aboard and calls out to no avail. Next day, his strength very low, Davie sees the boat heading for Erraid. When it draws near, the skipper tee-hee's with laughter at Davie's plight. He gestures and addresses him in Gaelic, until, at last, Davie understands he can get off the island at low tide and walk across to the mainland at the Ross of Mull.

All at once Louis stiffens at a sudden commotion below stairs. Fanny's voice in the hall - Bogue's mad barking - Fanny calling to Valentine. His pulse quickens. Fanny back! Her return signalled an end to unfettered time with Henry James. The Vandegrifter would whip him into what she called 'duties about the house'. Force upon him a routine, make him ill, drive him back to bed. At the same time, he felt a surge of relief, a pale echo of the desire he had felt on seeing Fanny for the first time at Grez-sur-Loing. A gutsy, cigar smoking American bohemian, would-be-artist and would-be divorcée, touchingly grieving for her child Hervey who had recently died in Paris.

Anticipating Fanny's imminent intrusion he writes fast - Davie runs across the islet as he's never run before, jumps over the trickle of water that lies between Erraid and the mainland - runs and runs until his feet sink into the boggy ground of the Ross of Mull, just as his and Bob's had done all those years ago.

End of chapter, he writes.

Then Fanny stands beside him, Bogue snapping deliriously at his shoes. He lays down his pen. 'Who on earth are you?' he jests, embracing her then holding her at arm's length, thinking her *unrecognizable, lean, brown and bloodshot, some London woman claiming to be Fanny*, as he later wrote to his mother. He clings to her, stirred by the familiar animal odour of her thick greying hair, the feel of her plump arms encircling him, her breasts, her bigness.

Then, wearied by the drama, he sinks into his chair. 'And what had the vet to say about wee Bogue?'

'Only that I must mix in a compound with his food twice a day. He put the lank condition of Bogue's coat down to the time of year. Human beings must eat green cabbage in the spring to clear the blood, he said, and dogs need extra minerals, too. You're writing,' Fanny says, briskly taking off her gloves.

'I'm deeply engaged with the ink bottle.'

'Valentine says you've been well.' Fanny fixes him with her sad stare. On account of the trials of her life, and bad teeth she refused to have pulled, his wife seldom smiled. 'She ignored my instructions to tidy out my wardrobe when I was away and offended Mrs Watts and Agnes with her superior airs. You didn't need her in your room?'

'I was well,' Louis says curtly. 'Ah, yes, wellness. A chapter a day, from now on.' He looks up into her galvanizing eyes. 'Hard going, but it's the schedule I managed with *Treasure Island*, remember?'

Fanny knew the bare bones of *Kidnapped* and he was the first to admit she had made helpful suggestions before leaving for London. But now, when she picked up the last page he had written, he wondered if he allowed her too close an interest in his work.

'Mind you don't smudge it,' he says irritably. 'You'll notice the ink's still wet in proof of this morning's industry and your cape is wet, too, in proof of your return from the rain-soaked world beyond Skerryvore.'

Fanny flattens the page on the ink-blotter then reads aloud: '"A sea-bred boy would not have stayed a day on Erraid, which is only what they call a tidal islet, and except in the bottom of the neaps, could be entered and left twice in every twenty-four hours, either dry-shod, or at the most by wading."' She laughs her grizzly laugh. 'In the bottom of the neaps? I thought neaps were Scottish turnips, Papa?'

'Different spelling, two "ee's" for the turnip,' he says,

pulling free of his wife and the chair. 'And Erraid is pronounced "Err-id", not "Ear-aid".'

His confused emotions over Fanny's return harden into something resembling resentment. These past days with Fanny away, he had felt pleasure in almost every moment. Now, would there be a return to the strife that punctuated their life together as surely as Old Faithful recorded the hours of the day?

The gong sounds in the hall below and, trailed by Bogue, they traipse downstairs. 'Neap tides, dear Dutchwoman, are low tides, and "the bottom of the neaps"- as in the extract you read - refers to the lowest point of the lowest tide.'

'So your shipwrecked boy Davie was not marooned after all. He could have walked off the island during this turnip tide?'

'Aye, that's right. It was all in the Balfour boy's mind. How he chose to see his situation was a reflection of his depression at losing by shipwreck his new friend Alan Breck and the relative security of the *Covenant* - notwithstanding the fact that the brig had been captained by Hoseason, a pillar of Presbyterianism.'

'Davie and Hoseason sound rather like you and your father,' Fanny says and Louis sighs, 'I wish you hadn't mentioned father. The morning's work was tyrant enough in forcing me to remember my own torment at Erraid in the summer of 1870.'

'Very well, we can change the subject. London was heavenly. Mr Tommy and I made many finds. The goods are to be delivered before our wedding anniversary.'

'Stolen goods! Faither means to pin us down with possessions,' Louis says, tucking his hair behind his ears. 'On the other hand it pleases me that you and Mr Tommy are so matey.'

Tomato soup steams in a blue-and-white tureen on the dining table. Fanny gathers up the folds of her dress and sits opposite Louis with Bogue at her feet. One of the boons of living with a literary man, she observes, is our shared love of words. She butters a bread roll and hands it to her husband.

Louis was impatient to know how Sydney Colvin and Frances Sitwell had received his wife in London. It riled him that his friends had been slow to accept Fanny, and even ridiculed her behind her back. Sidney Colvin, Charles Baxter and Henley - above all, Henley, who had once hurt him deeply by calling Fanny 'the Bedlamite' - belonged to this group.

In London, Fanny had invited Sydney and Frances to tea at the Buckingham Palace Hotel where she had been staying, bankrolled by Mr Tommy. The fiends had been friendly enough, she reported. She often referred to Louis' friends as 'the fiends'. As an American, Fanny found their over-refined manners difficult to comprehend, and she was well aware that they received her with surface politeness solely to maintain access to Louis. After visiting them at Hyères, Henley had concluded that Fanny - who had been on the verge of breakdown after long weeks of arduous nursing - always surrounded herself with alarms, lies and intrigue. Thus arose the 'Cassandra' nickname, which Louis found acceptable. There was a grain of truth in it, but Henley had gone too far when he called Fanny 'the Bedlamite'. He had been cruel to judge his wife when she was under such duress. 'The fiends' slipped into their conversation many times over lunch until Fanny put a stop to it. It was a trying subject, she said, and likely to bring on headaches or even one of her 'brain fevers'.

As Louis was well aware, he could never have called a 'lady wife' names such as 'Pig' and 'Vandegrifter', names Fanny seemed not to mind and even to enjoy. He sympathised with Fanny's sensitivity to the slights of 'the ladies' of his circle; Anna Henley, Frances Sitwell, Katherine de Mattos and Grace Baxter all regarded his marriage as an irreparable mistake. But the genteel insularity of the London group with their risk-free, stylish trips to the continent, made Louis value his dark skinned American wife's ability to live life on a dramatic scale. How dare they dismiss Fanny's past as beneath their consideration, as they might a gypsy's? He had noticed that his friends rarely attempted to draw her out on any subject. These days though, Colvin and his companion, Frances Sitwell (his 'first Fanny' who had infatuated him in the 1870s) received his wife and even corresponded with her. No doubt this was largely on account of Colvin's involvement in any future biography. Still, progress was being made and he applauded Fanny Van de Grift Stevenson's invincibility in face of the veiled hostility of the group. Certainly, no 'lady wife' would have had the power to save him from *the miasmas of the Styx* as his own weird wife had done last summer. How nearly he had approached death's door and been spared going through it solely thanks to the dedication of the valiant woman sitting opposite him at the dining table, earnestly wiping her plate with a bread roll.

After lunch Fanny declared, rain or no rain, she would go to Beaucox in the garden. Louis went upstairs for his nap. When he was well Fanny was happy, at least for a while. Apart from Valentine's failure to tidy her room as instructed, and the discussion about 'the fiends', the English weather had been the only fly in the ointment of her homecoming. When she had said 'rain, rain, always rain in Godforsaken England,' he had reassured her - they would not stay in England forever. One day, they would find a good climate to settle down in and, from time to time, they discussed their great escape. The China Sea, the Indian Ocean, even the South Seas featured in their dreams of elsewhere. No exotic land lay beyond the reach of their ambition to discover an earthly paradise where Louis would be well. He would swim in a high tide of black ink, the most famous writer of his day, and Fanny would create a paradisical garden out of fecund earth.

*

On the tenth of May, they were at a game of cards. In accordance with her ambition to make the drawing room 'the jewel casket of our home', Fanny had covered old oak chests with bright yellow throws, spread oriental rugs upon the brown-stained wooden floor and put up white muslin curtains to soften the midday sunlight. Their pictorial treasures leaned against a wall waiting to be hung: Turner's engraving of the Bell Rock lighthouse (the legendary achievement of Louis' grandfather) and two Piranesi prints. Louis' collection of weaponry that had served as inspiration when he wrote *Treasure Island* - swords, pistols and other buccaneering equipment - lay in a pile beside the artwork. (By 1886, after a visit to Auguste Rodin's Paris studio, a two-foot high plaster group, *Le Printemps*, had been added to their collection. It was a gift from the sculptor who was a friend of Teddy Henley.)

An assortment of side tables covered with lace, footstools, hassocks, and the embroidered fire screen, gave the room an artful cluttered look, but not so cluttered you banged into things, as Fanny declared. The arch-topped grate, kitted out with bellows, tongs, brushes and brass coal scuttle, cradled a modest fire most of the summer for the sake of Louis' health, and Bogue slept in a wicker basket beside it.

When Louis suddenly said, 'See what we have come to, Dutchwoman,' Fanny took him to mean their game of cards. But he referred to the room. 'You have made the drawing room look so beautiful, it positively gives me qualms.'

Yet again, he had been retracing in his mind how they had come to this respectability after their maverick wanderings in Switzerland, France and California. In this, of course, Thomas Stevenson had played the trump card, but tonight, with their fifth wedding anniversary looming, Louis felt inclined to enjoy his role as householder. His novel was progressing well, a circumstance that made him see sense in his kidnapping.

'Mind you, Pig, I'll have no stuffed birds under glass domes in this room, and no moths and butterflies pinned to boards either.'

Fanny cast him a tender look and dealt out a new round of cards. 'Oh, I'd hate stuffed and pinned things, too, Papa. As it is, the drawing room *is* delicious, and even one new treasure brings me the keenest pleasure. We are blessed with so many, thanks to Mr Tommy. Though I have to confess the hall displeases, I find it oppressive.'

The dark oblong of the hall was an entirely functional passageway leading from the entrance porch to the stairway and the upper floor. The kitchen door led off it to the left, flanked by the brass gong. The drawing and dining room doors were on the right with Old Faithful standing to attention between them. Captain Best had bequeathed the Turkey stair runner held in place with brass rods, the one cheery note that drew the eye of the entering visitor beyond the brown panelling of the hall.

On Fanny's instructions Beaucox had put up coat

pegs, and the obligatory mirror where lady visitors could arrange their hats. The hall was indeed dour, and Louis promised to put his mind to the challenge of enlivening it. The renaming of the house must be settled, too, and Louis seized the opportunity to put forward 'Skerryvore' as his choice.

'I haven't heard a better,' he said. 'When we viewed the house for the first time, I was struck by the sliver of sea view you get from the upstairs windows. I felt I was looking out of the lamp room in a lighthouse, and my immediate thought was this house will rescue us before we're shipwrecked again. A beacon to light our way out of the darkness of ill-health and poverty we've been floundering in these past five years of matrimony.'

'It's not a name I'd have chosen myself,' Fanny said soberly. 'But 'Skerryvore' would please Mr Tommy, and therefore I suppose I reluctantly agree.'

'Grand. We'll have a sign made and put up straight away, and advise the post office of the alteration to our address. That's settled then. Our lighthouse is ready for action.'

'A lighthouse without water, since B'cox advises against the dam. He says the stream will not always be there. It fills up then reduces to a trickle in no time at all, depending on the tide table and the time of the year.'

'It's a pity we won't have ducks,' Louis frowned. 'I, too, am fond of ducks.'

Suddenly the doorbell rang and Fanny raised her dusky eyebrows, 'a visitor at this time of night? It can only mean one thing.'

'The Prince!' Louis exclaimed, rushing into the hall where Henry James stood out of breath, waving a copy of *The Times*. 'I bring good news, Stevenson. Although it is getting late, I had to let you see this without delay.'

Louis drew James into the drawing room, where Fanny, languorous on the divan, received his customary kiss on her hand before James opened up the newspaper on Louis' desk.

'Here it is, Stevenson. A review of your story "The Dynamiter" from your volume, *New Arabian Nights*, and it is favourable . . . I'll read out the best bit: "We are much inclined to wish that Mr Stevenson may spin out his *New Arabian Nights* to the length of their immortal originals." *The Times*, Stevenson. This will do you a power of good.'

Louis peered over James' shoulder to read the article. 'The reviewer wants me to write a hundred more stories,' he exclaimed, turning to Fanny. 'Well, that should put some dollars in the bank. By Jove, this is encouragement that calls for a celebration. Poire Williams, don't you think, Fanny?' He took from the cupboard a bottle they had brought over from Hyères and filled three liqueur glasses.

'Sit on your chair, dear man,' Fanny drawled, pointing to the bergère that had belonged to Louis' grandfather. Their affection for Henry, who from their earliest acquaintance had been drawn to it, had prompted them to christen it 'Henry James's chair'. James did as bidden and Louis went to roll a cigarette at the mantelpiece. '"The Dynamiter" alone might sell between five and ten thousand copies by Christmas and make my name better known.'

Fanny sorted the playing cards into a neat pile. 'Longman, Green & Co. has commissioned Louis to write a shilling shocker for its Christmas 1885 number, but he struggles to come up with an idea.'

'Then you must help me, Fanny.'

Louis passed the cigar box to James, and when they embarked on a discussion about the vagaries of literary criticism, Fanny stifled a yawn. It was long past her bedtime and she was too tired to fight her corner with men intent upon barring her from all attempts to enliven their discussion. She made her excuses and, trailed by Bogue, retired upstairs.

Louis caught James' eye with a complicit smile. 'My wife writes, too, in fact she runs to keep up with me and intends to becoming a writer of crime fiction. She made up stories to entertain me when I was bedridden at Hyères last year - after the doctor took one look at my shuddering, skeletal self and pronounced me almost dead. A year ago you could have chucked a farthing for my life. Mrs Stevenson saved me from the jaws of death with her pills, potions, nursing skills and stories. I'm the first to admit it was partly from her stories that I got the idea of writing "The Dynamiter" - that and Gladstone's succouring of the Irish terrorists for Home Rule. At the time, if you remember, the London newspapers were full of the bomb outrages on behalf of Home Rule in Ireland.'

He slumped a little, remembering the awful time, the frightful pain and the haemorrhages at La Solitude. He had felt himself to be an object of pity, a terrible burden - and possibly a bore - to his family and friends. And, when his customary stoicism had deserted him, he had turned upon Fanny the most foul of rages. *The beast came roaring out. Why don't you get off my back*, he had railed. At times he had turned terrorist himself and wanted to kill Fanny and her stories. Once, in the thrall of drugs, he had grabbed and shaken her like a terrier with a rat. As long as he lived he would never forgive himself for displaying the devilish creature that lurked inside him.

James threw him a quizzical look.

'As you see, here at Skerryvore,' Louis said brightly, 'I am well enough.'

'Ah! Skerryvore. Mrs Stevenson has accepted the name?'

'She has; though she dealt me shrewd stabs over the matter. Nothing to be gained by turning life into King Lear, I said, especially over the naming of a house. Now it is settled - this lighthouse, this landlocked Skerryvore, will be a grand cradle for *Kidnapped* - the story I'm writing partly borrows from my own experience of the west of Scotland.'

'All authors do that . . . borrow, I mean, from past experiences. But to return to "The Dynamiter", nowhere is Mrs Stevenson's contribution mentioned in *The Times.*'

'That's true, and it's a misfortune I'll have to pay for at breakfast tomorrow. But, as you'll see when you get the book, my wife shares the title page with me. Mrs Stevenson riles when she feels slighted and I predict another storm over Sargent's plan to paint me again. She has set her face against a second portrait. And she's not in favour of admitting the small queue of artists waiting to draw me. I don't look my best, I'm far too thin and I tire easily, she reasons.'

Old Faithful sounded eleven chimes through the silent house.

'Good Lord, is that the time?' James said, easing himself out of the bergère. He laid a comradely hand on Louis' shoulder. 'Sargent is bound to do you justice next time. No doubt you'll bring Mrs Stevenson round to his visit as you have done with the naming of your house. And well done with that review, dear boy.'

Henry James slipped away and Louis climbed the stairs to Fanny's darkened room. Oblivious to the warning hoots of owls marking their territory above the trees of the chine, his wife lay snoring like a navvy. He pulled back the covers and got in beside her, contemplating a poem he might write for the Prince of Men.

Grit in the Oyster

As spring blossomed into summer, almost every day Fanny summoned Beaucox to dig and plant with her on the sloping bank of the chine. Fanny had been accustomed to reclaiming land in the American West. A born guerrilla gardener, she had exercised her talent in the rocky *garrique* above La Solitude where she had been inspired by the Mediterranean labyrinth of Zeus. By creating winding paths in the abyss of Alum Chine she saw herself as an Ariadne who would lead Louis to freedom from Bluidy Jack. Added to that, it was a pleasure to create for Skerryvore's visitors a direct route into Alum Chine and onwards to Bournemouth Bay. In her heart of hearts, she knew her plan to tempt Louis into her dreamscape was absurd. But when Fanny's passion was roused, nothing in the world could deflect her. Louis' comment that she might be getting too old for pioneering work was met with a proud toss of her head as she shouldered her spade and set off down the garden.

One damp May morning, Louis awakened with an attack of sciatica; *mezzo agony* on his scale for the affliction that regularly hit *the high reaches of soprano*. Not so bad, then, but the mezzo attack hit soprano after he and Fanny had a nasty quarrel during breakfast about his plan to rent a piano. Then Watts had arrived in the dining room complaining about cockroaches - 'dirty little things scurrying all over my kitchen when I come to work.' Louis had intended to get down to *Kidnapped*, but the quarrel and the cockroaches put Davie, Alan Breck and Scotland so far beyond the reach of his imagination he went to the drawing room desk and wrote a begging letter to his parents: *The drawing-room will soon be lovely, and we bankrupt. It will be a very quaint, but a very pleasing and harmonious room* . . . Then, when he was certain Fanny had disappeared into the chine, he ventured out to savour the day.

He enjoyed watching the action at the junction of Middle Road and Alum Chine Road while he sat smoking on the low wall fronting Skerryvore. A hansom might clop by, a maid carrying a basket hurry in the direction of the Westbourne market, an old boy in a blazer emerge from the villa opposite led by his King Charles spaniel. Bogue, who usually clung to Fanny's heels, might appear out of the blue with magnificent instinct and rush barking across the road. This particular morning, Louis' spirits lifted at the sight of Miss Boodle coming down Middle Road, a slender figure in an ankle length navy-blue suit edged with white piping. She comes to Skerryvore to rescue me from my wrecked emotions, he thought gratefully. They both enjoyed good-natured banter and Adelaide Boodle had become a frequent visitor to Skerryvore. Sometimes Louis tutored her in writing, sometimes the task fell to Fanny. It all depended upon the state of his health and Fanny's many preoccupations to do with the smooth running of the house and garden.

Adelaide sat beside Louis on the wall, listening to his account of the dramas of the morning: his sciatica, his quarrel with Fanny, and Mrs Watts' complaint about the cockroaches. Cockroaches were easily dealt with, the ever-practical Adelaide reassured her tutor. She would take it upon herself to fetch the remedy to Skerryvore.

'You've been writing and have come for criticism, I suppose?' Louis said.

'Yes; only I have done something so horrible I ought to be hanged on the spot. Pray do not be too severe.'

He played the game with a frowning face and tossed his cigarette butt into a bush. 'Come and be dealt with this minute,' he said, clasping Adelaide's hand and leading her captive all the way to the drawing room. 'Sit on the divan, Miss Boodle, and I'll be your judge and advocate in one.'

Their lips trembled with suppressed laughter, but neither wavered from the game.

'And now,' Louis commanded, 'unburden your conscience.' Daintily, Adelaide unlaced her portfolio and drew out a sheet of paper. 'I have written the exercise you asked of me.'

'Good.' He revealed a small smile. 'And how'd you find it?'

'I know you warned me against it, yet I found it impossible not to use the word "however".' After a small silence she said, 'I find the word "however" a valuable refuge from dead monotony in a poor sentence.'

Louis got up and drummed with his fingers on the desk, an ominous sign. 'Your favourite refuge, indeed! Your favourite refuge!' His Scottish 'r's' suggested rumbles of thunder. He turned to Adelaide with a severe look. 'However, indeed! For-r-r-sake it, woman! For-r-r-r-sake it forever! It is a r-r-refuge of lies!'

Adelaide pursed her lips, then said, 'I was writing about a certain type of Englishman.'

'Yes, yes - example, please? Read aloud if you will.'

'This is what I have written.' She gave a small cough and began: '"The Englishman might have been any age between twenty-five and forty. In reality he was midway between the two; he was barely thirty-three. He was short rather than tall, robust, but inclined to stoutness. It was this thickness of build that gave him an older appearance than was warranted by his face."'

Louis eyes danced. 'A bit long winded, but we can improve it. Please continue.'

'"However,"' Adelaide said with bold emphasis, '"he bore about him a fiercely swaggering, martial sort of air, as of a man who has had many a tussle with fortune."'

Louis' legs swung impatiently in and out of the kneehole of the desk. 'Enough, stop there! And how might *that* be improved? If I were a dominie in Scotland with a stiff ruler, I would swish it across your dainty palm for punishment.'

'I know you hate the use of "however" . . . However, try as I might for a substitution, that is, to use "but" or "nevertheless" or some such . . .'

'These too are refuges,' Louis growled and slid off the desk. 'You must dismantle your work, shipwreck sentences, entire paragraphs if necessary, and reconstruct boldly without recourse to refuge.' He snatched the page and gave it a cursory look. 'There's no point in continuing today. Come back tomorrow and let me see you've been brave enough to tackle the dismantling. And your next task will be to write a description of a place, any place you choose.'

'Oh, I'm hopeless at description.'

'Then you must learn.'

Adelaide tied up her portfolio. 'When does the piano come?'

'Any day now. Mrs Stevenson and I fell out over it this morning. She doesn't want a piano in the house. Says we can't afford one. Insists it will distract me from slinging ink and earning dollars and, though cheques are due from Holt in New York and Chatto in London, they amount to less than twenty pounds and we have need of ten times that amount.'

He paced to the window. ''Tis as well you understand the trials of the author's life, Miss Boodle, since to be an author is your aim. I'm a typical example; I have grown to live too much in my work and too little in life. 'Tis the dollars do it; the world is too much with us. Whenever I think I would like to live a little, bills come posting through the door, and I'm forced to plunge my pen in the ink again.'

There was no sign of Fanny, though dark clouds had made a grim landscape of the garden and threatened rain. Adelaide sat still, an attentive audience at Louis' confessional. 'My wife,' he said, clouding the window with his breath, 'that powerful steam press I call the Vandegrifter likes to rule the roost - I run the risk of getting caught up in her every day. This morning, for example, my little finger got into a quarrel with the machine and my whole body and soul went through after it.'

'Mrs Stevenson is perhaps a little overwrought with too much to do these days?'

'Very likely - she does take on too much - and the Vandegrifter gets knocked up by our theatricals, too - we both suffer in the process, and I come out as limp as a lady's novel.'

Adelaide got to her feet and turned towards the door. 'I don't mean you,' Louis said, rushing to her side. 'You could never write anything limp - we'll get your fiercely swaggering Englishman jumping beyond the confines of your story in no time. Forgive your poor mentor who has been wrung out almost more than he can bear, to the point of insensitivity?'

'You are forgiven; but only if you will stop calling Mrs Stevenson by such horrid names as "the Vandegrifter". She is your *sine qua non* and fellow breadwinner, your mainstay and friend.'

Louis suppressed a cry. Fanny a breadwinner when only one fairy tale under her authorship had ever been published and she had been working at her latest short story for over a year?

'Tish, tish, lass,' he said, going with Adelaide into the hall. 'You're right to check me over my nicknames for Lady Skerryvore. Only, it grieves me that while we are all in all to each other, there are times we might murder each other.' He took Adelaide's hand and patted it as he spoke. 'I'm going ahead with the piano. It comes next week and you will teach me to play, and you can criticise my poor attempts to your heart's content. I'm fond of Scarlatti and Schumann and I'm determined to play something by one of them before my birthday in November.'

'How about *Träumerei* from Schumann's *Kinderszenen*?'

'"Dreaming" from *Scenes from Childhood*? Since I do that most days - dream about my childhood, I mean - it'll be the very ticket if I'm up to the task.'

They lingered, exchanging small talk, watching rain spatter against the fanlights of the porch, while Adelaide silently committed the details of the tutorial to her prodigious memory. She fumbled with the catch of her umbrella. Then Louis opened the porch door and Fanny fell into his arms.

He turned pale. 'Fetch Valentine, Miss Boodle. She's about to pass out! Bring water, smelling salts and a cold compress.' He manoeuvered Fanny to the divan and covered her with the tartan blanket. When the salts arrived, he supported her head with a trembling hand until, suddenly, she revived.

'You must rest Mrs Stevenson,' Adelaide said before she went sadly away.

Louis drew up a chair and reached for Fanny's hand. 'Stockdologored, wife?' (Often, they used the slang he had picked up in California to lighten a mood. 'Stockdologored' described how he himself frequently felt when hit by a blow of ill fate.) He hoped the word would make his wife smile, even a little. She attempted a smile. 'I sure overdid it this time and got chilled into the bargain. I was digging up bramble bushes at the most perfect place for your writing seat.'

'You must stop it at once,' Louis admonished. 'I'm more than content with the writing desks in the drawing room and my bedroom - and to write with a board on my knees in the porch or the garden is a further pleasure. I appreciate your kind intention, but a writing place on the slippery slopes of the chine is an unrealistic prospect, Dutch, unless you'd want it for yourself? Why didn't you set Beaucox to the digging?'

'He was already digging! Digging out the edging for the new paths.'

Louis laid the compress on Fanny's forehead. 'Well perhaps this *petit mal* will remind you, you're a pioneer in the Wild West no longer. You're Lady Skerryvore. How d'you feel now?'

'A bit better, though I thought you might kill me this morning after breakfast.'

'I thought the same about you.' Louis brought Fanny's hand to his lips. 'You've such small fingers, let me kiss your poor little boy's hand and let's put the dramatics behind us. I approach your stockade flying a white handkerchief on the end of a pole.'

Tears sprang in Fanny's eyes, 'Oh, my dear, my lovely boy,' she said, fanning her face with her hand. 'A truce. Yes, let us have a truce, and let us remember how fortunate we are to have both been well lately. We have so much to be grateful for - Skerryvore, the servants, good food in our bellies, and the prospect of writing best-sellers before us.'

'All that's true, wife. Our marriage may not have been made in heaven - in my view it's all the grittier for that – and, as you know, pearls need grit to grow inside oysters.'

Their wedding anniversary on the nineteenth of May prompted Louis to recall the first time he set eyes on Fanny. Having arranged to meet Bob at Chevillon's Inn in Grez-sur-Loing, he arrived one balmy autumn evening, a weary traveller, dusty and footsore. Pausing to look through the window at the lively gathering of artists seated round the *table d'hôte*, he had been riveted by his first sighting of Fanny Van de Grift. There she was, the beautiful American Bob had raved about in letters, leaning back in her chair, smoking and talking nineteen to the dozen, her feet propped insouciantly up on the dining table. She wore a fitted bohemian jacket with a red kerchief knotted at the throat. How, he wondered nervously, could he hope to impress such a sophisticate? When the answer arrived in a flash, he vaulted into the room over the inn's half-door to the uproarious delight of the diners.

How altered his Fanny was, he thought, staring a little sadly at a recent photograph, framed in silver on a side table. Here was his bohemian lover, his pistol packing pioneer, in her new role as the corseted lady who fusses over the drawing room, straightens antimacassars and piles of books, rearranges footstools and flowers until he contemplates pinning her to a chair. Yet he could only admire her ingenuity in putting together so fitting a costume for her role as Lady Skerryvore. Her hair is arranged in the fashionable Grecian-style, secured with a headband. Her Empire-style ivory gown is embroidered with flowers and butterflies. It amused him to think of her outfoxing the fiends in her fashionable getup.

Henry James was the only guest at the anniversary feast. His gift of a Venetian mirror was a perfect choice, since mirrors fascinated Louis. James had a collection of Venetian mirrors in his London home, as he explained to his hosts. In Renaissance Venice, the well-arranged cityscape and the well-ordered government could be read as mirror images, he said, just as he hoped his ordered life reflected the meticulous prose he struggled to write in his novels.

Louis poured chilled champagne into Edinburgh crystal glasses, fluted in the shape of thistles. They caught the firelight and chimed a lovely note after Henry James proposed a toast. Then, when they were settled, Louis said, 'It amazes and amuses us to look round at the contents of our suburban home.'

'Our decoration might seem simple and sparse, Mr James, but I prefer it that way,' Fanny put in. 'It's comforting to know we have a home of our own we can count on.' She drew James' attention to the garniture on the mantlepiece: the carved figure of St Cecilia Louis had bought in a curiosity shop to represent his love of music, flanked by large Japanese vases sent as a gift from Katherine de Mattos. 'Skerryvore does not look much like other people's houses, but it pleases me so much more than if it did. I have never had such a chance to revel in colour before.'

Louis glanced affectionately at James. 'The mirror you have given us will shine out in the midst of it all. My own love of mirrors stems in part from the thrill of finding them in dimly lit curiosity shops. In my terror tale "Markheim" for example, I describe such a shop by candlelight, beleaguered by flickering shadows and rich mirrors, some from Venice and Amsterdam, where the hero - soon to be villain - sees his face repeated and repeated - infinitely - until his own eyes meet and make his nerves jerk like a hooked fish. Do you remember the passage, Fanny?'

'I do indeed: "He was alone, but conscious of some presence; it was a faceless thing and yet with eyes to see with." Louis does terror well, Mr James.'

'Dostoievsky, I admit, has influenced me. Reading his *Insulted and Injured* and *Crime and Punishment* revealed to me thrilling possibilities for my own tales. You'll see what I mean when you read "The Body Snatcher, James, and "Markheim" is to be published before Christmas, but, alas, I'm too preoccupied with *Kidnapped* to come up with an idea for Longman.'

'I don't believe I can help you there, Stevenson. Tales of terror are not my cup of tea.'

'Not enough gaiety, eh?'

Henry dimpled at the jibe, 'I am more concerned with observing reality.'

'Then George Meredith would applaud you, for he remarks in his latest novel that observation is the most enduring of the pleasures of life.'

'Quite so. The conceits and deceits of American exiles in Italy supply me with inexhaustible material, though as I have hinted, *The Princess Casamassima* is a departure.'

Henry James had recently returned from a short visit to Broadway with John Singer Sargent. There, the American artist, Everett Millet, had rented a charming house for the summer that was always filled with guests. Broadway, one of the most picturesque Cotswold villages, was a magnet for Victorian artists and writers. That summer the illustrator Edwin Abbey, Sargent's Philadelphian friend, was among the Millet community. (Abbey was instrumental in arranging the Stevensons' visit to America in 1887.)

As James reported to Louis and Fanny, Broadway was 'wondrously diverting and the Millets have a Bolognese cook who creates divine evening meals. Sargent offers to paint everyone, the Millet children, Gosse, Gosse's daughter. Gosse and Sargent are bosom buddies. Sargent and I often walk out into the countryside together, though we don't progress any great distance due to the weakness of my back that kept me out of the Civil War. I'm inclined to saunter rather than walk. We see every tortoise in England gliding past us and the wonder is Sargent stays as patient as he does with such a slow coach as myself.'

Fanny clapped her hands with delight. "Pon my soul. Tortoises!'

'I'd like fine to catch up with Gosse,' Louis said. 'He's a grand wit and a bonny talker. Gosse had a severe Darwin hating father; even more fanatical than my own if such a thing is possible. It amazes me that Gosse succeeds in holding together an impressive artistic network when he's so elusive himself.'

'Gosse is every bit as impressive as his network. I heard he gave Tennyson, Browning and Arnold as references when he applied for the post of Clark lecturer at Cambridge in 1883, and, of course, he's a close friend of Swinburne.'

'Of Meredith, too, and Leslie Stephen,' Louis said, staring thoughtfully into his glass. 'It was Stephen who first introduced me to Teddy Henley when he was lying in Edinburgh Royal Infirmary with necrosis of the bone.

That was a lifetime ago. Teddy had already had his left leg amputated below the knee, and was told his other foot was beyond cure until Joseph Lister's antiseptics stabilized his condition. We're all in Gosse's network, yet I wonder if we'll ever see him here at Skerryvore?'

'Did you notice, Mr James, we have hung up photographs of Louis' friends, Mr Henley and Mr Colvin? You have met them, I suppose?'

'I have, Mam, though I can't claim to have exchanged more than a greeting with Mr Henley at the Club.'

'Henley, he of the peg leg, was the inspiration for Long John Silver in *Treasure Island* - that is in appearance, not in character. Teddy is not a criminal,' Louis said. 'As for Sydney, it amazes me that he's Slade Professor of Fine Art at Cambridge when he started out as not much more than a literary hack. You know, at forty he's only five years older than me but he might as well be sixty-five.'

James smiled. 'Colvin is of a serious disposition. I meet him from time to time at the Savile.'

'He will consult with me one day on Louis' biography.'

Louis rose to refill their glasses. 'Let's hope that day's a long time coming for I've books still to write. Did I tell you, James, Miss Boodle is to give me piano lessons? Mrs Stevenson is not in favour of the plan but music, methinks, makes a home.'

'Music is a closed book to me since I cannot sing a note or tell one tune from another. I tell Louis that the last thing he needs is to be distracted from writing, but he pays me no heed.'

'My wife's envious of my long fingers, James. They're ideal for playing the piano, whereas Fanny's are stubby as a boy's. But let us have a tour of the room, wife, since that is of greater interest to our guest than a discussion about what I may and may not be allowed into my life, or the length of our fingers.'

Early in their friendship, Louis realized that Henry James studied Fanny. She fascinated the novelist, and the novelist's fascination fascinated Louis. He had a hunch it concealed the deep distaste for his wife shared by the fiends and members of the Savile. On the other hand, he was well aware that he occupied a special place in the Prince's heart wherein anything would be readily forgiven.

He imagined how Henry might slip Fanny into some future novel: *a short fat wheedling person with a moustache that was not a happy feature . . . a monkey in a spangled petticoat.* The 'two Fanny's' - the paramour he had fallen in love with and the matron she had become by 1885 - the 'Odalisque and the barrel organ monkey' - were ripe for characterisation in a story of his own.

Fanny had arranged a centerpiece of yellow roses on the table to complement their blue and white Staffordshire china. When Henry James wondered why he was the only guest, Fanny was ready with her reply. 'A friend such as yourself is worth more to us than the company of ten lesser mortals.' She had planned 'an American meal' to mark their marriage in California, and seated herself at the head of the table, determined to preside. Here was an opportunity to make herself heard above the male *basso continuo* that always threatened to drown her out. She lost no time in embarking on the memories anniversaries inevitably encourage.

Louis, she said, had to be smartened up for their wedding. Serious illness after he arrived in California had made him extremely thin, and his clothes were 'fit for the garbage can'. She insisted on the removal of his 'disgusting teeth - truly they smelled vile' and their replacement with false ones. It was strange that she neglected her own teeth, Louis said mischievously, but Fanny ignored him. 'I feel sorry for the poor who lose their teeth and thereby their digestion, Mr James. Teeth are the last thing they can afford to replace.'

Agnes served clam chowder from the Staffordshire tureen and, when Henry James expressed his surprise, Fanny said clams were easy to procure from stalls near the Bournemouth Pier. Then he must hear how Fanny's divorce from Sam Osbourne Senior had come through six months before Louis arrived, thus paving the way for their marriage. She and Louis had been living in East Oakland with her sister Nellie, son Sam, daughter Belle and assorted cats, dogs and horses.

'I arrived, a broken down Scotsman, and soon fell ill. I lay in a fever, coughing blood, fearing my congenital doom had come upon me. My forebears suffered from consumption. Then, as soon as I was fit, I moved into a room of my own in San Francisco and got down to work. It wasn't far from my obligations, mind you, that is, Fanny, Nellie, the children and the animals.

He had been writing a travel book, *The Amateur Immigrant*, and an essay on Thoreau for *Cornhill's*, when he fell ill again and Fanny fetched him back to the cottage at East Oakland. The news travelled swiftly and *The Glasgow Herald* reported, 'Mr Stevenson is lying seriously ill in America.' During his recovery, he planned new projects in the pretty cottage garden and, when his spirits and energy revived, he wrote a counterblast to Henry James' essay about Nathaniel Hawthorne.

'That was the first time I'd ever heard of you, James,' Louis smiled. 'I never expected to meet you, let alone have you as a guest at our table.'

They laughed over that, and Mrs Watts came in with a roasted ham spiked with cloves. Valentine followed pushing a recently acquired dinner wagon laden with dishes of roasted sweet potatoes, green vegetables, sour cream and American biscuits.

'I take *The Lancet,* Mr James, and have been reading about a diet sweeping England,' Fanny said. 'A chewing diet, reported to benefit the digestion. You must chew each mouthful thirty times to liquify the food before swallowing. Louis and I mean to practise it, but keep putting it off.'

Louis gave her an indulgent smile. 'And now is hardly the time for it, wife.'

He filled their glasses with a fine Sancerre. 'Let's return to our wedding day when we took the ferry across San Francisco Bay to the house of William Scott, the Presbyterian minister on Post Street. There, in that house, the twenty-nine-year-old groom and the forty-year-old widow, as my wife-to-be described herself on the marriage certificate, pledged their troth and placed wedding rings on each other's fingers'. Fanny dabbed her mouth with her napkin. 'I don't know what came over me, saying I was a widow rather than a divorcée.'

'Well, wife, it was understandable enough. No wonder thoughts of widowhood confused your mind at the time. There you were, newly divorced from Sam Osbourne with my poor skeletal self almost certain to die in your arms. Giuseppe Verdi could have composed an opera from our story. We were shipwrecked emotionally; ours was a marriage *in extremis* if ever there was one. Only your tender care revived me from a mere complication of cough and bones and transformed me into a bridegroom.' With glistening eyes Louis rose, glass in hand, to recite 'a verse from a poem I wrote for Fanny called "My Wife"':

Trusty, dusky, vivid, true,
With eyes of gold and bramble-dew,
Steel-true and blade straight,
The great artificer
Made my mate

A hush fell when Louis leaned over to kiss Fanny's cheek. Henry James observed.

Then Fanny was off recounting their honeymoon at Silverado. James said he had already read Louis' account in *The Silverado Squatters*, but she continued, undeterred.

'We had planned to settle at a ranch in virgin forest somewhere. That was our dream. Instead we were diverted to Silverado.'

'For the sake of adventure,' Louis put in.

'It was a totally unsuitable dump, knee deep in rubble and poison oak,' Fanny protested. 'A precipitous path led to the old mine where there were eighteen wooden bunk beds set in tiers and a platform running round the place with view of the Napa valley below.'

'Aye, it was a dump, to be sure, but I saw the chance to get a good story out of it,' Louis said, attacking his American meal with gusto.

'The surrounding ground was so muddy it was impossible to walk around the old mine. We had to keep to the platform, day in, day out.'

'Don't forget to mention we had Sam with us, Fanny - he was eleven at the time – as well as a dog. I often wonder what happened to that shaggy old creature.'

They talked of this and that until the light began to fade and, at Fanny's request, Valentine lit the gas lamps.

Before he departed, Henry James broke the news that he would have to return to London in July, and Louis' heart sank a little until a verse arranged itself in his mind. Not a very good one, but one that might be improved, and it gave him hope: despite Henry's impending departure, their friendship was bound to continue.

Now with an outlandish grace,
To the sparkling fire I face
In the blue room at Skerryvore;
And I wait until the door
Open, and the Prince of Men,
Henry James, shall come again.

A distraction lay on the horizon for them, too, Fanny said. Louis was well enough to travel and they were to be guests of Sidney Colvin and Frances Sitwell at Cambridge, with a few days in London en route. Louis' spirits rose at the thought of revisiting the Savile Club from which Fanny was barred. Fanny said she was looking forward to visiting Mr Dew-Smith's Cambridge studio where they had arranged to be photographed. Dew-Smith was the photographer of choice for the discerning of the land, she said.

When he heard about the Cambridge visit, it was Henry James' turn to feel disappointment. He had come to rely on the honeyed bubbles of communion with Louis that salved his anxiety about work in progress, fluctuating finances, and Alice's failing health.

'How I shall fill my days in your absence, Stevenson, I simply do not know.'

The American novelist marked his Bournemouth territory like a genial panther. Familiar haunts such as his lodgings, a favourite café near the Pier, Alice's townhouse, Skerryvore, and the tobacconist shop, formed the secure framework within which he tolerated long solitary hours wrestling with his art. He had noted R.L.S.'s penchant for rolling cigarettes with *Papier Persan*, and he called at the tobacconist's to get some as a gift. That very morning his landlord had handed him a telegram: *London damp and tiring, am returning to Skerryvore 9th June. RLS.*

The air was balmy and the sea so Mediterranean-blue it transported Henry James to his beloved Italy. Bournemouth struck him as almost American in its newness and ugliness, yet it did have saving graces. The expansive sea views to the Isle of Wight were particularly impressive. He selected a marble-topped table out of the direct glare of the sun and ordered a coffee to sip while he wrote a letter. When his visit to Alice could be put off no longer, he strolled through the Pleasure Gardens and paused at the flower stall to choose for his sister a bunch of white freesias, fresh from the Isles of Scilly. Then, irritated to find himself progressing uphill in time to the Italian Band's rendition of 'La Donna è Mobile', he quickened his step until he was well beyond its hearing.

Alice had scarcely got out of bed since her arrival in Bournemouth and Henry salved his anxiety with regular visits. Every visitor was a welcome object of fascination to his sister, much as moths and butterflies are to a lepidopterist. One afternoon, at Alice's request, he had taken the Stevensons in a hansom to meet her. Mrs Stevenson was decidedly a moth in Alice's view, and Louis, of course, a butterfly. After their visit, Alice declared Robert Louis Stevenson, though more than a little eccentric, almost her brother's intellectual equal. However, she never missed an opportunity to reiterate her low opinion of Louis' wife and Henry had to tread carefully lest Alice fuel his own ardour on the subject. Being attentive to Mrs Stevenson was the key to being admitted to Louis' company, as he well knew. Fanny Stevenson was, to be sure, a poor, barbarous and merely instinctive person who had raised herself up in the world by her association with Louis. He did not go so far as his sister, though, who held that Mrs Stevenson was positively simian and gave the strangest feeling of being in the presence of an unclothed being.

Henry raised the knocker on the painted black door of Alice's townhouse and braced himself before he let it fall. She always asked for news of the Stevensons, yet in their absence there had been nothing to report. Within the hour, having found Alice cheerful and in reasonable health, he found himself walking towards Alum Chine Road. Had Louis come down on an early train?

At Skerryvore, broody birds cooed in their cot, some of them pigeons, others doves, but otherwise the house was veiled in a silence never achieved when Louis was at home. Louis' presence had the effect of making everything gay. There was no sign of the servants either, so he proceeded to the end of the hushed garden and sat gratefully on one of the chairs, plotting his next visit to Broadway. Surely there was a way to take Louis with him? Stevenson would fit the company there like a velvet glove on an elegant hand, and it would do him the power of good. In spirit R.L.S. was one of them - Sargent, Gosse, Millet and the others - all alike in feisty demonstrations of their love of life, whatever its risks and trials. Yet it was no good. He could never hope to prise Louis from his wife's solicitous arms, and if she were to appear at Broadway the atmosphere was bound to lose much of its levity.

He sat back, tuning into the birdsong of the chine, and only a sudden pang of hunger prevented him from dozing off. A restaurant he knew in Westbourne teased his imagination. Fish and chips with mushy peas would serve well for luncheon. Then, suddenly, when the Skerryvore gates squeaked, he turned to see who would appear. Soon a young woman came towards him across the grass. She wore a dress of yellow and blue stripes, almost ankle length, with white stockings and shoes. Her auburn hair was emphasised by a fringe of kiss curls glowing above a sweet narrow face, and, for a second, he imagined he saw a heroine from one of his novels. When she drew closer he observed that her finely chiselled nose gave her an air of intelligent questing.

'Halloo!' Adelaide Boodle called out. 'Have you come to find the Stevensons? They are not at home, but can I help you? I am their gamekeeper in their absence. The servants are all away until this evening when Mr Stevenson comes back.'

With a degree of bluster they introduced themselves. 'It may not be proper, but there is no one else to do it,' Adelaide smiled, 'and besides we are both practically family here at Skerryvore. Mr Stevenson talks about you all the time. When they're not at home I look after the place, shoo rabbits away, keep an eye on sundry cats straying in off Alum Chine Road, feed the doves, that sort of thing. It's why they've called me their gamekeeper. To be honest, this is the first time I've played the role.'

Henry returned her smile. 'They speak of you too, Miss Boodle, and I'm delighted to make your acquaintance. I was about to go off and find lunch, but won't you sit a few minutes?'

Adelaide lost no time in confiding that meeting the Stevensons had been the best thing that had ever happened to her. 'For me everything at Skerryvore, except actual study, which is always in deadly earnest, resembles some transcendent game. Sometimes I feel our glorious friendship is too good to be true and might come to a sudden horrible end. To be welcomed into the Stevensons' magic circle is to be lifted out of the rut of ordinary things.' Adelaide spoke passionately, now and again catching the eye of her unexpected companion. 'Do you not agree, Mr James? To serve them in any capacity is to don a sort of magic livery, visible only to their eyes and one's own.'

'Well, yes; certainly they are unlike any other of my friends. And are you finding Mr Stevenson a suitable tutor? He has told me you mean to be an author.'

'Oh, I don't always get Mr Stevenson,' Adelaide said. 'Sometimes my work is first assessed by Mrs Stevenson, to see if it's worth passing to her husband. At other times he comes to fetch me from his wife's tutelage and claim me for his own.'

Henry was fascinated by this glimpse of life behind the façade of Skerryvore. 'And how does Mr Stevenson go about teaching you?'

'Oh, he gives me little exercises in the formation of style. He points out landmarks to help me to take my bearings if I find myself lost in a featureless desert of words. Mr Stevenson's rule number one is, never let a long sentence get out of hand; if it does tie it in a knot with a good strong inversion and swing it round on a pivot. He tells me David Hume is my finest model for study, and also well-written French books. The French are masters, he says, in the art of inversion and delicate balance. He reverts to Scots when the mere mention is made of Scotland, Mr James, or when he gets irritated or carried away by emotion. And French; a great deal of French is spoken in the house particularly by Valentine, though her English is not too bad.'

'What other advice does your tutor offer?'

'Rule number two, R.L.S says from his pulpit, don't work a simile backwards. Number three: don't bother your head about English grammar. Mr Stevenson says grammar is a poor study at best and that my fair grounding in Latin and French will serve me better in the formation of style. Number four: read every sentence aloud. Nothing my own ear is dissatisfied with must be allowed to stand. And, finally, number five: in dialogue never let the vulgar craze for realistic writing run away with you. Mr Stevenson holds that the highest art demands that while remaining true to the spirit of a speaker you should sift his language in your mind before committing it to paper and better it.'

'And what of Mrs Stevenson's teaching?'

'Oh, Mrs Stevenson is the soul of kindness, and her skill in all sorts of handicraft is far above the average.'

'And in writing?'

'Her criticism of my work is both ruthless and merciful, and she has an inspiring way of taking it for granted that even the best work one is capable of can generally, with thought and patience, be made infinitely better. Mrs Stevenson, though a brilliant talker, shines even more as a listener. To begin with, she shielded me from her husband until it was felt I could withstand the full blast of his criticism and not be killed outright.'

Here was a different slant on the character of Fanny Stevenson, Henry thought. Perhaps he had judged her too harshly? The soul of kindness. Was it possible that an altogether more endearing creature lurked beneath her bulwarks?

'On rare and enchanting occasions, Mr Stevenson comes into the room to read aloud some work of his own for his wife's immediate criticism. Last month he was reading to us an adventure story for boys, and I was encouraged to listen with pricked-up ears and even to ask questions of my own.'

When Adelaide fell silent, Henry observed a blush

stealing across her flawless cheeks. 'I confess I have read nothing of your work, Mr James,' she said at last, 'though I am eager to do so.'

'Then you shall. When I call on Mr Stevenson this evening I shall leave an autographed copy of *The Portrait of a Lady* on condition that you promise to reward me with your honest opinion of my effort.' He rose and consulted his pocket watch. 'Lunch calls, Miss Boodle, and I must be on my way. Will you walk me to the gate in your capacity as Gamekeeper of Skerryvore?'

When Henry James returned to Skerryvore that evening he found Louis engrossed in *Far from the Madding Crowd*.

'I'm reading it again in preparation for a visit to Hardy. After all, Dorset, where the man lives, is not far away; its border rubs shoulders with Hampshire at the head of Alum Chine.

'The novel's little short of a masterpiece. In my view, the man's a genius for making his characters live passionately on the page, and for creating suspense, and for depicting truthfully the ways of country folk, from the humblest shepherd to the owner of the manor. In this case, the owner is a lady who rejoices in the name of Bathsheba, and there's a character called Gabriel, too. Like me, Hardy knows his Bible from childhood drillings. He has wise things to say such as "we keep our secret knowledge of ourselves to ourselves." I intend to make Hardy's acquaintance this very summer.'

II

I am well in health, but not up to much intellectual effort; this last collapse was alarmingly complete; it even affected my conversation; this is not fancy - others observed it . . .
Robert Louis Stevenson to W.E. Henley, June 1885

The Mysterious Valentine

Louis wakened from his afternoon nap with the smell of Scotland in his nostrils: briny rocks, seaweed and tides mingled with the wild thyme, clover and grasses of his beloved Pentland Hills. Then he realized it was all in his imagination. The scents borne on a gentle breeze through the slightly open window of his room were Bournemouth scents of pine and sea. He got up to find his favourite red tie, his thoughts tinged with longing and sadness. His uncertain health prevented him from living in the *meteorological purgatory* of his beloved homeland. But, as he hoisted the knot of the tie to his throat and decisively got into his black velvet jacket, his mouth curved. If he couldn't have the sights and sensations of his native land, he would give them in abundance to the hero of his book. Now that David Balfour's feet were set firmly on Mull, he'd keep the lad out-of-doors for days on end, doing things he could never have done, even as a much younger man. Alan Breck was about jump back into the adventure, having survived the shipwreck of the *Covenant*. Now he would have Davie and the Pretender's chevalier hiding from the English troops behind rocky outcrops under the blazing sun. They would tramp the heather in chilly downpours, wander through sylvan woods of birch and pine, sleep rough at night with nothing but their woven cloaks for cover.

He pulled hard on the bell to get some tea and, seeing *La Bello*, felt a pang of disappointment. He had forgotten it was Valentine's day off. 'I'll take tea up here, Aggie,' he said. 'Are there scones today? I'll have them with cream and jam. After that, I'm not to be disturbed until supper time.'

Not a mile away, over on the Poole Road, Adelaide Boodle had asked her mother and sisters to leave her undisturbed in the parlour. Jane Austen was her model who had fended off her family half a century earlier in order to write novels in a similar small parlour. Entranced by her new friends, R.L.S. and Mrs Stevenson, Miss Boodle intended to capture their life in 'Flashlights from Skerryvore', essays written in the finest prose she could muster.

'There never was, and there never will be, another place like Skerryvore,' she wrote. 'Think of it under what aspect you will, that little home is wholly unlike any other. One of the villas innumerable that have laid waste all the poetry of Bournemouth, yet there is something about it which catches and holds one's imagination.'

Her 'Flashlights' would record visits to be tutored by the couple, or simply to sit at their feet. Whenever she imagined showing the Stevensons her essays at some future date, she felt the thrill of excitement that drove her on.

'Perhaps it was the little vane over the empty stables

that drew every possible ray of sunshine and flashed it kindly back upon the passers-by; perhaps it was the voice of the doves, filling the chimneys with their murmuring; perhaps it was the rich glow of the foreign-looking hydrangeas that prospered in such a surprising way in their shady corner near the entrance. These things were all to be seen at a glance from the road; the gateway once passed, the charm of the place took one's heart by storm.'

Mrs Boodle arrived to request her daughter's company during afternoon tea. The ritual must be borne. While her mother and sisters related the neighbourhood news, Adelaide considered how she might continue the 'Flashlight' she had concealed for safety's sake under a pile of magazines. As soon as the maid had cleared away the tea-things, she scurried back to her desk to write up her first meeting with the Stevensons and Valentine Roch.

'After some persuasion, my mother accompanied me to Skerryvore. Valentine (by some inspired mistake, as we afterwards learnt, for she had been charged to admit no living creature that afternoon) ushered us into a carpetless room, bestrewn with packing cases and straw. There R.L.S. and his wife, in happy security, were overhauling treasures to furnish the new home. Both were curiously clad. He had on the velvet coat and dark red tie that have become to many of us like a part of his actual personality; her garment was a mysterious looking overall (really, I believe, a painting-apron) admirably adapted to her needs at that moment. There was but one chair in the room. This was offered to my mother; my first resting-place in Skerryvore was a packing case.

'Valentine is an interesting creature. Wednesday is her afternoon off, and last week she went into Bournemouth to wander round the shops. A true Frenchwoman, she spied a sale at one of the few original shops still surviving in Bournemouth. There she had bought a very becoming jersey, such as fisher folk wear. Having made her choice, she was leaving the showroom when a lady entered, well known to the firm and a privileged customer. Valentine's choice, lying at the top of a pile, arrested her prompt attention. The lady pounced upon it with the eager exclamation that it was exactly what she was looking for.

"'That one,' said the attendant, "has been sold, and there is not another of the same pattern." Then, apparently, they tried hard to persuade Valentine to accept a substitute. But no; she knew what she wanted, stuck to her bargain, gave her name and address so that they might deliver her jersey and came galumphing back to Skerryvore.

'It chanced that I was there, having a tutorial with Mrs Stevenson, when the parcel arrived. We were working upstairs in Mrs Stevenson's room, to avoid, as we fondly hoped, any interruption by visitors. The door burst open and Valentine, aflame with righteous anger, broke in upon us and blurted out her tale. They had sent an altogether different jersey. "It is not what I chose.

Madame! I will not have it!" Valentine exclaimed. Madame looked up dreamily. "I cannot for the moment give you my attention, Valentine," she replied. "Go to Mr Louis and he will settle it for you."

'Like a whirlwind Valentine was gone, leaving Madame unruffled. But our work had not made much progress when a yet more impetuous entrance startled us. R.L.S. darted into the room brandishing in his hand a sheet of notepaper. "Listen to this," he cried imperiously. "It is a gem of literature!"

'He then declaimed, rather than read, a note addressed to the defaulting firm, a note which, as he joyously assured us, would infallibly bring the sinners to their knees. Alas! he was in such a ferment to dispatch it at once that I had no chance to transcribe it as a model for letter writing into my notebook. It was to go, he said, without a moment's delay; and Agnes went tearing off to the shop with such orders as to speed as Ariel himself might have found it hard to obey.

'Work was over for that afternoon, and while we awaited developments, R.L.S. and I consoled ourselves downstairs at the piano. Our suspense was of the briefest. R.L.S.'s ephemeral note worked like a talisman. Back came Valentine's jersey by express messenger, and with it the *amende honorable* which the conscience of the firm impelled them to offer.'

Valentine Roch flits through the rooms of Skerryvore, a mystifying yet omnipresent figure, and, by Robert Louis

Stevenson's admission, *very pretty*. A French-Swiss country girl. A photograph taken with the Stevensons after they arrived in America in 1887 shows her wearing a high-collared dark dress and white apron. To gaze at her image through a magnifying glass is to conjure up secrets from her almond shaped eyes, deep-set and serious under knowing arched eyebrows. Valentine was very pretty indeed, perhaps even a seductress. She was certainly a breath of youth at Skerryvore where, as Louis observed, Fanny often *sat and gloomed*.

Valentine had been in the Stevensons' service for two years before they came to Bournemouth. In France, although she had been hired as Fanny's maid, she had taken on nursing duties when Louis fell ill. At Skerryvore she was proving indispensable as the senior servant of the household. Louis' unease over employing servants was mollified by his *somewhat feudal view of our relation to servants*, as he wrote to his mother. This 'feudal' approach was practised in well-to-do households in Victorian Scotland where servants were treated as extended family. Louis' nursemaid, Alison Cunningham, enjoyed such status at Heriot Row. Now his elderly nurse was ministering to Sam Osbourne who had taken Louis' place as the surrogate son of the house. Valentine, though considerably younger than the legendary 'Cummy', wore the old Scotswoman's mantle at Skerryvore as companion, nursemaid and favoured servant of Robert Louis Stevenson.

When his mother suggested sending another maid to

Skerryvore, Louis rose to Valentine's defence: *Valentine has had the upper hand in our house, has done well by us, and is doing better; and I would not put her in a second place . . .The nemesis of the Bourgeois, who has chosen to shut out his servants - his 'family' in the old Scotch sense - from all intimacy and share in the pleasures of the house, attends us at every turn. An impossible relation is created and brings confusion to all.* The proposed maid never arrived.

Valentine Roch enjoyed the intimacy Louis referred to, but how far did it go? He had always felt more at ease with women of 'lower birth' (like Fanny and Valentine) than with 'well-bred' young women he met in Edinburgh's drawing rooms. And it is common knowledge that Louis 'frequented' prostitutes during his Edinburgh youth, and probably fathered a child by one of them. Intriguingly, Thomas Stevenson founded a Magdalen Mission for 'fallen women' in Edinburgh and supported it financially all his life. 'Was this a gesture of general philanthropy or some private effort at atonement for real or imagined crimes against women - his own, or those of his sex in general?' asks Robert Louis Stevenson's biographer, Claire Harman. 'Thomas's interpretation of chivalry did not lie anywhere on the usual axis between protectiveness towards women and the will to dominate them, but had a neurotic, slightly masochistic edge. It was taken on almost wholesale by his son.'

The truth about Louis' relationship with Valentine during the Skerryvore years remains undiscoverable in its well-sealed lair. There are only hints and guesses. There is the 1887 photograph, showing Valentine and another servant flanking the Stevenson party - Louis, Fanny and Sam, wearing furs and greatcoats against the New England winter. There are occasional references to Valentine in the Stevensons' letters and in Adelaide Boodle's 'Flashlights'. Margaret Mackay claims in *The Violent Friend*: 'A scandalous rumour arose in California because Fanny had written to friends that, when she was away, Valentine slept by the fire in Louis' room to be on guard against haemorrhages. After the story got round Bournemouth neighbourhood gossips claimed Valentine was the author's mistress.'

'Of course all the young women she knows believe there is only one interpretation of such behaviour,' Fanny wrote, apparently unconcerned. This can be read as perversity on Fanny's part, but it also reveals the lengths to which she was prepared to go to protect her husband: *My poor Valentine gives not only all her time and thought to Louis, but her reputation also . . . when I am away, if Louis is ill, or shows any signs of being ill, she sleeps on the hearth rug before the fire in his room, so that if a hemorrage* [Fanny's spelling] *takes place no time is lost . . . Once, I am sure, Louis was saved a serious hemorrage, if not worse, by her being there.*

Before she met Louis, Fanny Van de Grift led a sexually uninhibited life with several lovers and conquests. She had flirted with Bob Stevenson at Grez-sur-Loing, but it is unlikely they had time to develop a sexual relationship before Louis arrived on the scene.

From Skerryvore, Fanny wrote of Valentine, 'Though she is a French girl, she is as stiff a Puritan as ever lived.' Yet, several years later when they were sailing around Samoa, the 'stiff Puritan' was dismissed 'under a cloud'. Louis wrote to Charles Baxter that it had been *the usual tale of the maid on board the yacht*. Whatever interpretation is made of it, Fanny Stevenson's representation of her husband's relationship with Valentine, and her encouragement of their intimacy, seems willfully extraordinary. And it is telling that Fanny's relationship with Valentine deteriorated at Skerryvore even as she was nudging the maid into Louis' room. Sometimes maid and mistress were barely on speaking terms.

As a married man, Robert Louis Stevenson's strict moral code would have excluded extramarital relationships. But circumstances at Skerryvore were extraordinary. Fanny Stevenson had rewritten her job description; Louis' former paramour had become his literary adviser, homemaker - and sulky gaoler. The comely young Valentine was devoted to her master, who according to doctors was 'of a tubercular type' and thus likely to have been highly charged sexually.

In 1886 Valentine fell ill and was sent away to 'a farm'. The farm might well have been one of the 'baby farms' common in Victorian England, where illegitimate babies were born 'discreetly'. Pregnant women worked in the farmhouses and on the land before they gave birth, in exchange for their keep, a midwife to attend them, and adoption arrangements for their infants. If the farm was a 'baby farm', might Robert Louis Stevenson have been the father?

Looking ahead to a Thursday afternoon in 1886: Fanny is working with Beaucox in the chine, and Valentine is on duty. Louis asks her to bring up tea. 'Two cups, *s'il te plaît*, one for me and one for thee.'

He waits, leaning against the mantelpiece, rolling a cigarette. His eye catches sight of his favourite photograph of the bohemian Frances Van de Grift, feisty yet vulnerable. Taken in Paris soon after they met. While she was grand to cuddle up to on a cold night, nowadays Fanny's sheer bulk thwarted any ambition he had to satisfy her. Whenever they tried to couple, some phantom paralysed his futile attempts to function. Fanny forgave him in her way - he couldn't help it, she said, and, besides, they were soul mates on a plane far above the material world, and must settle for that. After years of frustration they had reached an accord: there would be kisses and cuddles, but beyond that, they must play solo parts. Fanny's lack of inhibition about this practise - where she came from pleasuring oneself was no crime - did little to reassure Louis. His infrequent solos filled him with irrational fears of eternal damnation. Guilt and pleasure were dodgy bedfellows. It grieved him that Fanny's irritability was, in no small measure, related to his inability to perform to her satisfaction.

When Valentine returns with the tea tray, he sees tears in her eyes and her hands covering her belly. He knows in a moment of fearful certainty, a life hangs trembling in the balance. He paces. 'Are you with child?' he says, and when Valentine nods and lowers her eyes, he's struck by several alarms. Who is the father? How would the Vandegrifter react? Would an abortion be necessary? Could they bring up the child at Skerryvore?

'Is the bairn mine?' he says, pacing.

Valentine sits uneasily on the edge of the bed. '*Non, non, peut-être, je ne sais pas.*'

'You've lain with someone since we came to Bournemouth?'

'*Oui, non,* I was lonely, and you did not call me to your room,' she whimpers. 'Madame will send me back to France. My parents will cut me off. I will end my days in the workhouse.'

Louis sits beside her and curves his thin arm round her shoulders. 'Madame couldn't do without you - why, who else could put up with her moods, who else could fix her hair or lace her stays? Nay, nay, *ma petite*, she will not send you back to France. She's got an awful temper but her heart's warm and I will protect you from the workhouse till my dying day.'

Valentine allows his hand to stray onto the mound of her belly, but when, after a small silence, he says, 'Could we not keep the child,' she flings it off like an angry cat. '*Tu es fou!* How can I be a mother and work in service?'

He staggers up to pour the tea. 'Here,' he says gently, 'drink this down, it'll do you good and so will the tears. There's nothing like a good weep at a time like this.'

Valentine reveals the hint of a smile and Louis says she must tell Madame right away. If she wants to stay at Skerryvore, she must not give rise to any suspicion that he might be the father of the child. 'But she *encouraged* us to . . .' Valentine says.

'I know. The Vandegrifter put temptation our way for the excitement of seeing if I'd fall for it, like God witnessing Adam's fall in the Garden of Eden. She wanted us to fall, and at the same time she didn't. My wife does not know what she wants.'

Valentine shivers. 'I am frightened.'

'Aye, that's natural. But it's usually wiser to confront a dilemma than flee from it. Tell Madame - but don't say you told me first, mind, she wouldn't like that - and when she comes to talk things over with me, I'll find a solution.'

Valentine dries her tears on a corner of her apron. 'We both need comfort, lass,' Louis soothes, determined in this hour of need to renew acquaintance with his friend sensuality. Prompted by Valentine's proximity, he was making a welcome comeback. He cradles her in his arms and they fall into a slumber on the bed until the sharp slam of the front door shatters their reverie.

'Get up, adjust your cap,' Louis urges. 'And remember, no *peut-être* or *je ne sais pas* when it comes to who's the father.'

Louis longed to be a father. When they lived at Hyères, he had been bitterly disappointed after Fanny had a 'false alarm', probably due to irregular menstrual periods at the onset of the menopause. Having mothered three children, the last thing Fanny wanted was to start again with a baby when she was over forty. After 'the scare', the Stevensons had been forced to conclude that ill health, relatively advanced age and poverty made them poor prospects as parents.

Even if she had connived in the possibility of Valentine's pregnancy, it would have been unthinkable to Fanny that Louis might father a child by the maid. Fanny's blind spots were glaringly obvious to everyone who knew her. She might even have victimized Valentine as no better than a common prostitute, in contrast to Louis' well-known sympathy for 'fallen women'.

'If you would only pause for one moment to consider all the depressing, demoralizing acts Valentine has to perform in our service, you might find it cause for wonder *not* that she has fallen, but that she is still as honest, kind and decent as she is,' he might well have said.

In August 1886 Louis wrote to Fanny in London: *We had Scott here; V. has just been moping; she is to have wine and tonics, and to go to a farm; no sign of disease anywhere; though Scott's opinion of her appearance at first was serious.* Arrangements were made to send Valentine to the farm. She was back in service by November.

News from Edinburgh

There were recipes to copy out from her treasured volume of Mrs Beeton, letters to write, and invitations to accept or decline as Fanny Stevenson saw fit. Old Faithful, chiming ten-thirty in the hall, emphasized how much there was to do before the morning vanished. The dining room - the *Blue* Room - simply must be finished before the summer visitors arrived. Fanny's inspiration was the Blue Room at Windsor Castle that had been Prince Albert's study until his death. She had seen it illustrated in magazines and read that Queen Victoria declared to the Nation, 'The Blue Room is not to be used again.' Shuttered up, it slumbered forlorn, whereas her own Blue Room would embrace the chatter and tinkle of dinner parties lit by the soft glow of twin candelabras.

The room was almost ready: the walnut sideboard on its massive carved pedestals, fitted with drawers and locked cabinets for silver and napery, and the dining table, large enough to accommodate the entire Stevenson clan plus one or two guests. A set of silver dishes Fanny intended to purchase would complete the scene, though she was inclined to agree with her favourite arbiter of taste that the best ornament for a dining room is a well-cooked dinner.

The House on the Chine

As she worked, Fanny must endure the racket from the drawing room next door. Adelaide was at her violin, Louis finger picking on the piano. She winced when, with inappropriate cheerfulness, he broke *alto voce* into the plaintive poem he had set to the tune of the *Skye Boat Song*:

Sing me a song of a lad that is gone,
Say, could that lad be I?

Bogue grunted, a somnolent heap of fur at her feet, and her mood softened. The little darling must be dreaming doggy dreams of chasing rabbits in the chine.

Merry of soul he sailed on that day
Over the sea to Skye.

Fanny held that her husband was sacrificing too much time at the altar of music when he should be at *Kidnapped*, or attending to the business of their lives together. This morning, after Louis had opened his post, she meant to pin him down with plans for the rest of the summer. As it was, the weeks were galloping away with no definite purpose.

Sing me a song of a lad that is gone . . .

Henry's mirror lay on its back at the centre of the table, a kaleidoscope playing with the sparkling glass chandelier hanging directly above it. It thrilled Fanny to imagine herself inside Henry James' London house, surrounded by his Venetian mirrors. Their bearded friend was such a feather in their cap. Lillie Langtry had the Prince of Wales and they had the Prince of *Men*, a distinguished fellow countryman. Perhaps it was her own American roots that drew him to Skerryvore so frequently? Unlike the snobbish fiends of Louis' English circle, Mr James - *Henry* - was truly refined and chivalrous.

Adelaide and Louis chorused - *All that was good, all that was fair, All that was me is gone* - before a profound silence indicated the end of the lesson.

Louis looked in. 'Just running upstairs to write a necessary epistle, Dutchwoman.'

'I need you here.'

'And I need time to execute a financial miracle.'

At his desk he wrote a swift note to his mother . . . *I gain flesh; but I am suffering from marine cachexia, which I used to call dry rot . . . I am in the necessity of begging . . . As you say, I fall always on my feet; but I am constrained to add that the best part of my legs seems to be my father* . . . He would get the letter off by the afternoon post. They were truly broke, and, yet again, Mr Tommy must bail them out. When time was on his side he would oblige his mother with a full explanation of *marine cachexia*, a disorder described by Dr Dobell in *Medical Aspects of Bournemouth*. This state of health - commonly seen at coastal towns, according to Dobell - was associated with digestive disorders and congestion of the liver. It fitted his symptoms, and it was a relief to have some idea of the cause. His digestive system was certainly out of sorts. Despite his jollity with Miss Boodle, he was not very well today. In fact, he felt like taking to his bed.

Fanny appeared in the doorway. 'Papa, I cannot wait

a minute longer. Come downstairs and attend to business *now*.'

He closed his inkwell with a snap of relief. He was in no mood to grapple with Davie Balfour, recently reunited with Alan Breck and on the run from the English army; he needed more energy to get the lad free of the Redcoats. He confessed as much to Fanny when they sat side-by-side at the dining table, his affectionate eyes signalling eagerness to please. He cut the air with the paper knife in a feisty demonstration of the sort of fray the hero of *Kidnapped* might soon be involved in, seeing off the Government troops.

Fanny handed him a cup of coffee and he studied the postmarks on his morning mail. 'All Edinburgh. From Baxter the lawyer, from mother, and - wait, what's this? - here's a letter, also Edinburgh, not from Fleeming Jenkin but from Mrs Jenkin.'

'It can only mean one thing,' Fanny said.

Louis went pale. 'Not Fleeming - I couldn't bear it!'

He scanned the letter then buried his face in his hands. 'He is dead. *Fleeming* has died when it should have been me. I who am *expected* to die.' He got up to pace the room, Bogue barking at his heels. 'Anne says he died suddenly after a *minor* operation - and dear Ferrier taken so recently, too - better and more loveable friends than these never existed - whereas I, worthless wretch, have been *expected* to die for donkey's years yet I linger on.' Bogue yelped when Louis gave him a sorrowful sideways kick and retreated to the safety of Fanny.

'Death has been a frequent visitor to the Jenkin family of late,' Fanny said. 'Anne Jenkin's mother was taken this time last year, and her father early in the New Year if I remember right. Then Fleeming's father shortly after, and his mother a few days after that. In February, I think it was. And now Anne has lost her husband. Terrible. So unfair. But do sit down, Lou, or you'll wear yourself out.'

'Poor Anne has lost everyone. Fleeming was only fifty-three. One of the last things he said when we met in Edinburgh was that bereavement had taught him to feel the goodness and support of God. That's all fine and dandy if you believe in God.' Louis paced from the door then back to the table, tugging a corner of his moustache. 'Fleeming's brainy correspondence with Darwin about *On the Origin of the Species* spawned his own version of Darwinism - and now Fleeming himself has been untimely felled by some bogey in his system Darwin might've called Natural Selection.'

Fanny studied Louis with anxious impatience. 'You must think about *your* health, Papa. Do not stress yourself unduly over a sad event you can do nothing about.' He strode towards the door, his eyes glittering with unshed tears. 'Send a telegram to Anne Jenkin offering our heartfelt sympathy and say we'll write soon? I'm going to lie down.'

'I'll bring up soup at lunchtime.'

'Let Valentine bring the soup. Please respect my need for solitude after this bitter news.'

He struggles out of his trousers and jacket, draws the curtains, and gets into bed. When he gives up summoning tears that refuse to come, he closes his eyes and there is Fleeming as vivid as he had been in Edinburgh last time they met. Fleeming's features are so distinct it gives him qualms. 'Come on, man, this life is a game for us to enjoy, and Hell take the hindmost,' Fleeming had said. Louis groans and pulls the covers over his head, too miserable to take up his friend's otherworldly challenge.

Rain patters on the window, soft southern English rain. Different from Edinburgh's *meteorological purgatory: snell, blae, nirly and scowthering.* He sees the words aligned on the page and feels their smarting kisses on his cheeks. Often, when he is ill or so upset he must lie on his bed, his imagination draws him home to Edinburgh. It is as if all the illnesses he has experienced since childhood have become inseparable from his visions of the Athens of the North where *the delicate die early, and I, as a survivor, among bleak winds and plumping rain, have been sometimes tempted to envy them their fate. For all who love shelter and the blessings of the sun, who hate dark weather and perpetual tilting against squalls, there could scarcely be found a more unhomely and harassing place of residence.*

Bournemouth rain patters on the window, comforting in its way - dependable rain, like the tears of heaven - and, from old boxes in the attic of his mind, scenes from his youth open up willy-nilly.

Days like great black blots on my memory.

Stage sets with Edinburgh for the backdrop.

Days living out my double life, the heavy metal of engineering crushing the life of my imagination.

Days of morbid melancholy, escaping into hashish or drink, hanging round Greyfriars churchyard for hours on end, sunk in the depth of wretchedness.

Louis pictures himself crouched like a tramp beside the old crypts and carved headstones, reading Baudelaire who, according to the orthodoxy of the Edinburgh establishment, would have corrupted St Paul himself.

Days of indulgence: intoxicating pleasures of imagination and flesh. Mary coming off her factory shift: coupling with her in Leith Walk's dark lanes before slinking away to charm prim-and-proper girls in New Town drawing rooms.

Days of terrifying entrapment at Heriot Row, days filled with ambivalence when I doubted my own sanity.

Edinburgh's architecture clashes in his mind. Its *barbaric displays of contrasts; Egyptian and Greek temples, Venetian palaces and Gothic spires, huddled one over another ... the brute mass of the Castle and the summit of Arthur's Seat ...*

He clutches his feather pillow for comfort, and remembers how Fleeming rescued him from despair almost two decades ago. Fleeming Jenkin, Professor of Engineering at Edinburgh University, had refused to give him the certificate of attendance he needed to pass his first year. Professor Jenkin had been right; his attendance at the science classes had been nil. And, though it was hard to see it at the time, Fleeming did him a great service. Failing the year paved the way for

Louis' confrontation with Thomas Stevenson that has haunted father and son ever since.

How is it that one incident in a man's past can seal itself so tightly in his brain it waits like a tick after blood for the first opportunity to haunt him again? Louis has in mind one evening after he returned from Erraid when his father proposed a stroll on the Braid Hills. They set off cheerily enough from Heriot Row. Father and son. How is it, that an hour or two in a human being's life can leave a bitter taste forever?

Lying on his feather bed at Skerryvore, Louis relives that episode; near the summit of the hill towards sunset, Thomas starts up a *tight cross-questioning* about my future.

Panting for breath, I climb behind him, my heart pounding at the cage of my ribs. The moment has come when I can, I will, I ought, I must tell the old blighter where to stick his lighthouses! I lean against a broken old fence and the floodgates open: why canna' you see ye'r flogging a deid horse that cares only for literature?

'Just a minute, young man,' cries Thomas. 'As I have said before, and say again, the devious and barren paths of literature are out of the question for a son of mine.'

'Listen to me, father! I've spent four years at the university and three summers on the lighthouse works, I've served time at a carpenter's shop, a brass foundry and a timber yard and still canna' tell one kind of wood from another, let alone make basic calculations.'

Thomas strikes the nearest bush with his cane. 'If it's not to be engineering you must follow another worthy profession like the law, or . . .'

Or I'll cut you off without a penny to your name. Is that what the old devil almost said? It was as if a bucket of icy water had been thrown over me. Father knew I couldn't survive if he cut me off. He had me trapped. Now I was to be kidnapped by the law.

We retreated home in silence.

With every haunting Louis feared his room might become transparent and reveal the wasps in the secret hive of his youth. Gradually though, kinder memories floated back: high-spirited appearances at the Speculative Club with Bob and his best friend at the time, Charles Baxter. *Let us be fools my friend, let us be drunken! Let us be angry and extremely silly!* had been their rallying cry.

At the club, and in the howffs of the Royal Mile, they chewed over everything from *Paradise Lost* to the effect of Covenanting persecution on the Scotch mindset. And of course, John Knox. Soon after his quarrel with Thomas, he had been invited into Fleeming Jenkin's social circle, an oasis in the desert of Edinburgh convention and prejudice. He threw himself into private theatricals organised by Fleeming and his bonny wife, Anne, at their home in Great Stuart Street. Anne Jenkin, charming and a little in love with him, had coaxed him through strenuous rehearsals, research and costume-making, in preparation for performances of the plays of Sheridan, Aeschylus, Charles Reade and others, all directed by Fleeming. Before long, Fleeming became his genial father substitute. An engineer like Thomas

Stevenson and a Christian, Fleeming also attended St Stephen's Church. Yet there the similarities between the men ended. Fleeming Jenkin's open-minded genius had replicated a phonograph similar to Edison's with only a report in *The Times* to go by, and it was Fleeming who had inspired Louis to study the new science of evolution spearheaded by Herbert Spencer and Charles Darwin.

'Ye have evolution on the brain, Louis,' Thomas the Rationalist jibed; 'I wish ye'd define what the word means.'

'Evolution is a continuous change from indefinite incoherent homogeneity to definite coherent heterogeneity of structure and function through successive differentiations and integrations.'

'I think, Louis, your friends Fleeming Jenkin, Mr Spencer, and Mr Darwin, must very skillful writers of polysyllabic nonsense,' said Thomas.

Louis woke up and saw a bowl of tomato soup on the bedside table. The soup was cold when he dipped his finger in it. He must have been asleep for some time. Then it hit him again - Fleeming was lying stone cold in an Edinburgh graveyard.

He shut his eyes to confirm his friend's presence in his mind. Sure enough, Fleeming was still there. Is my mind, then, a mirror for those I love? Louis wondered, struggling up to sit on the side of the bed. The swollen wellspring that had lurked inside him ever since he read Anne Jenkin's letter overwhelmed him. He might fall to the floor. His knuckles went white with the effort of anchoring himself to the mattress. He needed human company. 'Fanny,' he called out. 'Fanny!'

The sound of his voice calmed him a little, but when the silent house offered no response, he quivered on the brink of his bed until the fit passed over. He directed a spindle shank down a trouser leg, but the leg refused to leave the floor. He tossed the trousers aside and reached for his dressing gown. Fanny now bore the full force of his tetchiness: Where the devil's the woman got to? Oh, aye, it's stopped raining. She'll be out in the garden, enjoying herself wi' *le B'cox*, like Victoria and John Brown up at Balmoral, he thought waspishly. Then, with a frisson of remorse, he shuffled barefoot to the window and peered out through a gap in the curtains. There they were, tête-à-tête by the garden wall, Fanny leaning like a pet monkey against a spade, Beaucox holding out a plant for her inspection.

He half-opened the curtains and, hearing a noise in the hall below, 'Valentine,' he called, 'Valentine!' Her footsteps pattered up the stairs and when she put her head round the door, 'A cup of tea, *s'il te plâit*,' he said, 'and bring two cups and saucers.'

In respect of the memoir of Henry Charles Fleeming Jenkin, he decided, I will be the architect of his irrevocable past. And I'll mention his little-known correspondence with Charles Darwin after the publication of *On the Origin of Species*. By the time Valentine returned a page of notes lay on his desk.

Before dinner, Fanny arrived to find Louis whistling softly. She frowned down at him. 'Are you any better? One is afraid to open the post these days. Two cups on the tray? You took tea with Valentine?'

'I needed cheering with human company and you were occupied with Beaucox.'

'You do look better, though your eyes are overbright.'

'It's the shock of Fleeming's death.'

'If it brings on a relapse we'll send for the doctor.'

'I'm rather *disjaskit* but there's no sign of blood spitting,' Louis said dismissively. 'When I woke this morning I felt I was getting another cold but I don't need a doctor - if you fetch anyone let it be Scott, not Dobell - I've taken a fancy to Scott - and while you're at it, fetch my pen and paper - oh, and put up the wee bed table across my legs.'

Fanny sighed. 'Paper? Do you mean the manuscript of *Kidnapped*.'

'No, I don't. I want fresh paper. I've started a memoir of Fleeming, and Anne Jenkin needs a reply to her letter. I'm aiming to get Fleeming's obituary notice into the June edition of the *Academy*.'

'You're far too upset to write today, Papa. Have you forgotten, although you have been well these past days, you were not at all well the weeks before that, and now you show signs of being stockdologored again?'

He chuckled. 'You're a fine stubborn goose at telling me what's good for me and what's not. I'll get my implements myself.' Fanny made no reply, but she put up the bed table. 'Don't forget my bottle of ink,' he called when she made to leave the room. 'And come back and give your poor lad a kiss for comfort's sake.'

She did as bidden, then sat heavily on the bed. 'I fear the summer will be far too exciting for you. Don't you remember what the doctor said in Hyères last summer? For the next two years, no matter how well you feel, you must live the life of an invalid - if you are to see your fortieth birthday.'

'Aye, the doctor had some daft notion that if I reached forty I'd live to see ninety. Well, I'll be thirty-five this coming November. Not doing too badly, eh, old Dutch?'

Everyone went about on tiptoe after Fanny had a little talk with Valentine and Agnes. Hush, she said, is a requirement in every home where an invalid is being cared for.

'You must not make too much of this illness when you come into contact with Mr Louis, nor too little of it. He always fancies if too little is made of it people will think him an impostor. That said, please bear this in mind, he is unable to bear the least excitement when he is ill. He must be perfectly tranquil, trouble about nothing, have no shocks or surprises, not even pleasant ones. Must not eat too much, drink too much, laugh too much. For his sanity, he must work a little, talk very little, and he must never be crossed as anger is one of the worst things for him.'

The weather reflected the gloom inside the house with a show of persistent rain under pewter clouds. Louis lay burrowed into his pillows, damp hair clinging to his temples. Now and then he coughed and spat blood into a hanky. 'My speech is slurry, my vision blurry, and I'm in a hurry to find a cure,' he jested to Fanny who stayed close to her armoury of medicines. She placed a warm cloth on Louis' forehead and he gazed at her through narrowed eyes. 'I am *dim, dumb, dowdy and damnable*, wife. BJ means to get me.' Fanny stroked his forehead. 'Hush, my own, I beg you, lie still.' Louis smiled weakly. 'You're a fine seafaring woman married to *a somnolent son of a bedpost*. But, do not think me unhappy, wife; I have not been so for years.'

Agnes, tiptoeing into the room with a parcel, found them in a tearful embrace. Fanny tore off the wrapping and held up a maroon poncho. 'Someone of our acquaintance is anxious to replace your old red shawl,' she exclaimed and read the note pinned to the fabric. 'It's from your admirer, Lady Shelley. She invites us to Boscombe Manor.'

Louis inspected the garment. 'I like my old shawl better, but write a thankee note as my amanuensis, Dutch, and say we'll visit Boscombe as soon as I'm better.'

The following afternoon when Fanny was reading in the drawing room, Adelaide Boodle arrived. She held out a wickerwork basket covered with a rustic cloth. Fanny lifted a corner and clapped her hands, 'Louis must see it. Don't stay long, though. Remember the house motto: delight him but do not tire him.'

Louis, sitting upright against his pillows, played their game of severity. 'You're not expected until tomorrow,' he said darkly.

'I came early with a present for the household,' Adelaide said, passing him the basket. He lifted off the cloth and gave an amused start. 'Good God, I've never come so close to one before. What a queer marvel of nature, Miss Boodle - a hedgehog curled up asleep. Is it hibernating?' He ran his fingers lightly over the spines. 'Strangely soft, it must be a baby; but why have you brought it?'

'Why, for devouring the Skerryvore cockroaches.'

Louis looked baffled. 'But how does the wee thing get them?'

'Hedgehogs are *nocturnal*, Mr Stevenson. They wander around the kitchen during the night when the household's asleep and gobble up intruders. Hedgehogs are no trouble since they sleep all day. They're all the rage for clearing cockroaches in homes throughout the land.'

Fanny said beef tea was indispensable for invalids, and Louis tried a little while he waited for Dr Thomas Bodley Scott. He thought the doctor was *the very model for bedside manners*. Furthermore, Scott's prematurely balding pate and comfortable paunch brought to mind Henry

James' *old-world kindness of disposition.*

'Mrs Stevenson has filled me in,' Scott said, opening his medical bag and bringing out his stethoscope. Louis' skeletal torso rose and fell when he breathed deeply in and out. Fanny hovered, her eyes fixed to the stethoscope. 'Ever since we came to Bournemouth Louis has suffered from coughs, influenza and fevers, but there hasn't been much blood spitting,' she said. 'I thought by coming here we might leave all that behind, that he might be well.'

Scott kept silent until his examination was done. 'The lungs are a little congested, but I can find nothing seriously wrong.'

'Mrs Stevenson believes consumption is my condition,' Louis said. 'My parents and her son back this theory, though what a lad could know about medical matters is a mystery. The truth is, my family cannot bear uncertainty. They want the certainty of a definite diagnosis of consumption.'

'That is unfair and simply not true. Consumption is what we all dread,' Fanny said, taking a hanky from the night table. 'Have you forgotten how little Hervey died?'

Dr Scott frowned. 'It's unhelpful to dwell on a diagnosis when the treatment is what matters. Rest is the best medicine, Mr Stevenson. Rest will allow your condition to stabilize.' He wound up his rubber tubing and asked Fanny to show him the medicines she kept. Fanny wiped away hot tears for Hervey with her hanky and opened the cabinet.

'Well done, Mrs Stevenson, you have everything you need in the unlikely event of a severe haemorrhage when you can dissolve a grain of ergotine in water, inject two minims hypodermically, and send for me. As you probably know from past experience, the drug contracts the blood vessels and stops the bleeding.'

Fanny nodded. 'I did it in France. And laudanum for his cough?'

'Only if necessary, though it contains such a small percentage of opium, Mr Stevenson is unlikely to become a De Quincy.'

'I prefer tobacco to the poppy weed,' Louis said gruffly. 'I've dreams enough, and no need to induce them.'

Scott patted his shoulder. 'Work at your writing when you're able, but keep to your bed another few days and try to conserve your voice. You're fortunate to be in devoted and capable hands, but this wife of yours needs rest, too, and building up with iron and stout. We'll have you both fit as fiddles in no time and you might even entertain the idea of purchasing a tricycle, Stevenson, since gentle exercise would do you good when you're better.'

'Now there's a fanciful idea - me on a trike,' Louis laughed. 'Far better than walking with a stick, though, and I'd get further down the road.' Eagerly he turned to Fanny, 'write at once to the parents, they'll send one. They make grand bikes and trikes in Scotland.'

Keen to detain the doctor, Louis said he had read a

letter in the *Bournemouth Gazette* from a group of doctors concerned at the extent of tree felling by property developers in the town. 'A conflict of interests, indeed, Stevenson. As you know, our healing atmosphere depends on its unique mixture of sea breezes, pine essence and the dry air at the top of the chines, where, indeed, Skerryvore stands. The curative properties of pine trees in lung disease have been well known since ancient times. It is the reason you are here, and why I am here. I, too, am forced to live in an equable climate for my health's sake. It is ironic, is it not, that pine trees are felled to develop houses for new residents, many of whom suffer from lung disease, and yet the removal of the pines lessens the probability of their cure.'

After Scott's visit Fanny discussed with Mrs Watts the preparation of nourishing soups and light meals: broths of marrow bone and garden vegetables, omelettes, mashed potatoes, lemon sole with parsley, jellies and curds and whey for dessert. Watts sent Agnes to procure the ingredients. When his health improved, Fanny encouraged Louis to sit on the lug chair by the fire while she sat opposite, reading to him or crocheting. He enjoyed the sight of his wife at work, the white cotton spilling like snow down a hillside from her nimble fingers. One afternoon she tried to teach him to crochet, but several impossible tangles made him give up in frustration. 'The crochet hook's beyond me. It's the pen I'm born to wield - speaking of which, I have designs on a little activity. I mean to employ Boodle as my amanuensis - since I canna' play the piano 'till I'm well again, I'll dictate to her instead.'

'You mean to take up *Kidnapped?*'

Louis had no intention of 'taking up *Kidnapped*'. How could he when Fleeming's death had put inspiration to flight? Weary his body might be, yet a portion of his mind was sufficiently alert and cunning to write a memoir of his beloved friend. Admission of this would be like throwing a sparrow to Fanny's cat, so he let her believe *Kidnapped* was the target.

Fanny had ordered Valentine to stay downstairs and Louis fretted: his punishment for their little tea party. He missed Henry James, too, who must have gone to Broadway. When the front door bell rang sharply one morning, he hoped it would be the Prince before he heard the high, genteel voice of the parson and Fanny sending him away. He scribbled a note to Henry saying he was ill and had it delivered to his lodgings.

Fanny was far from well herself and took a little opium at bedtime for 'a woman's usual aches and pains'. Exhaustion, she claimed, was the cause of her stomach aches, and Louis was taken off-guard one morning when she sat on the edge of his bed and burst into tears. 'One can never count on *ordinary* days. If *you* are not ill, then it is I who am. If we are *both* reasonably well, then it is a friend who dies. I wanted an *ordinary* summer. A carefree, happy summer in our first real home together, when we might take a trip and visit friends and make literary acquaintances. We are invited to the Shelleys and must set a date when we're well, though us both being well at the same time seems an unlikely prospect, and *you* want to visit Thomas Hardy in Dorset. Meanwhile, they will all be *pouring* into Bournemouth, and will all arrive on the doorstep of Skerryvore.' Fanny wiped her tears on the mutton-leg sleeve of her purple silk blouse, recently purchased in London.

'They? *Who* will be pouring in?' Louis said handing her a hanky.

'You know perfectly well *who*. Sam is expected down from Edinburgh, followed a few days later by Mags and Tommy. Cousin Bob with his family, cousin Katherine with her daughter and Aunt Alan come shortly after them, and *you* want Henley and heaven alone knows who else.'

'Wheesht, old Dutchwoman, they don't *all* stay with us. Apart from the parents and young Sam, they'll have their own lodgings. Bob will keep Sam and I entertained with war games.'

'Sam has grown out of war games,' Fanny said sourly.

'Well, then, Sam will visit his chums in town, and I'll get Bob to decorate the hall with landscapes.'

Fanny's eyes sharpened with suspicion. 'What sort of landscapes?'

'You decide - it'll cheer up Bob to play the artist - he's facing a terrible time that recalls my own torment ten years ago when I was struggling against Mr Tommy to become a writer. Now our situations are reversed.

Bob has had to give up his dream of working as an artist to support his family. Remember, he doesn't have the backing we enjoy from Tom and Maggie. His own father's premature death left Aunt Alan, and Bob and Katherine, badly off for dollars. I mean to help by paying Bob handsomely for his work on the hall.'

Fanny was too overwrought to argue against the proposed mural that she judged herself capable of executing as skillfully as Bob. Katherine de Mattos and Bob had been Louis' favourite companions since childhood and, although this riled her to unreasonable jealousy, she had her own claim on Bob's past. Their flirtation had been heating up at Grez before Louis arrived. Occasionally she found herself wondering if she might have been better off with the healthy, impecunious Bob than the unhealthy, financially secure – albeit by proxy – Louis.

'We'll make the most of our visitors,' Louis said. 'We'll manage them all, Dutch, and take a trip or two, and make visits as well. And what do you say to a holiday at Dartmoor? We could call at Hardy's place in Dorchester on the way?'

The tricycle's arrival from Edinburgh encouraged Louis' dreams of cycling away from Skerryvore to experience, alone, the pleasures of central Bournemouth. A further gift came in the form of *A Canterbury Pilgrimage* sent by Joseph and Elizabeth Pennell. He had never met the authors, though he had long admired etchings by Mr

Pennell he had seen in various periodicals. Added to that, Lady Shelley had mentioned her high opinion of Elizabeth Pennell's book, *Mary Wollstonecraft Godwin*. The Pennells were a talented couple and Louis read their book at one sitting. When he turned to the dedication he felt so moved, he rang the bell for Fanny. 'The Pennells have been inspired by *Travels with a Donkey* to write their own travel book about a journey by *tricycle* of all things. What a coincidence, since my trike's just arrived from Scotland. Listen to the dedication, Fanny: *To Mr Robert Louis Stevenson, we, who are unknown to him, dedicate this record of one of our short journeys on a Tricycle, in gratitude for the happy hours we have spent travelling with him and his Donkey!*

Fanny's scrutinized the illustrations one by one. 'Its a handsome little volume and it gives me the idea that I could illustrate one of your stories in a similar manner.'

La Bello came in to help Fanny change Louis' bed linen. Then the girl cleaned his room until it smelled like a lavender field in the south of France. Everything was ready for Adelaide Boodle's arrival.

'All is at a standstill, Miss Boodle - my books are closed, my papers put aside, the voice, the eternal voice of R.L.S. has been well and truly silenced,' he said when she stood at his bedside. 'Are you ready to be the instrument for reviving my voice?' Adelaide nodded and said she was more than ready. 'Then sit on the chair, and we'll start without delay. You may learn much from taking dictation and you will discover no sentences beginning with "however".'

Louis and Fanny kept to their rooms until early evening when they cocooned themselves in tartan rugs beside the drawing room fire. Even in June, Agnes always lit the fire after the sun went off the house. Books stacked high on side tables vied with wonky piles of magazines for their attention. They were avid readers and wiled away the evening hours discussing the controversies of the day, sharing nuggets of news and gems of wisdom from the various publications they subscribed to. These included literary magazines put out by Scribner and Longman, *The Illustrated London News* and local newspapers, but Fanny's obsession with all aspects of human health inclined her to nominate *The Lancet* as the one periodical she simply could not do without.

'Fanny,' Louis said, looking up from the latest edition of *Atlantic Monthly*, 'you're glooming.' She glanced at him, her expression unchanged. 'I'm reading another report in *The Lancet* about Jean-Martin Charcot's latest research into hysteria and moral insanity at the Salpêtrière Hospital. I'm not so much glooming as thinking seriously about Charcot's work.'

'Ah, well, so long as you're not depressed.'

'I confess I am, a little. Sometimes I long to be in Paris, to be able to consult Charcot again about our little difficulties. There must be something he could teach us about controlling our terrible outbursts.'

'Tell you what; as soon as I'm up to a trip across the Channel, we'll go to Paris. We'll visit the great Rodin as well as Charcot. Henley's a pal of the sculptor and would be delighted to give us an introduction.'

'Rodin? That would be interesting, but, oh, to be in Charcot's milieu once more. I'll never forget the time we saw his live demonstration of hysterics - their paralyses, spasms and convulsions - and his celebrity hysteric, Blanche, in particular. They say Blanche has inspired paintings, sculptures, novels and newspaper articles.'

'It's a fascinating business, right enough, and I'm eager to learn more, for Charcot's interest in the subconscious - and his pupil Freud's for that matter - supports my first hand experience of my own divided self. As you know, the drugs I've had to take during my illnesses bring out the beast in me.'

'I know, dear. You can't help it, and if we could understand your experience better it might not seem so terrible.'

'I wonder if Charcot gives his hysterics drugs before he puts them on show in his public demonstrations?'

Fanny tut-tutted and rummaged in her sewing basket, 'surely not, Papa, since that would be against the ethics of the medical profession.'

'We'll never know the truth.' Louis shrugged then brightened. 'Tell you what, to cheer you up I'll read you the last chapter of *Diana of the Crossways*. I'm determined to finish it and return it to Sydenham's before the visitors descend. George Meredith's the one true genius of my acquaintance. I met him in 1877 at Burford where mother was holidaying. If Henry James would only stoop to do low life, Meredith might have a rival. I remember setting eyes on Meredith for the first time. He resembled a patriarch, I thought. At the time I was to-ing and fro-ing between Edinburgh and Paris, to visit Bob and, later, you yourself.'

Fanny nodded, her deft fingers threading beads onto muslin covers for her jam and pickle jars. She had read most of Meredith's novel, but not the last chapter. How would the exploits of Diana's sundry suitors, her flights between Ireland and England, and her struggle to become a novelist be resolved?

'It interests me that Meredith chose novel writing as the preoccupation of his strong-willed heroine. Perhaps he had George Eliot in mind?' Fanny said, and Louis replied that he hadn't the faintest idea. 'To be honest, I'm relieved that Diana's adventures are drawing to a close. Genius Meredith may be, but *Diana* has been a long-winded struggle to reach its conclusion.'

He read the last chapter aloud and, after a small silence, Fanny said, '*Diana's* not one of Meredith's best.'

Louis got up to pace the room. 'After I've made Hardy's acquaintance, I may reassess Meredith, since he goes all round the mulberry bush while Hardy cuts right to the chase. Hardy creates uncanny atmospheres and characters that *live* on the page by way of direct human speech. He recreates the dialect of life.'

Fanny bit off a red silk thread. 'Meredith does do women well, though I wouldn't want to read the book a second time. You'll easily outstrip Meredith and Hardy with your *Kidnapped*. You'll be the master of your generation, Lou, but you must practise writing realistic women.'

He froze and frowned down at Fanny. 'Dinna' be absurd, woman - writing's no mere competition, every author has a different mark to make.' Irritably, he took up the poker and prodded the dormant embers of the fire. '*Kidnapped's* mere juvenilia compared with *Far from the Madding Crowd*,' he snapped. 'That time I was telling you about - when I met Meredith - was a terrible time when you had abandoned me in Paris and bolted back to Mr Osbourne in California, with no thought of my feelings in the matter. You left me bereft, broken-hearted and embittered - I wondered if I'd ever see you again.'

Fanny set aside her needlework. 'Why on earth are you bringing up *that*? You know what happens when we get into these old stories of ours. This is exactly why I want to consult Charcot again. Out of the blue, you lay traps for me, Papa, but I'll not fall into this one. I have not the strength for an argument this time of night.' Setting aside her beadwork, she heaved herself off the chair. 'See you in the morning,' she said coldly. 'I'm off to bed.'

As soon as he heard Fanny's door closing upstairs, memories of the awful time in Paris raided the hushed drawing room. Meredith had praised *An Inland Voyage*, which had recently been published, and had sent Louis a letter after the Burford visit: 'I hope you will feel we expect much of you.' Here was encouragement worth its weight in gold that *annus horribilis* of 1878.

Louis stared into the fire, and a ghastly incident from that time seized his mind. Shortly before Fanny set out for California, they had been travelling in a curtained cab towards some Parisian entertainment or other. Was he in danger of losing her, forever? Was she was slipping from his grasp? Desperate to engage her full attention he had thrown her a childish challenge. 'See if you can bend my fingers back, Fan. Go on, I dare you!' He and Bob had played the game as children. Huffily, Fanny had refused, and her refusal enflamed his anxiety, so that a fit of hysterical laughter overcame him. In a fury he had grabbed Fanny's hand and threatened to break every finger on it if she abandoned him. He twisted her hand so fiercely, Fanny retaliated by sinking her teeth into his arm until it bled and he let go, begging her forgiveness in a flood of tears.

Why such melodrama all those years ago? He had needed Fanny with an unhealthy desperation; he understood that now, rising wearily to turn off the lamps. An unhealthy desperation. But why hadn't he marked their hysterical behaviour as a warning sign? He had been ill at the time, he gave himself that, and madly in love with Fanny who was grieving for Hervey, recently lost to consumption. They had both been in despair and they both yearned for love they could count on. He pondered that fact as he blew out the drawing room candles. - There has always been a disturbing undercurrent in our relationship, a lurking threat of violence - primitive and terrifying - waiting to burst through the surface at any moment. The mere thought of wanting to bend back Katherine's or Frances Sitwell's fingers, or anyone else's, made Louis shake his head sadly at the impossibility as he climbed the stairs to his room.

His thoughts raced as he undressed. - Tonight Fanny pre-empted my mawkish desire to provoke her. But why I wanted to, God alone knows. We stand firm together, reading Meredith, for example, then some trivial incident or remark, such as her harping on about my supposed inability to write women characters, causes the ground to shift beneath us in an eruption of Vesuvian proportions.

He felt like weeping until, the minute he lay down, his storytelling powers came over him like a tide. He took pencil and paper from the side table drawer and made notes. - Let it be a melodrama - Gothic - titled *Olalla*, the byword I wooed Fanny with in Paris - 'Oh-la-la' and a wolf whistle every time she opened the door of her garret to me. Let it be about a young man, a bit of an aristocrat and an English officer. Pride will be his fatal flaw.

A hero, Louis wrote, is sent to convalesce from war wounds at the home of a formerly grand Spanish family now sinking into ruin. Let this finca be situated in a wild, forested part of Spain - yes, let it be Spain. Call him 'X' for the time being - X discovers within the crumbling finca, a beautiful señorita (call her Olalla), and her mother, a hag of a señora, dusky and inclined to hairiness (cf. Fanny), two characteristics the officer dislikes intensely. By Jove, I'll do women in this story! Let there be a half-witted son, also dusky and hairy, sadistic, even bestial in his lack of self-control. A strain of insanity runs in the family. A series of sensational incidents culminates in a vampire-like attack on the hero by the señora. (She bites the officer's hand through to the bone! cf. cab incident with Fanny.) A wind in the forest - of a poisonous nature - fans the hero's ardour for the daughter, Olalla, whose breasts are emphasised by a split-bodice dress. The hag, in flashes of causeless anger and fits of sturdy sullenness, thwarts the hero's entrance to the mansion.

Louis let out a laugh. Why, that's Fanny all over - *flashes of causeless anger and fits of sturdy sullenness* - but I like the thought of breasts spilling from a split bodice . . . He drifted into an excited sleep. *Olalla* might be just the ticket for the shocker Longman was after.

The Summer Visitors

Every fortnight, the *Bournemouth Visitors Directory* updated information about arrivals in town so that visiting cards might be left in hotels and boarding houses to oil the wheels of social contact. Not to be outdone, Fanny wrote down the names and addresses of the Stevenson clan expected during the holidays, and sent Valentine to deliver it to the *Directory's* offices.

Before the summer invasion, conflicts between Louis and Fanny ruffled the peace of Skerryvore. Fanny's jealousy over some of Louis' friends and family, and his growing success, evinced by the small queue of artists waiting to represent him, was hard to placate. Theirs was a classic 'love-hate relationship', a one-way street with no exit. Each was tied to the other by psychological and financial necessity, and must make the best of it. A holiday might help. They replied to an advertisement in the local paper offering lodgings at a farm cottage on the edge of Dartmoor and, after Louis made sure that more than one bedroom was available - he was determined not to spend the entire holiday alone with Fanny - they booked it. They would visit Thomas Hardy on the way.

'But how shall we approach Mr Hardy?' Fanny said. 'We cannot simply *arrive*. We cannot suddenly appear on his driveway unannounced. After all, the Hardys, like us, have moved home recently. I have read all about the house they have built and named Max Gate. Where 'Max' comes from one can only wonder.'

'Of course we won't appear on their driveway out of nowhere. I'll write to Hardy nearer our departure.'

'We take some risk, Papa.'

'What risk?'

'That they may not receive us.'

'Brighten up, Vandegrifter. Let us not make a Shakespearian tragedy out of the supposition that Hardy might not welcome us to Max Gate. If we put our best feet forward he is unlikely to thwart us.'

'August will be perfect, Papa. We'll close up Skerryvore and give Valentine, Mrs Watts, Aggie and Beaucox their holidays. But who will keep an eye on Skerryvore in our absence?'

'Miss Boodle of course. She knows the ropes the ship sails by and proved her worth as Gamekeeper of Skerryvore when we were up at Cambridge in May.'

Sam Lloyd Osbourne was first to arrive. Westbourne Station, half-a-mile a mile from Skerryvore, was beyond Louis' reach. He longed to meet Sam off the train, yet he refused to allow the wheelchair out of the coach house. Fanny was all in favour of hiring a brougham to fetch Sam and his luggage, until Louis convinced her of their need to save money. Cheques were overdue from two of his publishers, Holt and Chatto, but until he received them they would have to tighten their belts. In the end, he hit on a satisfactory solution: Beaucox would accompany her with the wheelbarrow to fetch Sam's luggage.

The train steamed and clanked towards the buffers at the end of the line before it screeched to a halt. Sam Osbourne got off, doffed his cap and bent to kiss his mother's cheek. 'You've grown so tall,' she exclaimed; 'my soul, I scarce recognize you in that get-up.' Sam was wearing a three-piece suit of Irish linen, the trousers cut in the plus-four style favoured by the Prince of Wales. 'A parting gift from Aunt Maggie and Uncle Tom,' Sam said with a cautious smile.

'You must have been very good . . . to have deserved it, I mean; but, then, the senior Stevensons are generous to us all.' Fanny took Sam's arm. 'You'll go back to the parents-in-law in Edinburgh after your vacation?'

'Dunno Ma, can we talk about that later?'

'Margaret and Mr Tommy will be here soon. There will be discussions then. About whether or not, that is, you should return to university in Edinburgh or remain here in Bournemouth with a tutor as before. That is what *I* would prefer, and Louis would like you to stay with us.' When Sam fell silent, 'I noticed you travelled down in a first class compartment,' she said.

'Only from London, Ma; not all the way from Edinburgh,' Sam protested, guiding his mother out of the path of a coach and pair coming at a fast gallop up the Poole Road. 'Matter of fact, I had to stand all the way from Edinburgh to Berwick before I got a seat among the riffraff.'

Sam slowed his pace to his mother's, a gawky teenager, his long earnest face framed by dense, dark-blond curls. Fanny was wearing what she called her 'respectable gear': the feathered hat and shoulder cape she had worn for the portrait photograph Louis had sent to his parents from California after their wedding. All the way down Middle Road, their conversation came in short bursts interspersed with awkward pauses and the clunk of the wheelbarrow behind them.

'Has the tricycle arrived, Ma?' Fanny nodded. 'Phew, that's a relief,' Sam said; 'it would have cost a bit to hire one for the holidays. I don't suppose the Squire gets out on it much.'

Louis stood at the gateposts of Skerryvore waving a Saltire. 'Ahoy there, son of a seadog!' he cried when they came into view. 'War games in the attic after lunch, young Sam.'

Fanny felt embarrassed on account of the neighbours, and Sam said irritably, 'I'm too old for stupid war games.'

'That's what I told him, but it would cost you nothing to humour your step-Papa a little.'

Just as they were crossing into Alum Chine Road, Bogue burst through the gates with his usual performance of barking and leaping. 'The dog has terrible manners, Ma,' Sam said, stooping to make a fuss of him. 'He might bite the summer visitors.'

'Bogue has never actually bitten anyone, Sam. His

aggressive behaviour is but a showy demand for attention. As soon as he is acknowledged by strangers he's as good as gold.'

'Phew, Ma, that's a relief,' Sam grinned and, quickening his pace, he fell into the fragile embrace of his stepfather.

Thomas and Margaret Stevenson arrived next, bearing gifts for everyone in the household, as well as haggises and kippers. They passed Sam a letter from Edinburgh University and he ripped it open only to discover that, like his stepfather all those years ago, he had failed his first year examinations. Margaret planned to stay for a week, but Thomas could only spare three days. His pleas of business to attend to in London fooled neither Fanny nor Louis who knew the old man was determined to quit Bournemouth before the arrival of his nephew, Bob Stevenson.

Long ago, Thomas had discovered among Louis' papers at Heriot Row a note from Bob: *Ignore everything that our parents have taught us,* Thomas read and Louis returned home to find his father in a fury. Thomas already disapproved of Bob's artistic ambitions and 'loose living' and this note enraged him. More than once he had declared his nephew no fit companion for his son. Mercifully, another note escaped the elder Stevenson's rummaging. He remained ignorant of Louis' and Bob's involvement in setting up the L.J.R. Society. The society had been the cousins' *raison d'être* during high-spirited drinking sessions in the howffs of Advocate's Close. Despite the fact that Louis had been ill after an attack of diphtheria at the time, Thomas, aware - and afraid - that he was losing control over his son, started questioning him about his religious beliefs. When he heard that Louis no longer believed in the established Church or Christian religion, he was shocked to the core. 'Turning your back on engineering is as nothing to this act of disobedience to God,' Thomas thundered, and Margaret backed him up. To his fervently believing parents, Louis' atheism meant the eternal damnation of their only child's soul. After 'the inquisition', Heriot Row took on the atmosphere of 'a house where somebody awaited burial,' Louis wrote at the time. Thomas forbade him to see Bob that summer.

Whenever his father reappeared in his later life, Louis struggled valiantly against such painful memories. These days though, at Skerryvore, he celebrated the reconciliation his marriage had brought about. He delighted in Fanny's knack with the parents. She took pains to show them each and every improvement at the villa, thanks to their generosity. 'And when Louis and I are rich,' she said, 'and, if I am not too fat by then, there is a stable all ready for my horse.'

Fanny humoured Thomas by serving up his favourite dishes of roast mutton, potato croquettes, bakewell pudding and tipsy cake. She took him to see her excavations on the bank of the chine and read to him by the fire. She deflected Mr Tommy's attention away from

Louis every time the subject of his insufficient earnings introduced a sour note into the old man's conversation. When Thomas broke down in tears over his son's continuing ill health she reassured him, 'slowly but surely Lou *is* getting better.'

What to do now that Sam had failed his exams became a hot topic at the dinner table. Louis had been amused to learn that Sam slept in his former bedroom at Heriot Row, studied engineering at Edinburgh University, debated at the Speculative Club, and was considering joining Stevenson & Sons as an apprentice engineer. As if that wasn't enough of history repeating itself, Sam now voiced his ambition to be a writer, and had taken to wearing a velvet jacket similar to his own. It seemed unlikely, though, that Sam would trump his one and only contribution to Scottish engineering: a paper delivered to the Society of Arts in 1871 describing a device to make lighthouse lamps flash.

Louis and Fanny wanted to keep Sam at Skerryvore after the holidays; his youthful presence alleviated the tensions simmering between them. Louis felt relieved when Fanny's motherly instincts were deflected towards her son. The obstacle to keeping Sam was their inability to feed another mouth, let alone pay college fees.

'Young Sam's hardly ever at Skerryvore, where does the rascal go?' Thomas wondered one night when they were at dinner. 'Sowing wild oats in a brothel, nae doot.'

Everyone at the table froze. 'Bournemouth is *clean*, Mr Tommy, and so is my son,' Fanny said. 'There are no brothels here, besides Sam's mind's on cramming this summer.'

'All work and no play, eh?' the old man chuckled. 'Come, come, Fanny, young Sam's reached puberty, and every town in the land has its places of ill-repute. Bournemouth canna' be an exception. Why, when I was a lad, m'self,' Thomas began and Margaret stiffened. 'That'll do, Tom, this is not a suitable subject of conversation for the dinner table.'

Thomas put on a sulky face. 'I only wanted to tell them about my charity, the Magdalen Mission, set up to help fallen women in Edinburgh.'

'That has nothing to do with the subject under discussion which is Sam's future,' Margaret persisted. 'As Fanny rightly says, her son has other things on his mind, and we must take this opportunity before you leave, Tom, to discuss his academic future.'

'Aye, you're right as usual, Mags. Speaking of which, Sam can make up his own mind where to go, Edinburgh or Bournemouth. I favour Edinburgh.'

'Sam's rightful place is here with his mother and me,' Louis said sharply. 'The lad can cram and repeat his exams here in Bournemouth and help me to correct proofs, that sort of thing. He has an eye for the written word, though I doubt he'll ever make a writer.'

Thomas' fork clattered on his plate and he rose to his feet. 'Oh, and who's to pay for keeping Sam here when you don't earn enough from your stories to pay your own way? Me I suppose?'

'The money's not the important thing as you well know,' Louis said, fixing his father with a fierce eye. 'It's Sam's development we must consider above all else I assume the money so far spent on Skerryvore, the furnishings and fitments, etcetera, and all costs incurred in keeping Sam in Edinburgh, will be deducted from my inheritance at the end of the day. No doubt funds to keep Sam in Bournemouth would come from the same source.'

Thomas stared at his son, red in the face. 'Inheritance, is it? Inheritance? Well, we'll see about that.' He scowled and banged his fist on the table.

'Sit down at once, Thomas,' Margaret said sternly. 'Stop making a scene. We are *guests* at Skerryvore and what our son says makes sense.'

The entrance of Valentine at that moment with a moulded cream jelly took the heat out of the old man's temper. He thrust his plate forward and Fanny served him with a generous portion of the wobbly purple confection before she introduced a new topic of conversation: the Emporium recently opened in the Arcade.

Thomas left the next day, tears springing in his worn old eyes. 'God looks after his own,' he said, pressing a wad of notes into Louis hand. 'Take care o' yerself, my dearie.'

*

The 8 July 1885 issue of the *Bournemouth Visitors Directory* listed under Herbert Road (not far from Alum Chine Road) a guest house called the Claremont, and noted that Mrs de Mattos and family, Mrs Alan Stevenson and Mr and Mrs Robert Stevenson would be staying there. Ever the family man, Louis rushed to greet them when they called at Skerryvore. He tickled Bob's daughter, wee Pootle, kissed Bob's wife, Luisa, and slapped Bob on the back. Bob's sister Katherine, their mother, Aunt Alan, and Katherine's daughter Helen (nicknamed 'Snoodie') were all embraced into the villa they were seeing for the first time. Skerryvore was the perfect place for a family holiday. Croquet was set out on the lawn and thanks to Fanny's winding paths the beach was only fifteen minutes walk away through Alum Chine.

In preparing for the summer invasion Fanny had let herself be guided by Mrs Beeton. She willed her matrimonial home to run like clockwork so that Louis' extended family might witness how well their hero was catered for. *The Book of Household Management* offered advice about everything from hiring servants to the uses of beeswax polish and the preparation of joints for roasting. For weeks Fanny had been preparing à la Beeton and adding her own interpretation to menus designed to flaunt her mastery of French cuisine.

Extra provisions had been stored in an auxiliary larder. New dresses of sprigged muslin and white caps and aprons had been run up on the sewing machine for Valentine and Agnes. Mrs Watts' grey hopsack uniform would have to do since she rarely stepped out of the kitchen. After a good deal of persuasion, Beaucox agreed to attend in the dining room wearing a manservant's livery borrowed from the Shelleys.

It saddened Fanny that there were no raspberries to offer their guests. During her absence in London last spring, Louis had wandered into the kitchen garden and pruned the raspberry canes so enthusiastically he destroyed them. Fanny had to bite back the words, 'fools rush in.' After all, Louis only meant to be useful. When he realized what he had done, he begged her forgiveness and, as far as she knew, that was the last time he had set foot in her kitchen garden. Although it was a pity about the raspberries, there was plenty of other homegrown produce. As they sampled them one by one, the visitors declared Fanny's salads of herbs, lettuce and tomatoes superb. None of them had tasted sweet corn before, so she served it up with melted butter and was rewarded with the accolade 'divine'. 'All my vegetables are grown from seeds sent over from America,' she explained, adding diplomatically that, although vegetables tended to be bigger and juicier in America, they were not necessarily tastier.

In different ways, the sturdy, handsome children of his cousins resembled Bob and Katherine, so that Louis rediscovered in their company echoes of childhood days, running like the wind on the Pentland Hills. Pootle and Snoodie lost no time in demanding to go hand-in-hand with Uncle Louis to see the chine. The children made him bold. Step by careful step, for the first time he followed Fanny's winding paths until they discovered a wild raspberry bush concealed in the thicket. 'Our very own treasure, me hearties,' Louis smiled, waving his stick in the air. Then he pulled a face, 'Boo-hoo, boo-hoo, we don't have a swag bag to put the berries in.'

After speedy deliberation, Snoodie was sworn to secrecy and sent back to the house for a punnet. When she returned, Pootle's cupid mouth was smeared with raspberry juices. 'You have to be very careful,' Snoodie said in the tone of an elderly aunt, though she was not much older than Pootle. 'The thorns are very prickly.'

'Aye, and if we're to get berries with our tea, Pootle, you'll have to whistle,' Louis advised, 'since the human being has yet to be invented who has the power to eat berries and whistle at the same time.'

They picked the soft red fruit between snatches of song and bursts of impromptu poetry. When the container was full to the brim, Pootle was allowed to carry the treasure to Aunt Fanny who was supervising the dinner preparations in the kitchen, her brow smudged with flour. From the doorway, Louis returned his wife's broad smile. There would be no more mention of murdered raspberry canes.

Before Henry James was introduced to the family, Louis took him aside to confide, 'I'm plotting to get Henley here next week, only my wife sets her face against it.' Fanny was angry with the blustering, redheaded Henley for leading her husband into 'worthless collaborations' in the past, overexciting him on overlong visits, and encouraging him to drink too much. Like others in Louis' circle, Henley resented Fanny's self-appointed role as 'guard dog' and Louis for tolerating it. But Henley was determined to visit Skerryvore and Louis was equally determined to welcome him.

The dining table accommodated ten with its extension pulled out, and, after each guest had located their place by way of name cards decorated by Fanny, 'We are only nine,' Louis lamented. 'We are one guest short.'

'Yes, yes, I know you wanted Miss Boodle,' Fanny said, opening her cream brocade napkin with a flourish. 'But she has gone to Brighton for the weekend, so let us imagine your father is still with us. Pour out the wine and let's drink his health.'

'Aye, all right then . . . but let's say grace before we start?'

The Edinburgh matrons, Maggie and Aunt Alan, sat on either side of Louis, dressed in identical high-throated dark dresses and starched white mutches. His mother was taller, leaner and younger than his elderly aunt upon whom Louis cast a winning smile. 'Will you say grace, Aunt Alan?' His aunt looked down nervously and wrung her hands under the table. 'You do it, Maggie,' she whispered.

'Very well. For what we are about to receive, may the Lord make us truly thankful,' Margaret said crisply, and a chorus of 'amens' went round the table, swiftly followed by excited chatter.

Louis watched his mother start on her soup, her back straight as a ramrod, her pinkie stuck out at the side of her spoon. 'I do feel the presence of father tonight,' he told her affectionately. 'I'm heartily glad of our reconciliation these past years, though I still have to deal gingerly with him. His grievances against me simmer from all those years ago and it would please me more than anything in this world to be confident of true peace between us.'

'Why don't you consider going away for a few days with your father, just the two of you?' Margaret said. 'I've heard good reports of Smedley's Hydropathic Clinic in Matlock where all sorts of cures may be sampled. It'd do you both the world of good to be on your own for once.'

Aunt Alan was chatting with Katherine and, next to her, Henry James was listening politely to Fanny's opinion about the impact of the Civil War on America. One by one, the Squire of Skerryvore tuned into the conversations round the table. On Margaret's left, Sam was making an effort to get to know Luisa, and he wondered why Bob had married such a cold, standoffish woman when he had his warm-hearted sister and mother as role models. Then Fanny turned to Bob. Soon they were well down the memory lane of Hyères, back to the time when Bob had rushed over to help Fanny nurse him through the worst illness of his life. Snatches of their conversation reached him: 'Remember when we came back from Nice?' 'The lane to La Solitude was a mud slick.' 'We couldn't get the carriage up it . . .'

History takes queer turns, Louis mused; Bob's fortunes have sunk while mine have risen. Bob had arrived at Skerryvore, a pale shadow of himself, but now, after a few days on holiday, his cousin's banter enlivened the room like an old Scots tune.

Katherine was confiding in Henry her 'dreadful mistake' in marrying Sydney de Mattos. She had been taken in by his fine aesthetics during their courtship, she said, only to discover she had married a cruel misanthropist. Louis had heard it all before, and, when he caught Henry's eye, he was rewarded with a slow, knowing smile. He'll find a way to put Katherine and her plight into one of his books, Louis mused. The man's a lighthouse beacon sweeping the tumultuous sea of human follies and indiscretions for whatever flotsam and jetsam gets thrown up.

'I have two children, Mr James, but my boy has gone on holiday to Scotland with his father,' said Katherine.

'Some Scottish gossip, mother?' Bob called suddenly.

'Oh, we don't go in for gossip, son,' Aunt Alan said primly.

'Well, give us some news of the place, at least,' Bob persisted.

Margaret said, 'I can tell you about the Forth Bridge,' and the entire party turned their heads to listen. 'Only last week Thomas and I drove down to Queensferry to see the progress being made and, I can tell you, an astonishing sight met our eyes. The three gigantic cantilevers of the bridge have risen up out of the water, but they are not yet joined together. The effect is mystifying, and the noise is deafening. Men beating metal, hammering in rivets, putting all the bits of the bridge together on the shore, then shipping them out to the site.'

'I have seen pictures of the bridge's construction in *The London Illustrated News*. They say it is a World Wonder, the greatest engineering feat of our age,' said Henry James, and he remembered to add, 'with the exception of the Stevenson lighthouses.'

'We did that with the lighthouses, of course,' said Margaret and a small silence fell until Louis came to the rescue. 'Did what, mother?'

'The bits of the lighthouses were constructed on the island beaches before they were shipped out to sea and erected on the rocks for which they were intended.'

His napkin tucked under his chin, Louis tuned-into drifts and snatches of chatter rising and falling like musical phrases in the room. At times like this, he thought, it's a pleasure to be a householder.

After the last guest left and Louis had gone to bed, Valentine helped Fanny to lock away the silver before they went upstairs. Margaret had Fanny's room and she had been 'taken in' by Louis. The oil lamp had been turned down low, the fire was banked for the night, a solitary candle reflected its wavering flame in the dressing table mirror, and Louis slept in his bed.

'Mr Louis sleeps like a child while the rest of us worry,' Fanny whispered behind the scrap screen where she was taking off her dark blue taffeta crinoline. Valentine unlaced her stays and, with a sigh of relief Fanny slipped into her nightgown. They tiptoed to the dressing table. 'Having visitors is a great strain,' Fanny confided. 'Even Sam's being difficult. Caught between our middle-aged guests and Louis' young nieces, it's no wonder he sulks.' Valentine removed Fanny's tortoiseshell comb and took up the silver-backed hairbrush.

'Mr Louis' London editor is sending down an artist called William Strang soon, but I say he doesn't look well enough to be drawn. And Louis has invited Mr Henley to Skerryvore even though I've made it plain I don't want him. He keeps my husband up way past his bedtime, drinks all our whisky, spills out his ill-manners and . . .'

'I'll thank you not to insult my friend,' Louis suddenly cried out.

Fanny whirled round, clutching her heart. 'Good Lord, I thought you were a ghost.'

Louis was sitting upright in his bed with wild eyes. 'Henley is a man who lives in the moment. A man of passion and poetry who appreciates the great cry of green that goes up to Heaven out of the riverbeds. A brave soul who was dying of tuberculosis and necrosis of the bone when I first met him ten years ago at the

Edinburgh Infirmary and bears a peg leg to prove it.'

Fanny dismissed Valentine then shook her fist at Louis. 'What the devil got into you, scaring the living daylights out of me like that?'

'You deserved it,' he glowered. 'You don't want Henley at Skerryvore yet he is one of my oldest friends.'

'Henley leads you astray into worthless collaborations like the madcap theatricals we had to endure last year.'

'No doubt he will contribute to my biography - under your supervision, of course, after the reaper takes me - yet how can he carry out the task if you prevent us from meeting? Now, lower your voice woman, my mother is sleeping next door.'

'It's too soon to have Teddy Henley here, or artists to capture you for posterity. You're still weak after the shock of Fleeming Jenkin's death. And, you know what a boozer Henley is. Alcohol's bad for you, yet the man's never satisfied until he's got you drinking yourself stupid.'

'I won't have you acting as a guard dog at the gates of Skerryvore, admitting who you please among my friends and turning others away. I will have Henley, and that's the end of it. He'll stay at the Claremont with Bob and Katherine. And I will welcome all the artists who wish to come. A successful author must do the bidding of his publishers.'

Fanny rubbed night cream into her face. 'Sitting for graven images is a bad omen when your health fluctuates so wildly,' she told Louis by way of the mirror.

'You like your own captured images,' Louis said; 'the recent photograph of you in the dress you wore for our anniversary, and that other photo Dew-Smith took when we were at Cambridge.'

When Fanny got into bed, simultaneously they pulled the bedcovers up to their chins. But the outlook for slipping into sleep seemed grim until Louis produced a small sound of merriment. 'Lying so stiff as we do brings to mind yon effigies of Lord and Lady Such-and-such stretched out on their tombs in cathedrals. Let us not encourage time's winged chariot to draw near, Dutch. Let's be tender with one another.'

Fanny curled up with a weary sigh. 'I am too exhausted to be tender or to do anything but sleep. Goodnight.'

Art and Life

The day Aunt Alan left Skerryvore, Fanny offered to look after Pootle and Snoodie so that Margaret, Katherine and Luisa could accompany her to Central Station then continue on the branch line for a day out at Poole. Sam had gone up to the London Science Museum and Teddy Henley was due that afternoon. To humour Fanny, Louis said he'd go with her to the chine where she was showing their nieces how to construct a wigwam of branches and twigs. As the girls skipped ahead dressed in navy-blue and white striped dresses with sailor-style collars, Louis was reminded of the golden children on his scrap screen.

'Thanks for being a good sport about Teddy,' he said, taking Fanny's arm.

'I accepted what you said about his importance to your future biography.'

Pootle and Snoodie scrambled over the edge of the garden and Fanny called sharply, 'Girls, what is it you are forbidden to do?'

'Go into the chine without an adult,' they chorused, looking up at her with angel faces.

Fanny picked up the skirt of her Mother Hubbard and hurried after them while Louis paused at his sunbathing spot. It had been a long time since he had been well enough to enjoy it. When Pootle's excited child's voice rose up from the ravine he peered over the edge. 'Watch out the Brownies don't get you,' he called through cupped hands. Snoodie's voice echoed back, 'Brownies are *good*, Uncle Louis, you said so yourself!'

Just as he was about to follow them, Bob's cry announced the arrival of Henry James. He shouted to Fanny that the first of his Musketeers had arrived and punted back up the garden on his stick, wishing that he and Bob and Henry and Henley might never have to part. It's a queer thing, damned queer, that here at Skerryvore I'm forced to live without men, he mused. He felt keenly the paradoxes he would have to face this particular day. On the one hand, Henley would be here at last; on the other, he would have to say good-bye to Henry James who was leaving for London.

'Mr James tells me he has tramped the streets of London and visited the Millbank prison in the interests of researching his latest novel,' Bob said when Louis arrived.

'It is true, Stevenson; I have walked a great deal in London this past year. I walked in the day, for exercise, amusement and the acquisition of material. I walked home when the evening had been spent elsewhere, observing lives very different from my own.' Louis leaned forward attentively on his cane. 'And, as I moved as an observer through the thick jungle of humanity, possible stories and characters fluttered up before me like startled game until, gradually, out of all the dark mass sprung a sensitive individual with a fine mind. The hero of my book.'

'Hero?' said Louis. 'Didn't you say your book was named after a princess? Princess Casamassima, was it not?'

'It is, for the princess who made an appearance in an earlier novel obsesses me still. The central character is no aristocrat but a product of the slums, an anarchist and an artisan.' Henry gave his slow smile. 'I had better keep his name in the bottle.'

'And Millbank prison? You really went there?'

'I did. I needed a prison scene and I confess I got it up rather in the style of the French naturalists, Zola in particular. I wonder at my confidence now, given the extreme, the very particular truth and *authority* required in the writing of such a situation.' He paused, searching the earnest faces of Louis and Bob, before he gave a little chuckle. 'I *might* have pulled it off. Judge for yourselves when you read the book.'

Louis and Bob waited, but when Henry volunteered no more, they decided on a game of croquet.

After lunch, the ginger-bearded Henley announced his arrival with the clip-clop of two crutches much to the astonished merriment of Pootle and Snoodie. The children had been ministering to their dolls in the seclusion of the entrance porch. They ran out, swiftly followed by Bogue who fastened his teeth onto Henley's wooden leg and shook it so viciously he had to steady himself against the wall of the house. Fanny arrived in the nick of time to pull off the dog, slap its backside, and shut it in the porch. Then, securing the hand of each niece firmly in her own, she led Henley into the garden. The attack of the Skye terrier and 'Cassandra's' coolness failed to dampen Henley's bravado. Charged with vitality at the prospect of seeing Louis, he stomped bravely down the gravel path, and, as soon as he spied the friends at croquet, called out, 'What Ho, me hearties!'

Louis embraced his old friend, 'What Ho, Silver!' and Bob shook his hand vigorously. Then Henley must meet Henry James to whom they explained that, once upon a time in Edinburgh, there had been Four Musketeers, but since Ferrier's untimely and tragic death last year, alas only three remained - the very three who now posed with linked arms before the Prince of Men. Unanimously, they invited Henry James to become the fourth of the New Musketeers.

Linen jackets were the sartorial order of the day, except for Henry James who had on a navy-blue blazer striped with pink. Louis and Henley wore white sunhats with black bands they had bought in Nice on their infamous adventure two years earlier, when Louis had collapsed on the promenade. Everyone stood round listening to Henley's account of his merry journey down from London in a train filled with day-trippers. Then Fanny led the children back to the wigwam where she was teaching them a powwow dance.

The men eased themselves into striped deck chairs

set round a wrought iron table. When Fanny was safely out of earshot, 'We've done with tea,' Bob said; 'we're ready for whisky; after all, this is no ordinary day.' He vaulted inside through the open bay window and returned the same way with the decanter to a round of applause. After poetic toasts they settled down to discuss Henry James' idea that Bob, who was well versed in the history of Art from the Middle Ages to the present day, would make an excellent critic for an art journal. After all, had he not attended the recent Salons in Paris, and was he not familiar with the work of the new Impressionists? And, best of all, Henley added, any fool could bone up on any subject and be an art critic, whereas Bob was a rare beast who knew exactly what was involved in the technique of painting.

'As always, Teddy hits the nail on the head - you fit the profession of critic like a hand made glove,' Louis said and Henry nodded, 'so many critics these days are quick to judge without having any idea of how art is made.'

Smoking materials were passed round. Bob filled his Meerschaum, James and Henley settled for cheroots and Louis delicately rolled a cigarette. 'Speaking of the making of art, Sargent wants to paint me again,' he said. 'Fanny and I lost our hearts to him last November - he's got what I call an exhibition manner, but on closer examination he turns out to be simple, bashful, honest and, though he's American, he seems rude in a peculiarly inoffensive *English* way. He'd like to come soon, but

Fanny's against it.'

'Let him come, cousin,' Bob said impatiently. 'Stand up to your wife! Sargent's different from the rest of the moderns. It seems to me that most avant-garde painters are a rabble of pretenders who generate fads for their own dubious worldly purposes.'

'Mere cynics who seek only to shock,' Henry said.

Bob waved his pipe in the air. 'Aye, you're right there. Sargent, on the other hand, possesses a timeless body of knowledge and he employs it with taste and inspiration for the benefit of refined audiences. The man can draw to perfection and he's an immensely accomplished painter.'

'Sargent sees behind the surface of things,' said Henry.

'What do you say, Teddy?' asked Bob.

'Well, someone must play devil's advocate here, and it might as well be me. While I confess I've not seen much of the man's work, my impression is that Sargent lacks something basic to *genuine* modernity. Oh, he updates the past with flair, but he hesitates to challenge it and may well be destined to remain outside the charmed circle of the more daring artists of our time.'

'There, I cannot agree,' Henry frowned.

'The man's young, Teddy, give him a chance,' Bob said. 'We'll see marvellous things from him yet.' He turned to Henry, 'I hear you belong to the circle at Broadway where Sargent is one of the stars. I'd like to pay a visit there one day.'

Henry said everyone at the table would be welcome and he entertained them with the latest news from the Broadway colony until the voices of the children at the foot of the garden signalled Fanny's return. 'Heaven help us, comrades,' Louis said under his breath. 'Fill up your glasses before the bottle's snatched away.'

Pootle came skipping up and tugged Bob's shirtsleeve. 'Dada, there are Brownies in our wigwam,' she exclaimed, climbing onto his lap. Her cheeks and white stockings were smudged with earth. Snoodie followed more sedately. 'Not only Brownies, but Elves, too. I *saw* them. Phew! I'm exhausted,' she exclaimed, flouncing on the grass at Louis' feet. He smiled down at her. 'My Brownies have been with me since I was your age, Snoodie. And you're right, lassie, they're good spirits. They help families in their household tasks and writers to make books.' Snoodie studied him with an earnest face that reminded him so nostalgically of Katherine's he felt tears rising. 'Do Brownies help *you*?' she said with a hopeful smile. 'Aye, they do, and they've helped many a writer. Robert Burns knew all about them.'

'I know his poem about the wee mouse whose house was ploughed up,' Pootle said shyly.

'There you are, the Little People did Robbie Burns a service with that bonny poem.'

When Fanny brought out a plate of cucumber sandwiches Bob put down his daughter, gave Fanny his chair, poured her a whisky, and lolled on the grass at her feet. 'Like old times,' he winked. 'Hotel Chevillon meets Skerryvore.'

'If only,' Fanny said, attempting a smile.

Louis reached for her hand. 'My wife needs a holiday. Dartmoor is our destination and we'll visit Hardy on the way. Surely he will have heard of me?'

'Undoubtedly,' said Henry James. 'He is bound to have read *Treasure Island* at the very least. Perhaps even *Travels with a Donkey in the Cévennes*.'

Pootle started dancing. '*I* think he has read your *Garden of Verses*, Uncle Louis: *I have a little shadow that goes in and out with me, and what can be the use of him is* more *than I can see . . .*'

With mock-severity, 'Sshh Pootle,' Bob said. 'Have I not explained that children should be seen and not heard?' and Fanny sent the girls to Valentine who had laid out a tea party in the kitchen.

They embarked on a discussion of Hardy's work and turned to Henry for his opinion of *Far from the Madding Crowd* only to catch him in a doze. 'Henry's lost to this world,' Fanny said affectionately, and he wakened with a sudden lusty snore, consulted his watch and said he must be going. Henley struggled to his feet with the help of his sticks. 'Before we go our separate ways I'd like to propose a toast. Friends, lend me your ears! Rise up! I give you our beloved Louis!'

After that Louis lifted his glass to 'the guardian of my adult life'. 'I give you Fanny Stevenson,' he said and Fanny looked surprisingly coy.

'Mrs Stevenson,' the friends obliged and drained their glasses.

'The moment has come when I must leave you,' Henry said, bowing a little in Louis' direction. 'I'm going up to Broadway and I'll give your regards to Sargent and Gosse.' Louis clasped Henry's hands. 'Write to me often, and go quickly, for saying goodbye to a friend such as you is hard to bear.'

When James disappeared with Fanny towards the gate Louis started pacing the edge of the lawn where it meets the gravel path. A tightrope walker, he wondered, or a landlocked mariner? He paused and turned to Bob and Teddy. 'I love that man,' he said with sad emphasis.

'Aye, that's obvious,' Bob smiled.

'A more magnanimous soul I've never met.'

'Ye'll raise a cup o' kindness with him yet, cousin.'

'Aye, and maybe I'll discover the *grime* I achingly miss from his stories so far - what he says about walking the London streets and visiting the Millbank for the novel he's at gives me hope. So far he has shrunk from delving into the shadows that must lurk inside even a man as noble as Henry.'

'Aye they lurk in all men, especially artists. Artists have a *duty* to express the nightmare that is life, as well as its blessings,' said Henley, helping himself from the decanter.

The shadows of the trees had lengthened on the lawn, the doves were settling down with douce cooing and the friends had fallen silent when Fanny returned.

'Louis has had enough excitement for one day,' she said. 'Your coats are in the hall.'

July slipped by. Undeterred by spells of rainy weather, Bob, Luisa and Katherine took the children to the beach every day. They had hired a bathing hut near Alum Chine's opening into Bournemouth Bay, where they changed into bathing costumes, took shelter from sudden showers, and brewed up tea to drink with their sandwiches. Sometimes Sam joined them, after riding Louis' tricycle to the picnic spot by way of the corniche. Everyone else went by way of the meandering chine, laden down with picnics, towels, spades and pails. Pootle's and Snoodie's excitement mounted whenever they had their first glimpse of the sea. They skipped along, taking turns to sing out Uncle Louis' poem:

When I was down beside the sea
A wooden spade they gave to me
To dig the sandy shore . . .

Meanwhile at Skerryvore, on hot days that reminded them of Nice - and even on rainy days - Fanny constantly flapped her fan. It was made of pleated paper, fashionably Japanese in style, and she had chosen to display it in Dew-Smith's portrait of her. Louis had studied Fanny's portrait closely. He was fascinated by her resemblance to Olalla's stern mother, the hag in the story that had taken up residence in his mind. When Fanny first saw the photograph she protested, surely she didn't look so antique and dour? Louis niftily sidestepped her question by praising the artistry of the photograph.

One day, in preparation for Bob's painting, Fanny put on her painting apron and covered the hall floor with old newspapers. Beaucox fetched a trestle table where Bob laid out brushes and tubes of paint. Fanny read their labels with evident pleasure: 'gamboge, viridian, alizarin,' and Louis reminded them once more of Arcadian days at Grez-sur-Loing, when Bob and Fanny had painted landscapes and he had written 'Ordered South' for *MacMillan's Magazine*.

'I remember you painting the medieval bridge at Grez, Fanny,' Bob said. 'Have you painted much since?'

'I wish! There's no time these days, though I scribble a bit.'

'Ah, that's a pity since you'd a flair for painting. May I ask what you're writing?'

'A story for Scribner based on one of Louis' abandoned plays.'

Louis slipped an arm round her shoulders. 'I remember my first sight of the beautiful American in the rakish little cap of a *vivandière*, smoking with her feet up on a neighbour's chair, telling wild stories of the Nevada mines.'

'She cut a remarkable figure in her bohemian get-up, the waist-hugging jacket, the floppy bow-tie,' Bob agreed.

'Right now I'm more interested in what you plan to put in the mural, Bob. A lonely stag will remind Louis of

Scotland, and is quite the fashion these days. I'm thinking of Landseer's *Monarch of the Glen*. I dare say Queen Victoria sees scenes of nature every day at Balmoral.'

'And what about putting in the Skerryvore lighthouse as a memorial to Uncle Alan?' Louis said.

Fanny wiped her hands on a rag. 'The Skerryvore lighthouse is too much with us as it is. We are in danger of hitting the rocks. I'm off to town with Aggie. The urgent necessity to deal with the butcher's bill can't be put off any longer.'

As soon as they were alone, 'What's up with her?' Bob said.

'Mood swings, any one of a litany of ailments, the change of life - my wife finds it hard to bear - but let's seek respite from domestic alarms in the drawing room. Humouring a wife's a tiresome business.'

'Aye, your right there,' Bob said, stuffing his pipe.

Louis stretched out on the divan. 'Fanny puts on a good show as Lady Skerryvore, but she's a Navaho at heart.'

Bob laughed. 'Aye, maybe, and, as I've observed, Louisa and Fanny bear uncanny similarities. Neither is known for a sunny disposition. Fanny's much changed since our days at Grez.'

'She's a matron now, yet I'm still a boy. Once when we were staying at a hotel the receptionist took her for my mother.' Louis gazed palely at Bob. 'We have both lived to belie our natures, cousin. Yet all men do, all men

. . . and the disguise that grows about them stifles them.'

'Come, come, is it as bad as all that?'

'It's pretty bad and I'll wager you were done in when you arrived here two weeks ago. Now, by Jove, I begin to see a changed man. Suntanned and kissed by the waves of the sea, wearing the laurels of art critic-in-the-making. You're damned lucky to get out and about in the world, whereas I'm a prisoner here. Fanny's my gaoler. She visits my cave with tasty wee dishes, she wipes me down and reads me stories when I'm poorly. I am what she has made me, the embers of the once gay R.L.S. Still, even if I'm living half the life I'd like, I'm the first to admit it could be worse.'

'Aye, and you're fortunate not to know what it's like to struggle for a living,' Bob said gruffly. Louis looked away, thinking that he'd gladly trade his patrimony for good health. 'Uncle Tom would never let his son see the inside of the Marshallsea,' Bob went on. 'Yet I fear the debtors' prison every day. You've no cause to. You'll be rich when Thomas dies.'

'Stop right there cousin. I'm offended by your notion that I'd not pay off your debts to save you from the Marshallsea.'

'Aye well, that's as may be. But now I'll get back and draw out a scheme for the panels.'

He watched his cousin's retreat. Money has become a sore point between us, he thought sadly. Bob needs the money for the mural, yet he feels patronised by me. Money has come between us and wrecked the bosom companionship we once enjoyed. He lay back suppressing tears. *Damn Bob's tatterdemalion pride.* Damn the dreary truth that shadows must fall even upon the purest of human intentions.

The following day, Fanny kept to her room, catching up on overdue letters. Writing to Sydney Colvin was always taxing and made her feel like a Muslim praying to Allah. 'Best of Custodians, Our conduct, as usual, has been horrid,' she began, 'but you, as usual, I trust will prove forgiving.' She recorded that she and Louis were both suffering from ossification of the intellect. Sydney must know that they had had a good deal of wearing company lately, with Skerryvore full, and Bob and Katherine's party in the neighbourhood, and Henley coming down. 'It has been such a difficult party that I quite broke down under the strain.'

Meanwhile, downstairs in the drawing room, eager to begin his career as an art critic, Bob sat with Louis waiting for the artist, William Strang. 'I'm after the casual look of an émigré as befits *Treasure Island* so I've put on my poncho,' Louis joked and Bob said he looked dandy. He pulled a newspaper cutting from his attaché case. 'Strang's a Scot, about the same age as us, but listen to this, Lou. It says, "Mr Strang draws and etches with the mastery to be expected in a favourite pupil of Legros: a master of whose style - noble, simple, severe - sends forth some very honourable reminiscences."'

Louis winced. 'Badly written, I seldom heard worse,

but the sentiment is interesting.'

Strang arrived on the dot of eleven, a sturdy, handsome young man with curling sandy hair. The very model of the Davie Balfour of my imagination, Louis thought. He sat in the blue bergère while Strang got out his materials and Bob positioned himself near the bay window.

'I hear you're famous, Strang,' Louis said. 'You've exhibited at the Royal Academy.'

'Hardly famous, Sir, but, if so, I find myself in good company. I've read with great enjoyment your *Treasure Island* as well as *Travels with a Donkey*.'

'My cousin tell me you've bonny credentials and you've a bonny way with words, too. A Scot through and through, that's easy to tell, and it's a tonic to hear your native tongue. But what took you to London, rather than Glasgow or Edinburgh?'

'I left Scotland - Dumbarton to be exact - to study at London's Slade School of Art and when work came my way I stayed since I find the capital wondrously diverting. Are you writing at the moment, Mr Stevenson?'

Louis paced, cigarette in hand. 'I'm working on a yarn set in Scotland - or would be if my brain had not been turned to porridge by my recent infirmity.'

Strang paused, his pencil in the air. 'I'm sorry to hear that, Mr Stevenson, but I wish you would not march round the room. How can I be expected to draw you if you don't sit still?'

'See what you're up against, Strang?' Bob smiled. 'He's always been like that. Can't sit still for a minute. As for his face, why, it changes as fast as the Scottish weather. You'll have a devilish job catching him on paper.'

'Maybe, but Mr Stevenson's face is a pleasure to gaze upon. It has fine proportions.'

'I read an article about you recently,' Bob said. 'You were a pupil of the great Legros a few years ago?'

'A lazy pupil at that, with an eye only for the women. I worked two hours a day until the art of another student - H. S. Tuke was his name - struck me wondrously and I knuckled under with the intention of bettering him. These days I turn out etchings as if there was no tomorrow and paintings as well. And now, gentlemen, talk among yourselves, please, while I concentrate.'

Bob drew up his chair next to Louis. 'I've been thinking of putting a forest in the hall mural,' he said. Louis cast him a quizzical look. 'Funny you should suggest a forest, for I had a bogey dream last night that's left me haunted and distracted. A fragment is all that remains, though the scope of the dream was limitless. No doubt it included Shelley's heart and Mary Wollstonecraft's death mask; they've haunted me ever since I first saw them at Boscombe Manor last year. Yet, all I remember of the dream is a dark forest, densely planted, no sunlight reaching the floor, and me running feared for my life, chased by angry archers.'

'You escaped to tell the tale?'

'Aye, I woke up before one of them could send an arrow through my back. And I wondered when I woke up who in life might do such a thing. Thomas comes to mind, then Fanny in one of her darkest moods. Then there's the list of creditors fingering their quivers and publishers demanding shilling shockers I can't find the strength or the inspiration to write.'

The drawing swiftly accomplished, Strang turned down Louis' invitation to stay for lunch. 'I'll catch the next train back if I hurry, for I've an appointment in London.' From the gateposts of Skerryvore, they watched Strang's anxious dash up Middle Road before Bob went off to join his family. The postman arrived whistling on his bike and handed Louis a letter from John Singer Sargent. When he turned in through the gateposts, it came to Louis in a flash: Bob had been one of the archers in the forest of his dream.

He found Fanny writing in her room. 'Sargent comes again, I had this letter in the post. He proposes an overnight visit next week and intends to be with us in time for lunch. Don't be a killjoy, Pig. This can only do us good.'

Fanny swung round in her chair. 'Louis, why do you repeatedly provoke me so that I must repeat myself? Much as I like Mr Sargent, you know I'm set against another portrait for the simple reason that you've been ill and look far from your best. Posterity won't thank Sargent for another chuckle-headed image. Why you can't see the sense in postponing the portrait until we return from our holidays is beyond me.'

'An artist in the hand is worth two in the bush,' Louis jested, but Fanny didn't smile. 'I'm sick and tired of pampering you like a spoiled child,' she said.

'And I am weary of this pretence of a life, this confinement that turns me into a prisoner in my own home.'

'*Your* own home?' Fanny said coolly, and Louis slunk away.

A far grander house than 17 Heriot Row enthralled Fanny Stevenson during the Bournemouth years. Skerryvore was a paltry suburban plot compared to the stately home of their new friends, Sir Percy and Lady Jane Shelley. Boscombe Manor was set in wooded policies east of the town of Bournemouth. To Sir Percy, its situation recalled the Ithacan shores of the Gulf of Spezzia where his father had died in a boating accident. He purchased the estate in the hope that the climate of Bournemouth would benefit his crippled wife, and his ailing mother, Mary Godwin Shelley. Sadly, Mary had died in 1851 not long after they moved to Boscombe. Private theatricals, yachting and amateur photography kept Sir Percy entertained in retirement.

Fanny dashed off a letter to Sidney Colvin: *Lady Jane is delicious; naturally no longer young, suffering from the effects of a terrible accident that has left her a hopeless invalid, but with all the fire of youth, and as mad as some other people you know, and ready to plunge into any wild extravagance at a moment's notice.*

Sir Percy is an odd creature! Do you know him? He is the poet's son only in being so exceedingly curious. I think we will come to be very fond of him. They have a lovely little theatre at their place, and give very delightful entertainments, which will be pleasant for us. They have a bust of Mary Wollstonecraft done from a death mask, over which Louis raves.

Robert Louis Stevenson reminded Lady Shelly of Percy Bysshe Shelley. 'Why, he is Shelley!' she often said, and, as Margaret Stevenson recorded, 'when Lou comes into the room she gives a start and says "Shelley!"'

In the liveried coach-and-four sent to collect them, Louis, wrapped in his new poncho, was in high spirits. He chatted away to Margaret Stevenson, seated next to him in her Edinburgh costume. Thwarted and sullen after her trials as hostess of Skerryvore, Fanny sat opposite, now and then interrupting to complain of a migraine headache.

The horses galloped along the East Cliff road and Louis hung out of his window to catch the first glimpse of Boscombe Manor. When the coach suddenly veered into the driveway, Margaret had to steady herself on the hanging strap. It sped down the avenue of lime trees and delivered them to the marble steps fronting the house. Bradshaw, the butler, was waiting to help the party down. Under the portico they went and into the ornate Great Hall where Sir Percy leaned on his stick beside Lady Jane in her wheelchair.

'To be here again is like a homecoming,' Louis smiled, grasping their hands in turn. 'It comforts me to be with you, since I'm grieving sorely for Henry James who has abandoned us for London.' Prompted by Lady Jane he performed a twirl to demonstrate the charms of the poncho, then went straight to the urn containing the poet's heart. It stood beside a perpetually burning lamp in a silk-lined alcove off the drawing room. 'Percy Bysshe knew a thing or two about life's shadows,' he said. 'I remember a few lines from *Intellectual Beauty* that underscore my thought.'

'Tell us dear,' urged Lady Jane from her brocade settee, and Louis recited:

The awful shadow of some unseen Power
Floats though unseen among us - visiting
This various world with an inconstant wing
As summer winds that creep from flower to flower.

After a respectful silence Lady Shelley was the first to speak. 'Come. Sit beside me, Louis. It moves me to see you well, though still a little frail.' Then, with a cunning smile in Margaret's direction, she added, 'Louis is so much my son I wonder how he can be yours?'

Margaret, who had heard this before, sucked in her cheeks and straightened her back. 'If he is anyone's son now, Lady Jane, he is Fanny's. She gives him the care a child might expect from a mother. Not that his health has improved greatly since they came to live in Bournemouth.'

'You may borrow Louis any time you please, Lady Jane,' Fanny said darkly and Lady Jane said Louis would be welcome to come and live at Boscombe Manor.

Bradshaw served afternoon tea and everyone in turn must discuss their health and the remedies taken to improve it. Then the Shelleys heard about the progress of *Kidnapped*, the death of Fleeming Jenkin, and the summer visitors. As soon as tea was over, Sir Percy said, 'My wife takes Louis for her son to such an extent I would like to take a photograph or two this very afternoon if you have nothing to say against it.'

Louis sighed. 'Sargent has painted me and comes again, a Scotsman has been to make an engraving, my stepson threatens to photograph me at my desk. Does everyone who rushes to reproduce my image believe I've not long for this world?'

'*Louis!*' Margaret scolded. Had her son forgotten they were the guests of aristocrats?

'Will my death mask not be enough?'

'There, there . . . to please me, dear,' said Lady Jane, 'we *will* have you for posterity.'

'It would be a great favour, Stevenson,' Sir Percy broke in, 'since I'm a keen amateur photographer and portraiture interests me above all the possibilities of the art.'

'Aye, well, I cannot pretend to be less than flattered. I'll sit for one or two shots. I've not the energy for more.'

'Thank you, dear,' said Lady Jane. 'You know I have you as a Romantic poet, and you do bear a strong resemblance to Percy's father. Do keep on your poncho. It will add dramatic interest to Percy's portrait.'

Fanny, who had been sipping her tea more or less in silence, suddenly announced her intention to walk in the grounds if her hosts would excuse her. 'A walk will do me good. Skerryvore's a fine house of its type, but the grounds don't have the scope and expansiveness of Boscombe.'

'The summer visitors have exhausted Fanny,' Margaret said.

An affectionate, playful spirit seized the party after Fanny's departure. They discussed the proposed plan for a new Bournemouth Library, then Lady Jane presented several copies of *A Child's Garden of Verses* for Louis to autograph. Would he favour her by reading the last poem in the collection? Since she, too, was often ill and confined to bed, that poem was a great comfort to her.

'They're poems for children, mere juvenilia,' Louis protested, but obligingly looked up the poem. A hush settled in the room while he read aloud the first verse: *When I was sick and lay abed ...*

Margaret dabbed her eyes with her hanky. 'Louis was seriously ill in France when he wrote that.'

'There's more to come, Mother.'

'Oh, dear, I am *so* sorry to have interrupted.'

Margaret wept throughout the rest of the recitation:
I was the giant great and still
That sits upon the pillow-hill,
And sees before him, dale and plain,
The pleasant land of counterpane.

When it was over, Lady Jane patted Louis' hand,

'Truly, my dear, your art triumphs over the struggles of your life and inspires us all. How remarkable it is that even though you suffer tediously from pulmonary troubles, the voice, the eternal voice of the poet rings out.'

'Come, come, I don't deserve such praise, my lady,' Louis smiled. 'But I'm glad you like my wee poem. Let's get on with the photos, Sir Percy. Graven images my wife calls them.'

Sir Percy pulled on the fireside bell, and when Bradshaw arrived with Lady Jane's spare wheelchair Louis got in. 'I hoped I'd never have to put my poor body into one of these contraptions ever again, but, as I learned on our last visit, the corridors here are tediously long.'

On the way to the Sanctum, where the Shelley papers and other effects were kept, Louis' spirits rose. He had studied the collection before, and the prospect of seeing Mary Wollstonecraft's death mask again struck him as timely. A frisson of something like foreknowledge ran through him when Bradshaw steered him into the Sanctum. Surely inspiration would flutter back here?

The death mask of Mary Wollstonecraft, looking heavenwards from its plinth, shared the darkened room with Sir Percy's camera on its tripod; the death mask of a woman who had dared to claim equality with men, and had given birth to Mary Shelley, the creator of Frankenstein's monster.

The amiable Sir Percy said, before he disappeared

under his photographer's cloth, 'You will receive copies of the photographs, of course. It's as well for an author to have photographs to hand when newspapers request them. You have nothing to do but look into the lens and sit still when I say so, Stevenson. I'm using the dry plate method.'

Louis sat still. *Frankenstein* - now there was a feisty phantasm to spring from a maiden's mind. Mary Shelley's inspiration had served her well with the idea of a scientist creating a monster that, once out of the bottle, could not be forced back in. And Frankenstein desperately wanted it back in the bottle, for he realized the monster was a mirror of his own dark soul; *that man is not truly one, but truly two.* Louis' head slumped as he considered how it might be possible in his own fiction to unleash such a monster from within the being of the *same* man.

Sir Percy's genial voice boomed from his dark cave, 'Are you asleep, Stevenson?'

'No, no, I was away in a dream, thinking of your mother's genius.'

The aristocratic head reappeared above the camera. 'It *is* an unusual legacy for a son, but now's the time to look at the camera, Stevenson, and stay still. Try not to blink when the light flashes. I'll hold it out in a second. Now,' he mumbled from under the cloth, 'stay quite still! . . . still! . . . still! That's it! And we'll take another shot if you're ready.'

After the session, Sir Percy left the Sanctum. He

wanted to send off the glass plate negatives to a technician in town as soon as possible.

'I'll wheel myself back,' Louis said, but the minute he was alone he pulled himself out of the wheelchair.

He stood at the plinth, closed his eyes and ran his fingertips over the cool white curves of the death mask. Lady Jane had shown him a drawing of Mary Wollstonecraft, a pretty woman, and he struggled to bring that woman to life from under the chalk-white eye sockets, icy-smooth forehead and full plaster lips. A shiver ran through him when he considered again his narrow escape from death at Hyères and he wondered how his own face would have turned out in a death mask. How could voyeurs looking down on it ever succeed in resurrecting more than a semblance of the real R.L.S. when he hardly knew himself?

On the journey back to Skerryvore, Louis instructed Fanny never to permit his death mask to be taken.

No Mere Comma

Margaret left the following day to join Thomas on a harbour inspection tour in Ireland, and Louis and Fanny declared Skerryvore out of bounds to the family, except for Sam and Bob. They were exhausted after their visit to Boscombe Manor and must build up strength for the journey to Dartmoor. Sam was out during the day, cramming at school or loitering with his friends at the sea front. Bob was admitted solely to finish the hall mural. After consultations with Louis and Fanny he had decided not to paint the actual panels but to create a decorative tableau to hang over them. 'If you grow tired of it, or if you ever want to sell Skerryvore, you can take it down,' Bob reasoned.

The prospect of untrammelled leisure encouraged Louis' day long whistling of *Sing Me a Song of the Lad that is Gone* until Fanny shouted he was driving her mad. By way of apology he insisted he had been unaware of any whistling. 'You'll bring on my brain fever,' she yelled when he did it again, and he disappeared upstairs to whistle in peace.

He took out *Kidnapped*, glanced through the manuscript then shut it away in the top drawer of his desk. *Say could that lad be I?* He looked over his notes for *Olalla* and toyed with a few paragraphs until lunchtime when, in an attempt to lighten Fanny's mood, he tied a spotted handkerchief over his mouth. 'I can still whistle, Vandegrifter, but the 'kerchief reminds me not to,' he mumbled. Fanny's mouth twitched with traces of amusement. 'How will you eat your lunch, you daft lunatic?' He tore off the scarf with a flourish. 'At least while I'm eating, I can't whistle and annoy you.'

The Dartmoor farmer's wife had written to confirm their booking. Now they were in a position to consult train timetables and, after lunch, they got out a magnifying glass to study a map of Dorchester and pinpoint the location of Max Gate.

'I give up. The house must be too new to be on the map,' Fanny said at last.

'Give me a look.' Louis peered through the glass then admitted defeat. 'The cabby will know where to find it, though. We'll catch the morning train from Bournemouth to Dorchester, then after lunch at the King's Arms Hotel we'll hire a hansom to take us to Max Gate. According to Edmund Gosse, the house lies on the edge of the town.'

'We'll coincide with teatime. Perhaps they'll offer us tea?'

'Mind, it'll be a short visit as is only polite on a first occasion. A cup of tea - maybe they'll give us a bun with jam - then back to the inn to join Sam and Katherine for dinner. An overnight stay at the inn, then the train to Exeter.'

Fanny's eyes narrowed. 'Did you say Sam and

Katherine?'

Louis pretended to duck. 'Put off your pistol sighting look, Dutchwoman. I meant to tell you - I'm sorry if it slipped my mind - Katherine comes with us as well as Sam. It'll give her pleasure to see that part of the country.'

Fanny slumped on the divan. 'You've already *asked* her? How could you, Papa? What about my feelings in the matter? If *she* goes, you can count me out of the holiday.'

'Very well, I'll ask Valentine to collect *three* tickets for the journey and I'll set off next Tuesday with Sam and Katherine. But I hope you'll change your mind when you consider our reality - that is, we can no longer undertake such a journey alone - we can no longer be certain of managing our lives without help. We need Sam's strength and Katherine's companionship.'

Fanny lunged at Louis' legs with her fist when he walked past the divan. 'She's no companion to me, she hates me!'

He dodged the blow and retreated to his armchair. 'Come, come, Dutch, "hate" is too strong a word for the text. True, you and Katherine are very different in character, but that can't be changed and must be borne. Katherine is blood to me as Sam is to you, and you, of course, mean more to me than all the family put together. I dare say Katherine will distract Sam with long country walks and help you with the housekeeping. *Four* tickets, wife, I say. Let us get four.'

'If I agree to four it will be on condition the two of us go *alone* to Max Gate,' Fanny said, then added in a wheedling tone, 'it's only what I deserve, Papa, after the trials of the summer. I've been looking forward so much to going alone with you to the Hardys.'

'Katherine will explore Dorchester with Sam while you and I visit the Hardys,' Louis said patiently, and Valentine was sent to purchase the tickets.

The summer visitors departed, except for Katherine who stayed on at the Claremont waiting to accompany the Stevensons to Dartmoor. Sargent was due down and Louis looked forward to his visit, but Fanny said with dagger eyes, 'I'm sick and tired of being ignored by visitors who come only to see you . . . as if my life had nothing to do with yours. Why, I am hardly even a comma in our relationship, and a superfluous one at that.' She took to her bed with a nervous collapse.

Sargent had had an eventful summer. He travelled down to Skerryvore directly from Broadway where he had been living at the artists' colony. Fate had led him to Broadway, literally by accident. During a boating trip on the Thames with his friend Edwin Abbey, he had gone swimming at Pangbourne Weir and gashed his head. Abbey immediately took him to Frank Millet and his wife, Lily, at Farnham House in Broadway. The power and romance of the English countryside, as the American Millets perceived it, had led to their habit of living their dream for several months every year. They were practising artists themselves, with a gift for attracting fellow artists and creating 'a carnival atmosphere'. They belonged to an extensive network of English and American friends and acquaintances. One of the Americans was the super-rich Charles Fairchild, an early patron of Sargent who also admired Robert Louis Stevenson's work.

John Singer Sargent, purposeful, virile and young (he was twenty-eight in 1885) soon recovered from his head injury. At Broadway, he found himself transported into a magical world of bucolic days and convivial evenings. That summer the classical painter, Lawrence Alma-Tameda, joined Abbey, Sargent, Henry James, Edmund Gosse and the illustrator Frederick Barnard at Farnham House. Inspired by the garden and the children playing there, Sargent planned a large painting that would combine both elements. This was to be his 'big picture'. All summer he sketched the children gathering roses and lighting lanterns at dusk. He sketched lilies growing in a pot and, with Lily Millet's approval, transported flowerpots from one part of the garden to another to suit his purpose. Joseph Mazzinghi's hit song of the day became a favourite of the colonists. Sargent wrote down the lines that inspired his painting and tagged the note to his easel:

Did you see my Flora pass this way?
Carnation, Lily, Lily, Rose.

*

The morning Sargent was expected Louis smartened up. The poncho wasn't the image he was after for an oil portrait so he put on his velvet jacket, white shirt, red tie, serge trousers and brown shoes. His moustache and hair had been well trimmed by Valentine. He had shaved closely, neatened his eyebrows and pulled out a few stray nose hairs. When he was breakfasting in the dining room and reading *The Times,* Fanny appeared. 'Now here you are, come down at last. A sight to gladden the heart of any man,' he said, and enquired about her health. She was not quite well, but a little better, and planned to join Louis and Sargent at dinner that evening.

'I'll instruct Mrs Watts to prepare a buffet lunch in the dining room,' she said solemnly. 'You can help yourselves whenever you like.'

'Capital idea, wife. And I'll get Beaucox to put up the trestle table in the drawing room. The light's good, I've a hunch Sargent will paint me there.'

'Then get Beaucox to put an old sheet under the table. The last thing I want is oil paint spilled on the carpet.'

'Aye, all right. But I'd like you to join us for lunch and say a welcome to the man.'

When Fanny turned sullenly towards the door muttering 'it's you he wants', Louis vowed he'd give up humouring her forever. He felt very angry with Fanny and went outside to cool off.

Waiting for Sargent on the Skerryvore wall, his mind ran on carefree Paris days before he met Fanny. What a dash he and Bob had cut in bohemian circles. Scots dandies in peg-leg trousers, tam o'shanters and striped stockings: *Say could that lad be I?* Bob was already a Cambridge graduate, hailed as a 'university man' by the impressionable American art students he encountered in Paris. It must have been around 1874 that Bob had introduced him to John Singer Sargent at the atelier of Carlous-Duran. Sargent was a sophisticated American, brought up in Italy by rich, cultured parents.

Louis stubbed out his cigarette when he spied the artist halfway down Middle Road. Even from this distance he could admire the bearded fellow's handsome dress: hacking jacket, matching tweed cap, and plus fours of mustard corduroy. Sargent progressed slowly, deep in thought, part-bent under his painting gear and easel, his haversack bristling with long-handled painting brushes. Like a creature from a fairy story, Louis thought

'Velázquez, Velázquez, Velázquez!' Louis said when they embraced. 'D'you remember Carlous-Duran's chant from the Paris days: "Study Velázquez without respite? Execute the maximum by means of the minimum."'

Sargent lay down his gear. 'By Jove, Stevenson, you've a great memory.' He glanced at the villas flanking Middle Road. 'I say, this is a respectable part of the world. Can I safely assume you've said farewell to bohemian life?'

'Aye, I'm a householder now, though no doubt I'll soon be cast back on the dung heap where I belong - when the dollars run out and my wife runs away and

Father Tom refuses to throw his offspring any more crusts. But come and see the garden before we go in.'

They left Sargent's equipment in the front porch and walked towards the chine. 'Henry asked me to convey his warmest regards,' Sargent said. 'He often says his visits to Skerryvore saved him from abject boredom.'

'He is much missed,' Louis said wistfully when they stood at the edge of the garden. 'My wife, a former pioneer of the Wild West, has dug out a seductive little labyrinth of paths, stairs and arbours down there.'

Sargent went off to explore the chine, and, as soon as he disappeared, Louis rested on a chair and closed his eyes. – Sargent's an artist through and through; unafraid to show life as it really is. His so-called shocking portrait of Madame X merely revealed the hypocrisy of the Parisian bourgeoisie. The woman looked ready to step out of her dress and leap into lust, and why not? It's what most men and women secretly desire - lust with love, *le petit mort*. Sargent's a seeker after truth. I'll get a truer portrait from him than from any other painter in the land, and I'm in the mood for gritty reality. Not for nothing have I lain these past months listening out for time's winged chariot. To have suffered thus sets a keen edge on what remains of the agreeable in life - that much I've learned in the refiner's fire. If, as the Vandegrifter maintains, I resemble a wraith, then I'm content to be portrayed as one.

He had almost fallen asleep when a flash of inspiration made him open his eyes. Why hadn't he thought of it before? Sargent could paint the *two* of us - Mr *and* Mrs Stevenson - that would put an end to her complaining. Better to have Fanny captured within Sargent's frame than hanging about *like an unfed cur*. The words smarted his mind. It was increasingly difficult to feel generous towards Fanny.

'What a magnificent place, Stevenson. I'd heard of the chines of Bournemouth,' Sargent said, climbing back into the garden, 'but never expected them to be on such a grand scale as Alum Chine. What a find!'

As they strolled towards the house, Bogue arrived to growl at Sargent's feet. Fortunately, Sargent was a dog lover and after he had made a fuss of the terrier the Skerryvore bell must be seen . . . but not rung, Louis warned, since Mrs Stevenson was out-of-sorts and resting. The mention of Fanny reminded Louis - put her in the portrait? - but lingering ambivalence made him hold his tongue. On the one hand, wouldn't he resent Fanny's intrusion into his portrait, on the other, wouldn't it be worth it for the sake of a more contented home?

Louis led the way to the cold cuts, salads and breads laid out in the dining room and Sargent consulted his watch. 'Almost two o'clock already, almost past lunchtime, yet I'm keen to start work as well as eat.'

Louis pushed a plate into his hand. 'Let's do both, but let's not make a Lord Mayor's Banquet out of the need to sustain ourselves.'

They carried their plates through to the drawing

room where Beaucox had placed Sargent's belongings on the trestle table.

Sargent bit into a sandwich and looked around the room. 'I think I see the way to quote the Dutch domestic interior with post-Degas boldness. The large window lets in good light, diffuse rather than sharp. The Indian red walls suit my palette, and the Oriental rug lends a decorative touch to what might otherwise be too austere a portrait. It won't take long to execute the bare bones of it. I know exactly what I want, and I'll start with some quick pencil sketches.' He took a sketchpad and a small stretched canvas from his satchel.

'Is that for the portrait?' Louis said, taking up the canvas. 'It's a dinky size, I imagined something larger.' Far too small to accommodate the Bedlamite, he thought.

'These days, most of my portraits are twenty inches by twenty-four. I can execute them speedily, you see, and not charge much for them, or give them as gifts to my friends. I'm working my way through the Broadway set, the Millet children, Gosse and his daughter, Theresa. It's all good practise.'

Louis watched the preparations, his thumb and forefinger twirling the corners of his moustache. 'I've something to say,' he blurted out at last. 'I thought of Mrs Stevenson being in the portrait, but the canvas looks to small to hold us both.'

'Size is neither here nor there; but I understood Mrs Stevenson to be under the weather?'

'Aye, she is, though her malady might be remedied with a little attention. And, besides, she is all in all to me. I wouldn't be standing in front of you now if Fanny hadn't saved me from the jaws of death last year. I told you about my dance with death at Hyères when you visited our lodgings last November?'

Sargent looked thoughtful. 'You did. And I confess I came here with an idea for the composition. I wanted to capture you striding about as you often do, rather than seated as in the last portrait. Let me think over your suggestion for a moment . . . I see it's of great importance to you.' He rummaged in his satchel and laid a handful of paint tubes on the table. 'The two pictures hanging on the wall add a further decorative touch . . . and, perhaps I'll have the bergère below the pictures, all in shades of blue and green.'

Louis sat in the bergère. 'We've named it "Henry James' chair"', he said, patting the arms affectionately. 'Henry liked to sit in this chair above all others.'

Sargent laughed. 'I dare say he did, since the chair's button-backed and dear Henry's buttoned-up.' Then, 'Wait, don't move,' he said, studying Louis above a pencil held at arm's length. He went to open the drawing room door, inwards, so that Louis now sat behind the door. He returned to check the perspective from his original position. 'You want your wife in the composition, Stevenson? I believe there is a way. Go and stand on the other side of the door? Yes, that's right, and Mrs Stevenson can be in the bergère. There will be two *foci* of interest in the portrait . . . the main focus will be you, striding about on one side of the open door. There will be a view into the hall with the stairs rising up. The rest of the canvas, roughly a third, will show your wife on the other side of the door in Henry's chair. I'll set out my colours while you fetch Mrs Stevenson.'

Louis went upstairs, and, when he returned smiling broadly, the room smelled promisingly of turpentine and oil paint. 'We have made her happy as a skylark,' he said. 'She'll be down shortly.'

Sargent placed the canvas on his easel and took up his sketchpad. 'Then let's make a start. I'll do a few drawings while we're waiting . . . I don't suppose you'd consider removing your clothes?'

Louis mimed a shiver. 'I do it every day - take my clothes off - naked I go to the world of dreams, naked I return each morning, unless it's chilly and I have on my nightshift and long johns.'

'When my sitters are unclothed, it's easier to see the structure of their bodies. Might I make a quick drawing of you in the nude as a preliminary to the painting?'

Louis shivered again, 'I'd do it, only I'm shy of the world seeing me as a skeleton - and, even though the fire glows in the hearth, I'd likely catch my death of cold.'

'Will you *stride* then? Get some interesting theme into your head and pace up and down. And each time you walk away from the door, turn a little and gaze at me.' Louis tried a practise run. 'Yes, that's perfect; and hook your thumb over your trouser pocket if that feels comfortable and natural. You often make that gesture, you know.'

Louis paced uneasily. Why had Sargent's request to draw him naked discomfited him to the extent that his heart was pounding in his chest? He wondered what Sargent saw when he observed him so keenly and made rapid marks with his charcoal stick. I pace, and I look at him as I turn, and he looks up at me as if we reflect each other in an invisible mirror. He's the large man I might have been but for my sickly constitution. I'm a wraith compared to Sargent, yet we're a match for each other as artists. Will he capture the worst of my faults, *a certain impatient gaiety of disposition that conceals a multitude of duplicities?*

Louis went to the open door, turned, then walked back gazing at Sargent. Now and then, when Sargent looked up, their dazzled eyes met and Louis knew a powerful desire to embrace the man and dance with him, round and round the room in a glorious sweeping waltz. He could even hear the music. It was *The Blue Danube*.

Back and forward he paced until curious thoughts silenced the music in his head: *though a profound double-dealer, I was in no sense a hypocrite; both sides of me were in dead earnest . . . I thus drew steadily nearer to the truth. Man is not truly one, but truly two.* What sort of a character might say that in a story? The words didn't fit *Kidnapped* and they didn't fit *Olalla*, but what about the Christmas shocker? It was hardly surprising, he thought, that double-dealing was on his mind since, at that very moment, he and

Sargent were deeply engaged in an act of duplicity. Their eyes met again, and suddenly both men froze.

Fanny made a theatrical entrance in a sleeveless orange silk shift under a lustrous lace shawl embroidered with gold thread. Her feet were bare and the shawl was draped Odalisque-style over her head. She's got herself up in fancy dress like something abducted from the seraglio, Louis thought, perplexed yet admiring. *This* was how Fanny wanted the world to see her. The exotic wife of Robert Louis Stevenson was no mere comma after all.

Fanny had refused to let Katherine stay at Skerryvore before their departure to Dartmoor, and, having scored on that account, she could scarcely turn down Louis' wish to invite Katherine to dinner during Sargent's visit. Fanny retired to her room directly after the meal, leaving the others drinking coffee.

Louis pushed his cup away. 'I shouldna' do this.'

'Do what?' Katherine said.

'Drink coffee late in the evening. It'll keep me awake into the wee small hours. When I was a sickly boy, Cummy, my old nurse, would give me coffee to soothe my frets in the middle of the night.'

'Coffee in the middle of the night, cousin? But coffee is known to be a stimulant.'

'Och, Cummy meant well and knew no better. When coffee first came in it was hailed as a miracle drug by the middle classes, but the combination of coffee and the airlessness of my nursery brought on feverish nightmares. The parents had it sealed up against draughts, and the little room swelled and shrank during terrible long nights when I lay awake, a hacking cough for my companion, praying for sleep or morning. Sometimes I wondered if some spirit flew out of the cabinet made by Deacon Brodie that stood in my bedroom.'

'Deacon Brodie, the body snatcher?'

'Aye, the same.'

Sargent puffed on a cigar, silent but attentive, his keen brown eyes following the cousins' exchange.

'I remember you had nightmares when you were a student,' Katherine said. 'Presumably coffee was not to blame then?'

Louis smiled at Katherine's snare. 'Oh, I still drank coffee, though not in the middle of the night. Drink and hashish brought on the night terrors of my student years. Nightmares that reflected the double life I was leading - but I'll not go into detail about that, except to say there were times when I feared for my reason.'

'You could have confided in me,' Katherine said softly. She was wearing a dress of gold tussore with a neckline cut low enough to set off an amethyst necklace willed to her by their grandmother. She had high cheekbones, a shapely chin and deep-set, intelligent eyes.

Although she's a matron now, Louis thought lovingly, her bonny face remains undiminished by the ravages of divorce and single motherhood.

'Aye, there were times when I thought of coming to

you, Kate. But that's all in the past. Come now, friends, let us not sink into the gloom of missed opportunities. Let's rejoice in the present when you, Katherine, are the mother of the exceptional Snoodie and her wee brother, as well as a translator and author; when Sargent here is a talented painter; and me? Well, I've lived to tell a few tales, and no doubt there will be more before I'm done. Mr Sargent might be interested to hear about your work, Kate.'

They made a striking pair, Katherine de Mattos and John Singer Sargent, but as Louis well knew, handsome Sargent's preference was for his own sex.

'Cousin Kate's a woman of independent means,' Louis prompted, and Katherine said, 'without the full support of a husband I have had little choice. My mother takes care of Snoodie and her brother when I'm writing for the *Magazine of Art* edited by Mr Henley, our family friend, and other periodicals.'

'In addition to that, Katherine's a competent translator, and she publishes short stories under the pseudonym of Theodor Hertz Garten.' Katherine and Sargent laughed aloud at Louis' pompous pronunciation of the German name. 'You make it sound ridiculous,' Katherine protested.

'It's a fascinating pseudonym, Mrs de Mattos. Theodor means "Gift of God" does it not, and Hertz Garten "garden of the heart"? I'd be happy paint you in either of your guises.'

'Then you shall. My cousin will give you my address

in London where you'd be most welcome. But tell us what you're working on these days, apart from the portrait of Louis?'

Sargent winked at Louis. 'The portrait is to be called *Robert Louis Stevenson and his Wife.*'

'Aye, it's true, Kate,' Louis said. 'Fanny's crept into my picture, but more of that another time. Let's hear about our friend's work.'

'I'm working on a large painting at Broadway called "Carnation, Lily, Lily, Rose". It's not a commission; it's very much my own thing - a risk, since I can ill afford to do unpaid work. In effect, it is an exploration of dark and light on a large scale: seven feet by five feet. And you, Stevenson? What have you in store for us? Something to rival *Treasure Island*?'

'I've put another adventure story called *Kidnapped* away in a drawer until my mind comes up with a melodrama for the Christmas market. You could say I, too, am exploring the theme of dark and light, though not so much in the external world as in the soul of man.'

'"Carnation, Lily, Lily, Rose" . . . that's an entrancing title for a painting,' Katherine said and when she hummed a few bars of Joseph Mazzinghi's popular song, Louis and Sargent joined in.

'Last year I began studying the effects of twilight at Broadway,' Sargent said at last; 'making notes, small oils, etcetera, in preparation for the big canvas. I have the children in white dresses and Japanese lanterns strung above a plot of rose trees and white lilies. The lanterns will be lit up when I paint the scene at twilight. I started practising with the children last summer and learned to fill my pockets with candies to reward them for posing.' He stretched and pushed his chair back. 'And now, friends, if you'll excuse me, I need to work on this afternoon's oil sketch before I turn in. All the marks and colour notes I've made will be amplified and perfected at my studio in Tite Street.'

After breakfast Sargent asked to be left undisturbed 'to tinker with the portrait'. When he appeared in the hall a little after noon, 'I'm expected at Broadway this evening and must catch the next train out,' he said. 'I'll send the finished portrait down soon. I'm a fast worker, you won't have long to wait. Mr and Mrs Stevenson may not *like* the final result, but I hope they'll find it honest.'

'Aye honest, that's the main thing,' Louis smiled.

In the afternoon he wrote to Thomas Hardy: *Dear Sir, I expect to arrive in Dorchester tomorrow or next day; and if I shall be strong enough, I shall do myself the pleasure of calling on you - if not, I shall let you know at what inn I put up, and perhaps you will be kind enough to call on me? I think you must have heard of me from Gosse from whom, if time had served, I could have got an introduction; but my acquaintance with your mind is already of so old a date, that I scarce felt such formalities were needed, and if you should be busy or unwilling, the irregularity of my approach leaves you the safer retreat. Yours truly, Robert Louis Stevensonn.*

III

The world is too much with us; and coin it grows so sparsely on the tree! I am pouring forth a penny dreadful . . . they call it Doctor Jekyll, but they also call it Mr Hyde.
Robert Louis Stevenson to Sidney Colvin, autumn 1885

Interlude with Sam

Skerryvore lay closed and silent when Sam went through the gate with the dog. His key clicked in the lock, Bogue strained at the leash, and the floorboards echoed Sam's footsteps when he headed for the kitchen. After he set light to the stove, he put out a bowl of slops for Bogue and poked the sleeping hedgehog with a spurtle. It let out a screech so baleful Sam faltered, his hands covering his ears as he pictured a great army of cockroaches scurrying all over the kitchen, pursued by the spiky hedgehog. How strange it was to be alone at Skerryvore with a dog and a hedgehog, he thought, hastily stuffing ship's biscuits and a hunk of cheese from the pantry into his pocket. Then he went sprinting across the garden and descended into the chine by way of his mother's winding paths, made slippery by recent rain.

Slithering downwards, now and then he clutched a bush or a damp limb, and when his feet touched the even ground of Alum Chine, he set off in the direction of the sea. There was no one about on this dank autumn day when the first brassy leaves of autumn had fallen. The sweetish metallic scent of mouldering foliage hanging in the dark ravine intensified his anxiety over Louis, fighting for his life at Exeter. His poor mother had been at breaking point from nursing him. He started to run fast, hoping his anguish might lessen when he got beyond the murky chine to the sea. Sure enough, when the chine opened out the air became lighter and purer and he paused to calm his throbbing heart. Then a final sprint transported him into a world of pastel sand, and sea and sky in various shades of grey.

Not the weather to be out, yet he noticed a few eerie souls strolling in dark coats along the front. He threw himself down on the sand. Rain threatened but weather was the last thing on his mind, gnawing at the cheese, crunching the biscuits in his mouth, wondering if he had done the right thing to abandon his mother at Exeter. Yet she had insisted he leave: Louis is over the worst, Sam, he remembered her saying. I don't need your help to lift him anymore. You must return to Skerryvore, go back to the crammer, and when we come home we'll discuss whether you should stay with us at Bournemouth or repeat the first year at Edinburgh University.

Louis might have a relapse and die, Sam worried, lifting his head in hope of a response from the threatening clouds. He's not out of danger yet. If the Squire were to die, I'd be responsible for Ma. Well, that wouldn't be so bad. I'd give up the university lark and be a writer like Louis. Tom and Maggie would see us right for dollars and as soon as Tom dies, well, I dare say we'll be rich as Croesus. He let out a laugh and the first drops of rain spattered his forehead. His hands played in the damp sand for a few moments, then on an impulse he threw off his clothes and raced to the sea. It was as if the icy sea wrung his troubles out of him. Dive after dive, he plunged through its salty waves.

Goose pimpled and shivering, he dressed quickly. What a plunge! he chuckled. *That* was daring! I could have been arrested for swimming in the altogether like that. When he thought about it, he concluded he had never in his life done anything so . . . well, against the law. And that made him think of his father. Sam Senior had disappeared without trace in California and was forever breaking the law. That much he had gleaned as a youngster from snatches of conversations between his mother and Aunt Nellie. Maybe I should go out West and search for Pa, Sam thought urgently. But then, well, wouldn't that set the cat among the pigeons? I mean things're settled here. The Stevensons are mighty strange but they're all me an' Ma have got.

He ran back to Skerryvore, a frown etching his brow. When he arrived in the kitchen, Bogue was snoring beside the hedgehog's basket. Still shivering, Sam peered into the dark drawing room where the furniture had been covered with white dustsheets. It was all so dim he suddenly thought maybe I've got opthalmia like the Squire at Hyères? He remembered the Squire, lying sick in his bed with the added irritation of an eye infection, after the corporation dumped a mound of putrid refuse on the road near La Solitude. Louis had to stay in the dark wearing bandages over his eyes and strange green goggles shaped like a pig's snout. It had not been funny, though, and slipping between the ghostly white shapes to throw open the shutters, Sam felt alarmed by the memory.

Having decided there was no point in opening up the dining room before the parents' return, he trudged upstairs. When he threw open the shutters of Louis' room, he caught sight of himself in the cheval glass and laughed with relief. I can see! I don't have opthalmia after all. I won't be forced to wear goggles like the Squire. Still, maybe I need ordinary glasses? He did have to step right up to the mirror and peer through narrowed eyes to see what he looked like after his swim. His fingers combed sticky sand out of his curly hair. Not that there's anyone to see me, he thought, and I should get warm.

Nervous and excited, he wrapped himself in his stepfather's tartan blanket and took possession of the room during a swift inspection. So many objects and furnishings he had never felt free to examine before. There was Louis' flute, and he tried out a few notes. He smelled Louis' lavender shaving soap in its hand-carved bowl, he saw Louis' view from the window, the long sloping garden and the chine. He went to Louis' desk and toyed with the worn label attached to the key that had been left in the top drawer. Decisively, he opened the drawer and saw, neatly stacked, the manuscript of *Prince Otto* with a note: 'To be edited'. Underneath it he discovered the draft of *Kidnapped*. Ma said it must be almost finished by now, Sam thought, turning to the last pages. *Chapter XV*, he read: *The Lad with the Silver Button*.

He sat in Louis' armchair, and read the introduction. 'Memoirs of the Adventure of David Balfour in the year 1751': *I will begin the story of my adventures with a certain morning early in the month of June, in the year of grace 1751, when I took the key for the last time out of the door of my father's house. The sun began to shine upon the summit of the hills as I went down the road; and by the time I had come as far as the manse, the blackbirds were whistling in the garden lilacs, and the mist that hung around the valley in the time of the dawn was beginning to arise and die away* . . . Sam read on until David encountered Uncle Ebeneezer and was kidnapped aboard the *Covenant*. Spellbound, he immersed himself in the drama of the shipwreck.

When the front door suddenly banged, Sam's heart lurched. He held his breath, listening to soft footsteps tracing the line of the hall below. Why didn't Bogue bark? He tiptoed out to the landing and peered over the bannister. 'Who's there?' he called nervously.

'Only me, back from France, Master Sam,' came Valentine's timid reply. He raced downstairs, rehearsing his mother's admonition to keep his distance from the maid. When Valentine said she would take her bags to her room, Sam returned to *Kidnapped*. He had read to the point in the story when the Squire has Davie swimming for his life towards Erraid. He couldn't wait to discover the fate of the stranded boy.

Valentine came up to say she had opened the

shutters in the drawing room and did Master Sam need anything? He said he would like tea, and followed her downstairs with *Kidnapped*. Before he settled down to read again, it occurred to him that the hero of the story was a lot like him: around the same age, sensible, strong, and conservative in his opinions

Just as he was wondering if Louis had modelled Davie on himself, a queer tapping sound drew him to the window. Adelaide Boodle was peering inside, her hands a shelf over her eyes. 'Has the family returned? I didn't expect you for another two weeks,' she said when Sam opened the window. 'How was Dartmoor?'

'You had better come inside,' Sam said, sounding more like Thomas Stevenson than Davie Balfour. Still, he was the temporary master of the household and he meant to show his mother he could carry off the role. He stood up when Adelaide came into the drawing room, swiftly followed by Valentine with the tea trolley. 'Fetch two more cups,' he said.

They sat down, teacups in hand, Adelaide all smiles to be back inside Skerryvore, Valentine nervously perched on a drawing room chair.

Adelaide was first to speak. 'Did you go to the sea near Dartmoor? Were there any signs of the Wreckers?'

Sam studied his feet. 'There was no holiday.'

'Why ever not?'

'Mr Stevenson fell ill - too ill to travel. Ma sent me back to get Skerryvore ready for their return.' Sam looked towards the window, uncertain how to continue.

'They were to visit Thomas Hardy at Dorchester on your first day away,' Adelaide prompted.

'Yep, they did, and the next day on the train to Exeter, Louis talked non-stop about Mr Hardy - my mother was less committal - and he was in fine fettle until that evening at the New London Inn he started spitting blood.'

'God preserve him,' Adelaide murmured. Valentine covered her mouth with her hands.

'He is seriously ill,' Sam said. 'He almost died.'

Adelaide took out her handkerchief. 'Tell us everything right from the beginning. Tell us what Mr Stevenson said about Thomas Hardy.'

'Well,' said Sam, rising to take the chair at the drawing room desk, 'to begin with we were a merry party with several rooms set aside for us at the inn. As soon as our bags had been brought up, I set off with Mrs de Mattos - Katherine - to explore the city. During dinner that evening Louis talked about Mr Hardy and how Hardy's early manhood had been similar to his own; that is, Hardy's feet were set on a very different road from writing. The Squire was to be an engineer and then a lawyer before *he* became a writer, and Mr Hardy was articled to architecture. Mr Hardy lost his religious faith like Louis and only after the success of *Far from the Madding Crowd* was he was able to give up architecture. Ma gave Katherine and me a hilarious description of the house he built called Max Gate and we all laughed, except Louis who had gone white as a sheet. He said he felt a peculiar longing for his bed.'

Sam paused to assess through narrowed eyes the emotional state of his companions. 'Do I tell you too much detail?'

When Adelaide and Valentine shook their heads solemnly he continued, 'I remember the Squire saying he knew this longing well, and that it often preceded illness yet it filled him with tenderness for all humanity.'

'Fancy that,' Adelaide whispered, and Sam said never in his born days would he forget Louis saying it. 'Then Louis staggered to his feet and asked me to help him up to his room.'

Adelaide gave Valentine a wan smile and impulsively took her hand. 'My heart's in my mouth to hear what comes next.'

'Well, the parents' room was comfortable and pleasant with a dormer window, and I was glad to see it had an extra truckle bed that would serve should the Squire and Ma have a fight. They do, you know, fight.'

Adelaide and Valentine exchanged sad conspiratorial glances.

'Louis asked me to draw the curtains and the next moment his voice was strangled by a haemorrhage. I whipped a bowl off the washstand just in time to catch a torrent of blood. Then I supported his head until the next burst of blood practically filled the bowl. I couldn't leave off the bowl to shout for mother, but thankfully she came in anyway and I raced down the corridor to the bathroom to fetch it back clean.'

Sam paused, hearing stifled sobs from the women. 'If it's too upsetting?'

Adelaide blew her nose. 'No, no, please go on. Tell us everything.'

'Well, if you're sure. When I got back the bleeding had stopped and Ma and I got the Squire into his nightshift. He was limp as a rag doll, but his eyes darted madly from side to side. Ma said it was a signal he wanted pencil and paper.'

'What did he write, Sam?'

'I refuse to die in summer.'

Adelaide smiled through her tears and turned to Valentine. 'Do you understand everything Sam says?'

'*Presque tout.*'

Sam curved his arm over the back of the chair. 'Valentine has seen it all before, Miss Boodle. She helped Ma to nurse Mr Stevenson when they lived at La Solitude. At this stage Louis requires ergotine and prefers to dose himself. He thrust out his hand for the minim glass Ma had taken from the medicine chest she always travels with. Make the first dose a small one, she begged the Squire, for you know its effects. Ma's hand trembled when she helped him to measure a dose, swallow it and sink back into his pillows, and no wonder since the ergotine makes him crazy.'

'R.L.S. crazy? That's impossible!' Adelaide protested, but Valentine said softly, '*C'est vrai*, I saw this at Hyères.'

'Strong drugs do terrible things to people, Miss Boodle,' Sam said, a note of authority in his voice. 'The next thing was, Ma and I went to get hot water to wash him. But when I turned on the hot water tap, the plumbing system started up with such unearthly creaking and groaning it terrified Ma and she burst into tears.'

'Her nerves must have been on edge, Sam. She thought R.L.S. might die, and so far from home. How terrible.'

'When we returned to the room, the Squire's eyes were sunk in their sockets, yet it amazed me how expressive they were, following Ma's movements about the room with signals of distress or appeal which she immediately understood. They communicate in a sign language all their own when he's ill. Ma washed his face with lavender soap, and I remember the relief when she whispered, the ergotine's done its work, Sam. It's stopped the blood bursting in his lungs. She wiped the perspiration from the Squire's brow and stroked his cheeks with the scented cloth. Then she measured out laudanum to Dr Scott's prescription. We'll get the local doctor first thing tomorrow, she told the Squire, but take this for now, then we can both go back to sleep. As he swallowed the laudanum off a spoon, he held Ma with his eyes and gave her a strange sad smile. Bluidy Jack, he mouthed, but she shook her head. I'll see he doesn't get you and I'll leave the lamp turned low for comfort's sake, said Ma. Then she said goodnight to me. I waited till she stumbled to her truckle bed before I went to my room along the landing.'

'It's a mercy you were there, Sam,' Adelaide said.

'Hell, yeah! And next morning I found Ma in a private parlour the innkeeper set aside for our party. There she was, tucking into her breakfast of tea, toast and eggs while the innkeeper's daughter fetched mine. Prudence is her name. The New London Inn is a family business. As we ate, Ma told me she had wakened to see Louis lying like a cadaver and feared the worst, but when she put her fingers on his pulse, the faint beat, beat, beat was there, so she hurried downstairs to ask the innkeeper to send for the doctor. The doctor arrived when we were still at breakfast: quite a young man in an old-fashioned frock coat with a pale face and a thatch of red hair. You know how Ma is with new acquaintances? She never stands on ceremony, and soon she was telling him the Squire's medical history in great detail, from his sickly childhood to all the times he had nearly died in her care, in California, Hyères, and now here. Do you remember, Valentine? The London doctor who came rushing out to France said we must keep Mr Stevenson alive until he's forty. After that, like a winged bird, he might live to be ninety. The implication is that for five years, between now until he's forty, he must live as though he were walking on eggs.'

Valentine nodded, '*Mais oui, c'est vrai.*'

'It's true that some men outlive their illnesses,' Adelaide said pulling her shoulders back. 'I've heard that said more than once.'

'When we went upstairs, the Squire hadn't stirred.

The House on the Chine

We stood looking down at him for a few seconds before the doctor had a stethoscope at his chest. When he bent down to listen, there came a little groan and the Squire opened his eyes. He was overcome with fits of coughing. He writhed about, struggling for breath, until the doctor supported him bodily and I grabbed the basin again.'

'He needed more ergotine,' Valentine said.

Sam nodded. 'The doctor injected him then asked Ma what medicines she kept. A second seizure gripped Louis. Blood gushed into the bowl. At least a pint, and, after it was over, the doctor took Ma aside while I held the Squire's hand. Ergotine is likely to make him behave in a peculiar manner, the doctor said. Ma replied she knew it all too well and nothing scared her more.'

Valentine shivered. 'It is *terrible* to see, yet *l'ergotine* is the best thing, maybe the only thing, to stop the bleeding.'

'The doctor gave him a dose of morphine and Ma rearranged his bedcovers. He fell asleep and we all went downstairs.'

Sam asked Valentine for more tea. After a small silence Adelaide said, 'Was the inn a pleasant place?'

'Nothing special by way of luxury, Miss Boodle, but friendly and comfortable. The private parlour was cosy. Prudence kept a fire going and lit the gas lamps every time we came in. But, where was I? Yeah, the doctor . . . Ma took the fireside chair and sat still as a stone for a few seconds before she burst into tears. I put my arm round her shoulders and the doctor said Ma was to be congratulated. If she had not brought the ergotine along for just such an emergency, her husband might well have died. He advised us to send for Dr Scott whose good relationship with Mr Stevenson might help his recovery. Meanwhile we were to send for him any time of day or night.'

'Where was Mrs de Mattos while all this was going on?' said Adelaide. 'I expect she was sitting upstairs keeping watch over Mr Stevenson.'

Sam shook his head. 'No, at first Ma wouldn't let Katherine near him. The doctor wanted to give Ma St John's Wort to calm her nerves but she refused saying she'd need all her wits about her for what was yet to come. To cut a long story shorter, the doctor said we should prepare to stay at Exeter for a few weeks. I had said very little all this time, but now I said, Bournemouth is not far away; perhaps my stepfather will be able to travel there sooner? The doctor replied that the patient lay at death's door and was in danger of flying through it if he was disturbed in the least.'

Sam covered his face with his hands, concealing tears, and Valentine said, 'I must go to Exeter.'

They were silent for a few moments until Sam recovered. 'Katherine came into the parlour after the doctor left. Ma told her the holiday was over, a terrible disappointment we must all bear for Louis' sake. She said Louis' fit was less bad than the one at Hyères last year. It didn't last so long, but was more violent, and if it had it continued it would certainly have strangled him. Then, Valentine, do you know what Ma said?' Valentine leaned forward eagerly. 'I remember her very words: "I wish Valentine had come with us. Valentine shared the nursing with me when Louis was at death's door in France. Day and night she took watch with me and in his strangling coughing spells she lifted him, pillows and all, in her strong young arms. I would send for her if she were not in France."'

Valentine pulled free of Adelaide's hand and stood up. 'I will go to them *immediatement*.'

'Well,' Sam began, 'but Ma didn't think you'd be up to another journey.'

Adelaide's eyes flew from Sam to Valentine. 'Have you and Mrs Stevenson quarrelled again?'

Valentine stared at the floor. An awkward silence fell. Then Sam burst out, 'C'mon, Miss Boodle, let's get a breath of fresh air in the garden.'

The clouds that hung about the house dispersed, leaving the garden bathed in hazy sunshine. Adelaide helped Sam carry out cake and lemonade to Louis' sunbathing spot. 'Ma said it was a relief to know you were keeping an eye on Skerryvore in her absence, Miss Boodle,' Sam said when they had settled in the garden chairs.

'Oh, it was nothing. I would climb the mountain of Everest for the sake of your parents. But tell me what happened next?'

'Ma went up to unpack the travelling cases into the

chests and wardrobe. When, at eleven o'clock the Squire still slept she slipped down to the private room, but soon Prudence arrived saying terrifying shouts were coming from room seven. We rushed upstairs and found Louis writhing on the bed, shouting nonsense and rolling from side to side. Katherine stood weeping by the door. She said it frightened her to see Louis like that. Ma said, then go away, then added that his agony was caused by sciatica. Ma was so brusque I felt sorry for Katherine. She and my mother find it hard to see eye to eye at the best of times, but there's never any need for rudeness.' Sam broke off abruptly, 'I'm not sure I want to go into any more details, Miss Boodle. In fact, I feel suddenly weak myself. Most probably got a chill from sea bathing this morning.'

'Then you must take care of yourself, Sam. Perhaps you might tell me more tomorrow? In the meantime, may I depend on the Squire being out of danger?'

'Unless he has a relapse. All we can do now is pray he does not and wait for the telegram Ma promises to send as soon as the doctor gives them permission to return home. I suggest we play a game of croquet every day until they return.'

Sam's chill kept him in bed for the next two days and Valentine left trays of soup and light meals on the landing. He dropped notes outside his door when he needed something, such as a hot toddy the first evening and a washing bowl filled with warm water next morning. Over and over again, he relived in his mind what it had been to nurse the Squire at his mother's side. Vividly the nightmare repeated as if to convince him his place was at his mother side, rather than in Edinburgh playing the role of the perfect grandson, or setting off for the Wild West in search of his father.

Scenes from the New London Inn he had been unable to share with Adelaide haunted him: helping his mother to lift Louis into a kneeling position when he started shouting, watching as he lay still for a few moments then started roaring like an animal in pain as he struggled to reposition his body. The Squire needed to be constantly moving. Help me to lift him round again, Sam, yes, that's right, on all fours, Ma would say. Let his face rest sideways a moment on the pillows. Then we must lift him again to take the pressure off his legs. What a relief it had been when the groaning stopped.

Vividly Sam recalled lifting his stepfather what seemed like a hundred times over the next few days: Louis' shanks flaying weakly in the air, his withered body sinking into his arms. When he laid the Squire gently onto his pillows, his face had been the colour of wax. Sam would never forget the feel of his stepfather's shoulder and arm bones under his hand, hard, almost without flesh, like a skeleton's. - We will witness this weird performance again, you can be sure, Ma said. But don't be frightened, Sam. It is all to relieve the pressure on his bones from lying in the bed, and at least his lungs have stopped bleeding.

Sam remembered going to look out of the window, his eyes blurry from unaccustomed tears he managed to wipe away before his mother called him. He heard himself saying, you've been through too much, Ma; first, little Hervey dying, and all the Squire's emergencies ever since. The clattering of horses' hooves and the voices of children out in the street had risen up to the room where his mother was folding clean linen. Ma closed the linen closet and reminded me I had been there to support her in California and Hyères when Louis was sick. A son like you is all the support I need, she said. Yeah, he remembered replying, but I'm always at a distance from the drama, Ma. I can lend you my strength, lifting and laying the Squire, but I wish you had a best friend or someone else to comfort you. His mother had given him a strange look. She was putting up the photograph of herself taken in California after her marriage. - Louis is my duty now, Sam. I give daily thanks that you are a healthy young man whose support I have always been grateful for.

Sam searched his mind for what had happened next: the gong sounding for lunch, Katherine waiting in the parlour for him and Ma. Over the summer holidays he had come to love Katherine with a passion that alarmed him and made him hope to find a wife like her one day - but much younger of course. Huddled by the fire, she had looked so pale and frightened he longed to reach out and touch her. - The innkeeper suggested we take luncheon here rather than in the dining room,

Katherine had said. - She always tried to make things agreeable. Sam remembered them eating the roast beef dinner in silence until his mother said, I'm not so cast down as I was when Louis was ill in America and France, strangely enough. I dare say it's because this illness is taking a familiar course. And Katherine said she thought Ma was very brave and that she wanted so much to help her.

His mother explained to Katherine that heavy doses of ergotine made Louis behave like a mad animal. Yet he must take it to stave the bleeding from his lungs. Ma and Katherine were picking at their dinner when he had made things worse by saying the Squire had been so tormented at Hyères, he almost killed his Ma.

Upsetting Katherine was the last thing he had intended, yet her knife and fork had hit the plate with a clatter. - Louis could never in a million years even *think* of killing anyone, she protested. He was trying to calm Katherine, to explain, when Ma looked Katherine straight in the eye and said, Louis shook me like a terrier with a rat at Hyères. Katherine shook her head, disbelieving, and Ma went on, kinda' angry. Well, she said, wouldn't *you* get a little violent if you were forbidden to talk, were nearly blind and were confined to bed, dependent on others and their fussiness and inability to meet your needs? When Katherine wept into her handkerchief, Ma suggested a course of action. She would nurse Louis that day then, if all went well, they could share watches. Katherine cheered up at the chance to be helpful. - I'll need Sam's strength to turn and lift Louis, that is all, Ma said. Louis' pattern is to sleep like a dead man, with intervals of madness in between. After a few days, the worst should be over and you and Sam can sit with him and read to him a little.

They lingered in the parlour with its guttering gas lamps and cheery fire. One of the things he loved about Katherine was her predictability, but suddenly she brought up a painful subject. Now why had she done that, so out of the blue? - Sam has told me about the dreadful time when your son Hervey died, Katherine said, and I didn't know where to look, in case Ma thought I'd been disloyal. - Swiftly I said, I wasn't there, but my older sister Belle was, forgetting that Belle was another sore subject for Ma. - Belle has gone her own way in America, Katherine, Ma said curtly. We have no use for each other at this juncture of our lives. - He had only been trying to oil the wheels of the conversation when he had added, Ma don't approve of her husband Joe, but he knew from the tone of his mother's voice, he had not succeeded. - *Does not*, not 'don't' approve, Ma said sharply, then gave her dry laugh and said, Belle flirted outrageously with Katherine's brother Bob when they were at the artists' colony near Paris. Now why Ma had chosen to raise this, God alone knows, but Katherine was interested. - Grez-sur-Loing? Bob sent me letters at the time, she said. According to Katherine the letters had been about Ma, the 'bohemian American woman', and Belle, and how both of them flirted with

Bob at every turn until Louis came on the scene and fell for Ma's charms.

When Katherine said it must have been such fun at Grez-sur-Loing, I don't believe I have ever known fun like that, Ma replied tartly, she wouldn't call it fun exactly since Hervey died not long before I met Louis. He lit the darkest hours with his wit and *joie de vivre*.

Prudence arrived with Eve's pudding covered in custard. Wow! The innkeeper's daughter was some beauty, with her blond ringlets and dimples! He had fallen on the pudding with gusto, saying between mouthfuls that his little brother, Hervey, weren't much more than knee-high to a grasshopper when he'd been taken and how he'd been in California with his Pa at the time. Then he had turned to Katherine and blurted out, Pa's disappeared. No one knows where he is, could be in prison for one of his fiddles, or married again, or dead for all we know. Ma thinks I should take my middle name Lloyd 'stead of Sam, so no one will confuse me with rascally Sam Osbourne, my Pa. He had only been trying to lighten the mood, but Ma didn't like him speaking of Pa like that in front of Katherine. - Hush, Sam, she said, folding her napkin into a neat oblong. This is neither the time nor the place to discuss your Pa.

The day Mrs Watts and Agnes returned from their holidays with a clattering of pots and raucous bantering, Sam got out of bed. The best part of being well was his reunion with school chums at Café Florentine near the sea front. Adelaide Boodle's arrival for daily croquet cheered him up, too, and between games they rested on the garden chairs while Sam continued the Exeter story.

'Shortly after lunch one day, alerted by a note from Ma, Lady Shelley arrived by carriage from Torquay where she had been on holiday. The innkeeper found a room on the ground floor to accommodate her wheelchair and another for her footman in the servants' quarter. In addition to her trunk, Bradshaw fetched up Lady Shelley's gifts for "my dear Louis": invalid aids, including a backrest and a bed table, so he could write comfortably the moment he was well. Then Dr Scott arrived on an overnight visit, Miss Boodle. During his examination, the Squire lay drugged and impassive while Dr Scott confirmed the advice of the local doctor: on no account must the patient be shifted. That evening Ma and Dr Scott took dinner together. His aim was to boost her morale and encourage her to continue to act as she always had, in the best interests of her husband. The crisis was over, Ma had handled it superbly, he said, but they both knew the ergotine might provoke further alarming episodes. I came into the parlour at that moment and Ma took my hand saying, I have my son to assist me, and Dr Scott retired for the night saying all we could do was wait and pray for the Squire's recovery.

'Lady Shelley was far from well herself and kept to her bed, determined to stay in Exeter until the Squire was fit to receive her. Now we had two invalids to occupy us, and we took turns to visit Lady Shelley, whose wit and charm were like a tonic to our spirits until, that is, Ma discovered from the night porter the extent of the old lady's anxiety about Louis. Any noise in the house or street during the night, he reported, sent the old dame wandering, candlestick in hand, through the lower reaches of the New London Inn, wittering on about Mr Stevenson dying.

'Ma said she could not have Lady Jane's collapse on her hands and that she must return to Sir Percy at the earliest opportunity.'

'Lady Jane has such character. I should dearly love to meet her,' Adelaide said, and Sam offered to arrange a visit to Boscombe Manor.

He swung his croquet mallet back and forth under his chair. 'What Ma and Dr Scott anticipated came about. For several days, Louis lay half-conscious, occasionally moaning in his sleep then waking up suddenly, roaring like an animal so that whoever was on watch over him must rush for help. This went on for several days until, one morning, Louis opened his eyes and looked up at us with a beatific grin. Ma said the worst was over. The sickroom was disinfected and sprayed with lavender water and I carried Lady Shelley upstairs in my arms. She's just a perfumed old bag of skin and bones, Miss Boodle. Their audience was private so I waited outside the door. Louis was too weak to speak, though he could communicate by signs, and, after a few minutes, Ma said I should carry Lady

Shelley back downstairs. We were all near to tears at the tenderness of their leave-taking. Louis is like a son to Lady Shelley.'

Adelaide nodded, 'Mr Stevenson tells me she takes him for a reincarnation of Percy Bysshe Shelley.'

'It *is* touching,' Sam said, getting to his feet and shouldering his mallet. 'Lady Shelley returned to Torquay the following morning. And now that Katherine and I could stand in for her, Ma began to go out a little herself.' He shouldered his mallet and invited Adelaide to take first shot at the ball.

A Weevil in a Biscuit

Fanny tried not to dwell on the miserable fact that their holiday had been lost to them. Slowly, Louis was improving, and she had sent Sam, who had been mooching over Prudence, back to Skerryvore. Sometimes her thoughts returned to the days before they reached Exeter: the excitement of packing the holiday trunks, the train journey to Dorchester through open countryside with distant vistas of the sea, their curious reception at Max Gate, and the first night of their holiday - the *only* night of their holiday - at the King's Arms in Dorchester. When Louis was asleep, she wrote letters to friends who must know of their enforced detention. And, with an eye to the future, when biographers would be anxious to trace every footstep of Robert Louis Stevenson and his wife, she must record their visit to Mr and Mrs Hardy.

'What strange marriages literary men make!' she wrote to Sydney Colvin *à propos* the Hardys. Sidney would appreciate the intended irony, since the Colvins judged her own marriage to Louis extremely strange. Margaret Stevenson was due a letter, too, and to prevent her from flying down to Exeter if she heard of Louis' illness - appalling prospect - Fanny dissembled with an account of their visit to Max Gate: *Thomas Hardy is a pale, gentle, frightened little man, so that one felt an instant tenderness for him, with a wife - ugly is no word for it, who, when we arrived, said "whatever shall we do". I had never heard a living soul say that before!*

The solemn Sabbath spread below the window, so hushed and soothing Fanny imagined she might be in the countryside. Then the cathedral bells chimed the hour of four, a distant locomotive clanged and huffed into Exeter station, and the spell was broken. She started a letter to Teddy Henley: *It is now a week since we left home, and we are no farther away than Exeter. We stayed one night in Dorchester where we saw Hardy, a most loveable creature, and then here, where one night Louis was taken with a dreadful haemorrhage* . . . She threw down her pen when Louis groaned in his sleep, and when he whimpered, 'oh, oh, please don't!' she fetched a cool cloth for his forehead. 'Sssh, Papa, you are safe. Do you need a drink?'

'Don't break in . . . I dreamed,' he stuttered. She lifted his head to the water glass and he took a few sips. 'I was alone in an abandoned room with high ceilings and a grim narrow bed.' Fanny kissed his forehead, 'Hush, my own. I'm glad you can speak again, but tell me the dream when you're stronger.'

'I'll forget it. Hear it now.' His voice was so faint Fanny's ear was almost at his mouth. 'The room was in a once great house, now a cobwebby ruin. Grey and empty. A terrifying presence lurked within. I tried with all my might to close the room door, but a tremendous force countered from the other side. Just before I managed to turn the key in the lock a creature, neither man nor beast, leered in at me.' He turned his solemn head to look at Fanny. 'It was the face of evil.'

Fanny said nothing.

'I said, it was the face of evil!'

'Try not to think about it, dearest. The drugs encourage these nightmares. The important thing is you can speak again.'

'It might be the tale for Longman.'

'Louis,' Fanny admonished, 'you have been so terribly ill, you almost died. I beg you not to think up bogey tales. That's the last thing you need if you are to get better. And Mr Tommy has sent money. There is no need to worry about the Christmas market.'

'I want to go home to Skerryvore.'

'Then make an effort to get strong.'

Sometime later, Katherine arrived. 'Come and comfort me with your presence, Kate,' Louis whispered.

Katherine approached his bed with an affectionate smile and asked Fanny if she would like to be relieved.

'Yeah, I sure would. For a lifetime!' Fanny snapped and hurried out of the room.

Louis asked Katherine to get him beef tea and a cigarette. In her absence he lay willing the *nuggets of felicity* he had depended upon since childhood to return. Even in the worst of times, somehow he managed to dredge up the otherworldly treasure that made life worth living. A letter to Henley took shape in his mind: *I have been really ill . . . haemorrhage, weakness, extreme nervousness that will not let me lie a moment, and damned sciatic o'nights . . . It is not often that I suffer, with all my turns and tumbles, from the sense of serious illness, and I hate it as I believe everybody does. And then the combination of not being able to read, not being allowed to speak, being too weak to write, and not wishing to eat, leaves a man with some empty seconds.*

Katherine came back and found Louis asleep. She had in her hand a letter addressed to her from Teddy Henley. 'I am heartbroken for Louis' new breakdown,' she read, and gave way to her pent-up tears. She sat at the bedside until Louis wakened and reached for her hand. 'Read to me from Ida Taylor's novel *Venus' Doves?* She's the daughter of Sir Henry Taylor, a Westbourne neighbour, and I'd like to catch up with her progress.'

He lay still for a few pages into the reading before he grimaced, 'Drivel. Sheer drivel, Kate, yet it entertains me. Read on, if you please'

Katherine took a deep breath, 'I need to pause, dear. My voice is becoming hoarse.'

'Aye, well, pause. Miss Taylor should have taken a leaf out of Miss Boodle's book and come to me for lessons. That would have prevented the world from being bombarded by such verbal refuse.' Katherine laughed and he brought her hand to his lips. 'You saw me at my worst, Kate. Illness makes a monster out of me, yet I canna' help it. Dark forces prey on me in its worst manifestations as they did in my boyhood at Heriot Row. I'd wake from a nightmare, screaming bloody murder and clinging to the iron bedstead, knees to chin, until Cummy or father came to my rescue.'

'I didn't know you suffered so terribly.'

He smiled wanly. 'I'm happy now you're here reading to me.' In the silence that fell between them, Katherine's eyes slid to the photograph of Fanny on the bedside table. 'That's my lady wife,' he jested, following her eyes.

'She has the look of a woman who bears much yet does not love herself,' Katherine said.

Pretending not to hear her, Louis riffled through the pages of *Venus' Doves* to see how long it was. 'Fifty-thousand words, at a guess,' he said. 'Far too many.'

Katherine persisted, 'Do you love Fanny?'

Louis glowered. 'You know better than to ask that. You know I love *you*, the rest doesn't matter.'

As soon as the Exeter doctor decided Louis' condition had stabilized, Katherine left for London. Her children needed her and she had an important translation to finish. Louis' memory was improving and Fanny assisted the process by reminding him of recent events. They laughed over the exploits of the summer visitors. 'Aye, Henley came down, I mind. That was a great afternoon.' 'And Bob started the tableau for the hall and took it away with him to finish,' Fanny encouraged. 'Aye, and I wonder if he's finished it yet . . . and Sargent was down to paint me again.' 'He painted *us*,' said Fanny. 'Aye, so he did. You were slumped in Henry's chair - now why did you do such a thing?' Fanny chuckled, 'Sargent insisted on it for the sake of balance in the composition. When we get the painting we'll hang it in the drawing room next to Henry's mirror.'

Fanny finished her letter to Henley. He must know what she had endured and she would not diminish the impact by mentioning that Sam and Katherine had been on hand to help her through the worst of it. Louis couldn't get Sargent's painting out of his mind. He pictured himself, pacing back and forth, gazing at Sargent then pacing again, and the words he learned by heart that day came back to him: *I thus drew steadily nearer to the truth . . . that man is not truly one, but truly two.* A kernel of felicity. He lifted his head to tell Fanny about its providential return.

When Louis was well enough to travel, the date was set for the following Saturday. Fanny Stevenson, though not conventionally religious, visited Exeter Cathedral where she lit a candle to give thanks for her husband's deliverance. At the bookshop she purchased novels to entertain him during his convalescence. A fedora caught her eye in a shop window and she bought it to keep his head warm on their journey back to Skerryvore.

Saturday came at last. The bill for their stay had been settled and their trunks taken down to the hall. Louis stood at the window admiring the golden trees in the park opposite. 'We arrived in summer and leave in autumn,' he said, wistfully. His step fell lightly and oddly on the wooden stairs. There was a swing to his gait, as if he had been a prisoner suddenly let out of jail. Fanny lumbered behind him, his warder in a crinoline.

The innkeeper was waiting in the hall with his wife and Prudence. 'It's not often we have famous folk staying here,' he said, waving a copy of *Treasure Island*. 'It would be a great honour, Sir, if you'd sign your book before you go.' Louis wrote his distinctive signature on the title page, then blurted out, 'I am so happy to be alive! And now I'll sign your Visitors Book.' *I cannot go without recording my obligations to everyone in the house,* he wrote, *if it is your fate to fall sick at an inn, pray heaven it may be the New London!*

'He has borne the journey wonderfully well,' Fanny announced to Sam, Valentine, Mrs Watts, Agnes and Beaucox, all lined-up at the gateposts to welcome them home. The steaming horses champed on Alum Chine Road and Sam rushed to help Louis down from the carriage. At the sight of the Squire, so pale and thin, so dwarfed by his ulster and having to lean against Sam, everyone's eyes filled with tears - except Beaucox's. They burst into applause and Fanny showered the delirious Bogue with promises never to leave him again.

When Sam helped Louis into the hall, the first thing he noticed was Bob's 'tabloo'. 'It came by post,' Sam said, 'and I hung it to welcome you back.'

'Abstract, in tones of red,' Louis said. 'Very strange. He's used a lot of alizarin, the colour of blood.'

Fanny was removing her hat at the mirror. 'It

brightens things up, and looks fashionably *avant garde*.'

As soon as he was alone in his room, Louis looked out at the garden where the chairs still waited above the chine. The sight of them made him ache for Henry's company. For flashes of silken wings. Undressing behind the scrap screen, he plotted how to get the Prince down for a visit. He pulled on a fresh nightshift, weak yet strangely charged with a sense of the ineffable. He had been saved from Charon's rowlocks, and for a purpose. *The Bedlamite has saved me once more*, he imagined writing to Henry James, then let out a laugh. Bedlamite! As if he would write that of his nearest and dearest to Henry of all people.

Quiet days followed, 'getting back to normal,' Fanny was fond of saying as she bustled in and out of the room where Louis dutifully kept to his bed. 'We must prepare for our first winter at Skerryvore.' She came in with Valentine, their arms laden with winter clothing sent down from Edinburgh. 'See, here's a fine Harris Tweed.' Fanny held up on a wooden hanger a lovat green three-piece suit. 'Now show him the coat, Valentine.' Valentine held up a dark brown greatcoat. 'I like the suit,' Louis declared. 'It'll give me the look of a dominie. The coat, I'm not sure of. It resembles the coat of a criminal, and, besides, it would stretch to my ankles.' Neat piles of clothing soon filled the wardrobe: several pairs of the woollen socks Scotsmen wear with their kilts, thick vests and long-johns Margaret Stevenson had purchased at a mill sale in the Scottish

Borders, winter shirts in muted checks, cardigans and tweed waistcoats.

Louis loved the comforting bustle of women attending to his every need: the rhythms of the day, from the setting of the morning fire to snuffing the oil lamps at night; the cups of tea, soup and cocoa that arrived unbidden on his bedside table; the nourishing meals served to him every four hours. The downstairs gossip that came via Valentine, and even Fanny's complaints that Valentine and Agnes were at each other's throats again, entertained him. His sciatica had shifted down the agony scale to alto, and he gave thanks that he could turn himself and arrange pillows under his legs to relieve the pain. When his spirits drooped he called in Sam for a man-to-man. It was important to stress that he couldn't hang forever on his mother's apron strings, doing nothing much in Bournemouth now that he had repeated his exams. He called for Valentine. Together they roamed in their imaginations the streets of Hyères and Nice, rejoicing in honey coloured stone, azure sea and tumbling perfumed flowers. He had only to close his eyes to be returned to the South of France.

When his spirits sank beyond cheering, he fell to judging himself *a beastly infirm householder, of no real use to anyone*. One dark afternoon, when the sky beyond his window glowered under autumn clouds, he found himself dredging up Edinburgh and a tartan biscuit tin his mother had purchased at Jenners in Princes Street many years ago. It had on it a scene of Edinburgh Castle and the Mound. Hoping for a handful of biscuits, he had opened the tin - it must have been at Heriot Row - to find there was only one left. As soon as he put his hand in to get it, he spied a weevil gnawing away at its centre. Lying in the comfort of his featherbed, the centerpiece of the house around which everything else revolved: *I'm but a pallid brute,* he thought, *a weevil in the biscuit of Skerryvore.*

One morning Valentine brought up the latest edition of *Atlantic Monthly* with his breakfast tray, and he was delighted to find the first instalment of Henry James' *The Princess Casamassima*. After he had adjusted to the name of the first character, Miss Pynsent - 'Pynsent'? - what possessed Henry to give so obvious a name to a dressmaker? - he was drawn deeply into the drama of that lady and her young charge, who had an equally quixotic name. A few paragraphs later, it was as if Louis stood with Miss Pynsent and the boy, Hyacinth Robinson, at the gates of the Millbank prison, at 'the threshold of this dreadful place,' as Henry himself must have done. 'It seemed to her an adventure as dangerous as it was dismal,' Louis read, chuckling to think these must have been Henry's very thoughts the day he had visited the prison himself: 'This particular penitentiary struck her as about as bad and wrong as those who were in it; it threw a blight on the face of the day, making the river seem foul and poisonous and the opposite bank, with a protrusion of long-necked chimneys, unsightly gasometers and deposits of rubbish, wear the aspect of a region at whose expense the jail had been populated. She looked up at the dull, closed gates, tightening her grasp of Hyacinth's small hand . . .'

'Aye, and no wonder,' Louis exclaimed so loudly that Fanny rushed to his side. He flapped the magazine in the air. 'I'm reading Henry's latest work. Henry can do it after all, it seems. He's had the courage to descend into the murky regions of the dismal city where most of mankind is forced to live.'

Fanny stayed to hear the rest of the chapter, in which Hyacinth comes face to face with his real mother, incarcerated at Millbank. A former beauty become a 'hollow, bloodless mask' and 'cruelly misrepresented by her coarse cap and short rough hair, dying after years sealed up in that dreadful place.'

They were both in tears before Louis reached the end. 'Henry does children well, though why he's called the boy Hyacinth, and where the Princess Casamassima fits into the story, we must wait for the next instalment to understand.'

Fanny dabbed her eyes with her hanky. 'How I am to wait is quite beyond me.'

During her recovery from the Exeter ordeal, Fanny kept to her room as much as the supervision of the household allowed, with Adelaide Boodle her only visitor. One afternoon, hearing laughter through the adjoining wall, Louis struggled into his dressing gown and went to spy through Fanny's door. She was propped up on her daybed wrapped in colourful shawls. Adelaide sat on the rug, hugging her knees and gazing adoringly at the storyteller.

'We ate a hurried lunch at the King's Arms and hired a brougham - Louis was thrilled to recognize Dorchester as the model for Casterbridge in *Far from the Madding Crowd* - and we asked the driver to take us to Max Gate. "Oh, thon's a strange, haunted-looking place," said the driver shaking his head sadly, "but the folk in it seem nice enough. Born hereabouts was Mr Hardy, at Higher Brockhampton." We discussed the fare with the cabby and directed him to set us down at the gates and return to collect us an hour later.

'Max Gate cannot *actually* be haunted, I whispered to Louis, for it is a new house wherein, as far as we know, no one has yet died. And when we reached the house on the edge of town, I remarked with relief that the gate was open as if they expected us. I took Louis' arm, and we proceeded up the drive towards a symmetrical frontage of plum coloured brick with corner turrets and a central gable topped by a broad chimney stack. The cabby was right. I never saw a stranger place. It looks so unwelcoming, said I, drawing back a little before I added, it would benefit from having some trees planted around it.'

At this, Louis burst into the room. 'As I said then and must now repeat, Max Gate is *new*, wife. Hardy has not had time to plant trees.'

'The house has no architectural merit whatsoever,' Fanny went on coolly. 'I greatly prefer our Skerryvore. I am telling Miss Boodle about Max Gate and you're welcome to join us, but only if you'll stay quiet and listen.'

Louis smiled fondly at Adelaide and kneeled on the rug beside her. 'I don't like to be silenced,' he said and Fanny frowned, 'Stop behaving like a child, Louis.'

'My name is Loo-is, not Loo-ay,' he protested. 'It's near ten years since we met and why you persist in using the American pronunciation of my name is beyond me.' Fanny gave an exasperated sigh, 'Look, do you want to join me and Adelaide or not?' Louis nodded vigorously, 'Oh, I do, I do, I do.'

'Well, let me speak. We were walking up the drive when I tugged Louis' arm. Quick! Take a look, said I, for there's a face at the window. Louis looked but saw nothing. He said the face was a manifestation of my overworked imagination, and we proceeded to the front door.'

Louis raised his hand, 'Might I say something?' and Fanny gave a reluctant nod. 'At the time, I was rehearsing in my mind all I wanted to say to Thomas Hardy by way of praise for *Far from the Madding Crowd, The Return of the Native* and other works of his I'd read when Mrs Stevenson said, perhaps they didn't get your letter, perhaps they will not receive us, after all? I gave her a withering look and pulled on the bell.'

'After a few moments we heard a movement within,'

Fanny said, 'and the front door opened to reveal a small, nervous man, a mere shadow of the giant I had anticipated. Are you expecting us, Sir? Louis said pulling back his shoulders. I am Robert Louis Stevenson and the lady at my side is Mrs Stevenson. "I go-ot your letter," Thomas Hardy stuttered. "We don't get many visitors and you are among our first . . . you had better come in."'

'Continue, Fanny, if you please,' Louis said with a tolerant smile.

'We were an odd trio standing silently in the hall, embarrassed as actors who have forgotten their lines, until a thin, frail-looking woman emerged from the gloom of the passageway. Hardy said, "ah, at last, here is my wife, Emma." Mrs Hardy wrung her hands and looked nervously at her husband. "Whatever shall we do?" she said.' Fanny let out a chuckle at what was to come next. '"Why, I expect we should take our visitors inside, my dear," Mr Hardy replied. "As I have already explained to the Stevensons, we are not much practised in receiving visitors. Come now, Stevenson, Mrs Stevenson, tea awaits you in the parlour." A maidservant came with a tea trolley and the door closed behind us. It was the queerest parlour I have ever seen.'

'Aye, maybe, but it must be a grand thing to design your own house to live in,' Louis broke in. 'Hardy and I spoke a great deal of literary matters, Miss Boodle. Emma, that is, Mrs Hardy, and Mrs Stevenson hardly said one word to each other for reasons best known to themselves.'

'Emma Hardy is a nervous, shy woman,' said Fanny.

'Aye, maybe so, but Hardy and I saw eye to eye on most matters - except Balzac. Hardy and Henry James have Balzac as the greatest of novelists on account of the breadth of his vision and so-called vitality. A load of tosh, I say. Balzac never found his method. He was, in my opinion, an inarticulate Shakespeare, smothered under feeble detail, yet when he surrendered to his temperament, how good and powerful he was. Be that as it may, Hardy and I agreed to collaborate on a theatrical project sometime in the future. It would be a great collaboration. The man's finishing off a book now, *The Mayor of Casterbridge,* a mighty drama set in Dorchester. Now that I've met the man, I put Hardy equal with Meredith in the top rank of the geniuses of my acquaintance.'

Gradually, Louis grew sufficiently strong to take up pre-Exeter tasks where he had left off. Adelaide returned to assist with Fleeming's memoir, still under oath not to spill the beans to Fanny. His strength wasn't up to the piano so he took up the flute and managed to pick out a few tunes. Fanny protested so vigorously that the piping provoked her headaches, he was limited to practising when she was out of the house.

The Exeter crisis led him to reconsider his will in a series of letters to Charles Baxter in Edinburgh; . . . *it is all very well if Sam outlives us all, I think; but I really have not yet made up my mind what to do if he does not; I shall consider of it.* And he must make plain to Charles that if Fanny wished to write his biography after his death she must do so, but that the account of his previously designated biographer, Henley, must be incorporated, and emoluments shared in proportion to their respective contributions. Further, he stipulated that Sydney Colvin must be consulted about the biography.

Fanny came to Louis' bedside from time to time to discuss Sam's future. After cramming all summer, he had failed the science exam again. Louis blamed himself for misjudging Sam's ability, and told Fanny that the prospect of having to wheedle money out of Mr Tommy for Sam's keep at Skerryvore was more than he could stomach. The lad would have to return to Edinburgh, but he could help him to correct the final proofs of *Prince Otto* before he left.

When the task was complete Louis dictated a covering letter. 'Sign it thus, Sam: *Excuse the hand of an amanuensis as I am out of sorts and in bed, Yours very truly, etcetera;* and make sure it goes with the afternoon post? I consider *Prince Otto* to be my first novel for adults. I have not held back from describing fuck-stresses as you may have noticed. I suppose you know what they are?' Sam coloured but kept on writing. 'Whores my boy. *Prince Otto* will bring us pennies from heaven before this year is out.' He studied Sam signing the letter. Fanny's boy was too much of a goody-goody. High time he sowed his wild oats. 'There was an earlier adult novel that might have made my fortune if your mother hadn't burned it,' he said.

Sam squinted at him through narrowed eyes. 'Ma wouldn't have burned anything valuable.'

'Oh, the story was good. It was the subject your Mama didn't favour. She burned the manuscript. In those days she had power over me.'

'You wouldn't let her now?'

'Damned right, boy, I would not.'

'What was the book about, Squire?'

'About prostitutes, so-called fallen women. I was friends with some in my Edinburgh days. Grand lassies all, and the heroine of the destroyed novel, *Claire,* was modelled on a particularly fine specimen of a woman.'

Sam's head retracted a little into his shoulders. 'I should not like to know any fallen women. I shall save myself for the girl I marry.'

'The destruction of *Claire* grieves me still. It's as if I've lost a child,' Louis said, watching Sam addressing a large buff envelope to Andrew Chatto. Sam slipped in the manuscript of *Prince Otto* and said he would catch the post if he went straight away.

Louis threw him a wink. 'Not a word about *Claire* to your mother, lad. Nothing to be gained from stirring old porridge, eh?'

One day, Louis put on his coat and wandered down the garden to the edge of the chine. When the sun poked out between scudding clouds, he risked sitting down.

The House on the Chine

He laid his hand on the neighbouring chair as if to make Henry magically appear, his footfall scrunching on the gravel near the Skerryvore Bell. How, he wondered, could he lure Henry James back to Bournemouth? He sorely missed a male confidant, since wasn't a dilemma shared a dilemma halved? Blasted decorum had prevented him from opening his heart to Henry earlier in the year when he'd had the chance.

He glanced over his shoulder to make sure no one was spying from Skerryvore's windows, then shifted into the chair Henry had sat in last spring. He felt terribly small and alone in that long garden where a gentle wind made the autumn leaves skitter at his feet. Decorum take the hindmost, he muttered, poking the leaves with his stick, and, after a few moments it was as if he sat in Angel James' lap. He envisioned something eminently human beaming from HJ's imaginary eye, like an invitation to open his heart.

First, about young Sam: whenever he comes close, I surge with a peculiar longing. I love the boy, yet the way he wanders in and out of my room gives me qualms. He keeps an eye on me as if to say, one day I'll be the dominant male of Skerryvore. He vies with me to possess his mother whom I love betimes, and detest as many. We face acute lack of dollars, and I'm loath to ask the aged parent for more, Mr Tommy's very generosity being a form of possession. And then, there's the Vandegrifter. I've observed you watching her, watching us together. A queer kind of marriage, I agree.

Maybe I'll start a diary about it when I'm better. The diary of a fellow lurking in his lair, sinking deeper and deeper into a vortex, strength sapped, brain no longer connecting. Others serve him, change his nightshift, empty his piss pot. That man's me and the nurse's name is the Vandegrifter. When she's ill with one of her brain fevers, or her change of life, she damns us both to Hell - turns into a sullen, staring ape, silent for long pauses, then raging fit to kill. The neighbours overhear our rows.

With a sorrowful shudder, Louis thrust his walking stick into the earth. I must bear it all, Henry, for I am mortally dependent upon my weird wife. Fanny's the sort of dame you might one day characterize in a novel of manners, exaggerated, of course, to make the point. And since, we're on the subject of novels, Henry - well done, so far, with *The Princess*. I've sent off a manuscript to Chatto. Even though I've laboured over it for more than three years, my heart tells me *Prince Otto's* a dud. But given the public taste for duds, I've a hunch it'll make my fortune.

Fanny called loudly from the house, 'Are you out there, Lou? Come in this minute or you'll catch your death of cold.' A posse of terrified rooks fled from the beech tree overhead.

Even under his ulster, Lady Shelley's poncho and his velvet jacket, he felt chilled. But he resented Fanny's imperiousness and stayed where he was. If he closed his eyes he might come up with a way to keep HJ close. He might transform him into a character in a future novel. Portly, bearded and balding - a fine bedside manner - let him be a doctor. Let the doctor's Christian name be Henry, and he'll have something fine and upstanding beginning with 'J' for a surname. When Louis looked upwards for inspiration, the pattern made by the shifting clouds and the slanting sun suggested a stained glass window. A shiver went through him as he recalled himself as a young lawyer recently brought to the bar, sitting in the Middle Temple of London's Inns of Court. Everywhere he looked in that dim interior he had discovered something to spark his imagination. The huge table made from a single oak tree barged down from Windsor on the orders of Elizabeth I. The portrait of Charles I on a white steed, painted by the studio of Van Dyck. And the window - above all, the window - the stained glass window, depicting two shields - one for a Josephus Jekyll and the other a Roburtus Hyde. For a long time he had stared up at that window and, though he never discovered who Jekyll and Hyde were, what mattered now was that he had retrieved their names through the long lens of history and might write them into a story. Yes, HJ could be Henry Jekyll.

A fit of shivering forced his retreat to the house. The last thing he wanted was to catch his death of cold when he'd a story to write.

He leaned his cane against the lug chair opposite Fanny's and stood warming his hands at the fire. 'A perfect scene of bourgeois respectability,' he said. 'How is it wife we have come to this?'

Fanny ignored his bait. 'Have you lost your senses, sitting outside in this weather?'

Louis sat down wearily. 'I was conversing with Angel James. I miss male company. And you? You've got on your pistol sighting look.'

'Joke if you must, but I'm the one who'll have to nurse you if you get a chill.' Fanny handed him his tea, already milked and sugared. 'Have you forgotten you almost *died* at Exeter a few weeks ago?' She passed him a scone on a plate.

Louis rejected the scone with a flick of his wrist. 'My objection is that you won't leave me alone for a minute even when I'm well.'

In a fury, Fanny grabbed the walking stick. Deftly he caught the other end, but her hold was so strong it brought him to his feet.

'Let go this minute!' he shouted, wrenching the stick from her grasp.

Fanny lost her balance and fell to the floor with a horrified look. 'If you won't obey me in matters concerning your health, I will no longer answer for the consequences,' she said indignantly, and he rushed to help her up.

He returned to his chair with fiery eyes. 'Don't start lecturing me again,' he railed, brandishing the stick.

'I'm sick of being on the sidelines, your bloody nurse, housekeeper and minder.' Fanny's voice grew shrill. 'Does my life count for nothing? My talent goes virtually unrecognized while others arrive to sit at your feet.' She made to grab the stick again.

'Careful wife, leave off that cane,' Louis growled. 'It could do you an injury.'

Fanny made balls of her fists. 'In your hands? I doubt it,' she mocked, and Louis took aim with the tea plate. It flew over Fanny's head and knocked one of Katherine's vases off the mantelpiece. It shattered on the grate.

'Oh, no,' he wailed and fell to his knees in a fumbling attempt to fit the fragments together. 'Now look what you've done!'

'What I've done?' Fanny shrieked, towering above him. 'You did it yourself, and it's high time you took responsibility for all you've done to bring us to this sorry pass.'

'Aye, wife,' he said looking up at her. 'It's a bleak high mountain pass, right enough. Pitch black at night, and infested with bandits waiting to leap out at any poor unsuspecting traveller.' Fanny put her hands over her ears and ran from the room.

Shortly after six, Valentine brought up Louis' dinner. 'Miss Boodle called at teatime but refused to come in. 'She heard you and Mrs Stevenson fighting from the other side of the street and begged me to call the police.'

Louis sighed. 'It's over now, lass. Bank up the fire and leave me in peace.' Valentine bent towards the fire.

'Mrs Stevenson sits crying in her room,' she said, shaking coals from the hod. Louis reached out and pulled her onto his lap. 'Then tell her to come to me when she's eaten her supper.' He tickled Valentine until she squealed and broke free, protesting she must go at once to the mistress.

Darkness was falling by the time Fanny stood before Louis in her Oriental robe.

'Don't take on the role of a Japanese warrior, wife. Our tussle was but a storm in a teacup. We both went mad this afternoon.'

'The drugs that made a monster of you at Exeter are still in your system. You can't help your moods,' Fanny said sadly.

'Let's not bandy words about so mischievously in future, nor walking sticks, nor tea plates. Get in the bed beside me and let me woo ye wi' poetry - but, first, could someone fetch me a supper of bread and jam?'

'Someone? I suppose you must mean me?'

A Fine Bogey Tale

The moon approaching fullness hovered beyond the slumbering windows of Skerryvore. Its eerie light entered the room through the gap between the velvet curtains and fell on the sleeping author. When he cried aloud Fanny jumped out of bed shouting, 'Wake up, wake up!'

Louis came to with a crazed look. 'Why did you waken me? I was dreaming a fine bogey tale.'

Fanny calmly lit the candle on the bedside table. 'You mean a nightmare? Usually you require me to waken you from nightmares.'

He drew the blankets around him. 'This one was different. I was deep in the grip of Morpheus - it scared the living daylights out of me.' He lay ashen for a few moments before he swung his legs over the side of the bed.

'Where are you going?' Fanny demanded. 'Get back in bed at once or you'll catch your death!'

'Don't keep mentioning death, don't tell me what to do, don't interfere. Be quick, light the lamps, stoke the fire, bring paper and ink, then leave me and go to your room. I must write down the dream.'

He sat shivering on the edge of the bed, following Fanny's eerie shadows, now gigantic, now dwarfish, on the walls, the ceiling and the scrap screen, as she moved around the room. He struggled for breath, clinging to the dream, until the lamps and the fire had been lit and the shadows put to flight.

'Please open the curtains, Fanny. Moonlight's a fine amanuensis in the middle of the night.'

After he pulled on his poncho and got into bed, Fanny arranged his table. 'I have the tale for Longman,' he said. Silently she left the room. She's furious, he thought, but no matter. The dam against my imagination's burst.

For some time, he stared beyond the fire lit room at the ghostly smiling moon, taunting the world behind her diaphanous veil. Then he took up his pen:

I was coming home from some place at the end of the world, about three o'clock of a black winter morning, and my way lay through a part of town where there was literally nothing to be seen but lamps. Street after street, and all the folks asleep - street after street, all lighted up as if for a procession and all as empty as a church - till at last I got into that state of mind when a man listens and listens and begins to long for the sight of a policeman.

In the morning Valentine found Louis asleep. His work of the night littered the bedcovers. A few drops of ink had run together on the invalid table in a queer shape. Like the face of a water sprite Valentine thought with a shudder. She set down his tea with deliberate clamour and when that failed to waken Louis she touched him. He felt cool but breathed steadily so she tucked the bedcovers closely around him and went to fetch the mistress.

Fanny woke him and urged him to drink his tea. She mopped up the ink spill and gathered his work into a neat pile. He smiled broadly. 'That's the start of a fine melodrama, my dear. The plot I've been racking my brains for arrived in the night.'

Fanny sat solemnly on the edge of the bed and said she hadn't slept a wink all night.

'Are you fit to hear the dream, though?'

She nodded wearily.

'It was a fragment, like the one at Exeter, remember? The ghastly presence on the other side of the door tries to break in? Yet this one's different. I dreamed a scene split in two in which a good man - I've christened him Henry Jekyll - presses himself into a cabinet and swallows a powder. The drug changes him into another being, a monster I'm calling Edward Hyde.'

'What you describe replicates your horrific experience of your own divided self, let loose by ergotine at Exeter.'

'Aye, it's true; the beast in me came roaring out as it does in this story. After you left me last night, almost every detail came clear to me.'

Fanny hesitated, then said, 'I've been so alarmed by your spasms and hallucinations, I've been doing research on the drug.'

'Go on. It would interest me to know more.'

'According to *The Lancet* and other sources, ergotine is derived from ergot, a potentially deadly hallucinogenic fungus. The mould affects rye and wheat and caused mass poisonings during the middle ages. Victims suffered vivid hallucinations and convulsions, just as you did, Lou. In the old days, these symptoms were taken as signs of demonic possession. Many witch trials, including those at Salem, Massachusetts, in 1692, are believed to have resulted from outbreaks of ergotism. Nowadays, ergotine is used to stop bleeding in the lungs, as we do. But I wonder if at Hyères and Exeter the doctors prescribed too much of it.'

'My symptoms were induced by an overdose?'

'That's my hunch. You lived through the appalling experience of an altered state.'

'An Edward Hyde state. The roots of inspiration are mysterious indeed. But what's important to me this morning is I've the energy to work for the first time since Fleeming's death. I'll work on this story until it's done, even if it kills me - no arguments, wife. It'll be a double-life story, describing the transformation of a reasonable man, Jekyll, into a deformed troglodyte, Hyde, by means of the drug. Not exactly the same as last night's dream but with the same malignant atmosphere. I'll start work right away.'

He swung his legs off the bed and Fanny put out her hand to steady him. 'Suits me down to the ground since I've work of my own to be getting on with and letters to write.'

He looked into her eyes. 'You're still angry with me? But I'm depending on you to read over the first draft.'

'I'll help you if you try not to be so moody.'

'Aye, I promise I'll be a good boy, and I'll take a wash and start work again without delay. I don't want your criticisms until the first draft's done. Let the household know there are to be no disturbances for the next few days.'

He crossed the room to his rose patterned washing bowls. Fanny followed and caught his eye in the shaving mirror. 'On another subject, Sam leaves for Edinburgh soon and after that I'm going up to London.'

He soaped his cheeks for a shave. 'Good news on both counts. First, we can't afford to keep Sam here, and, second, you, wife, deserve all the pleasures London life has to offer when your Louis is nothing but a pest and a driveller.'

The house beyond his room took on the solemnity of a religious institution. Meals and washing bowls stealthily brought in were the only disturbances. Whenever Agnes attended the fire and left the door ajar, Sam peered in to watch his bedridden stepfather filling page after page without a pause: . . . *I thus drew steadily nearer to that truth, by whose partial discovery I have been doomed to such a dreadful shipwreck: that man is not truly one, but truly two.*

When he fell into a dwam between bouts of industry, Louis concluded that he was writing something elemental, rude, violent and savage that mirrored his own recent derangement. And Walter Ferrier's too, he thought. The *awful smash and humiliation of Ferrier's descent* was Jekyll-like in its intensity. Ferrier was *the best gentleman, in all kinder senses, that I ever knew.* But under the influence of drink *the lunatic brother* of good true Ferrier burst out. That a man with rich qualities and faculties like Ferrier could be *wrecked and aborted from the very stocks* had deeply troubled him when news of his death reached him in France in 1883. Now it returned to haunt him with the thought, *it's uneasy gold I'm mining here.*

The first draft was swiftly done and he rang the bell for Fanny. 'I value your opinion, Dutch, but you know how it tires me to go over any editing you might suggest verbally, so, as usual, I'll thank you to put your comments in writing. Longman will have its penny dreadful and we'll have the dollars by Christmas.'

She left with the draft and he burrowed under his blankets, tormented that he had swept aside the Hyde he wanted to write.

All at once, I saw two figures: one a little man who was stumping along eastward at a good walk, and the other a girl of maybe eight or ten who was running as hard as she was able down a cross street . . . the two ran into one another naturally enough at the corner; and then came the horrible part of the thing; for the man trampled calmly over the child's body and left her screaming on the ground.

That bleak dark night in the story, the Hyde of his imagination hadn't *trampled* over the child's poor, helpless body, he had *raped* her.

The next day Louis wrote again to Charles Baxter: *I ha'e been faur frae weel this whylie, but I keep pushin forrit. I have sent Sam a draught on your firm. I am generally all there, what there is o' me, includin a skyatica . . .* and after that he found the strength to put on the Harris Tweed three-piecer.

Fanny was smoking in the drawing room with Bogue curled up at her feet. Silently she pointed to Louis' manuscript spread out on the desk, and he went to gather it up. Fanny's comments stood out in bold black ink in the margins.

'Well, Dutch, what d'you make of it?'

'You said we were not to discuss it. But since you ask, Edinburgh's Old Town not London, is the true model for the city in the tale?'

'Aye, maybe, but with an eye to the market, London serves more readers than the northern capital. And, what more?'

Fanny tossed the stub of her cigarette into the fire. 'Either you want a discussion or you do not. Which is it to be? I have been up most of the night writing pages of criticism and now you ask for my *verbal* opinions.'

'Did the story appeal to you? Is that too much to ask?'

'Of course I liked it, in the sense that you are incapable of writing badly, but the barely concealed sexual references scare me. You know you must be ultra-careful, Lou, not to fall foul of the law of the land. You might consider diluting Dr Jekyll's "disgraceful pleasures" - masturbation and, or, homosexuality, I suppose? - and his confession of "a career of cruel, soulless and degrading vice" might be too much for readers seeking confidence in their amiable doctors, as we do in Dr Scott? I detect echoes of "The Body Snatcher" and "Markheim", and of *Crime and Punishment* in your story - and, of course, Mary Shelley's *Frankenstein.* Also, Sigmund Freud's studies he calls "Strange Cases" and Charcot's latest research at Salpêtière Hospital on hysteria and moral insanity, which we read about recently in *The Lancet.*'

'How astute you are, Dutch.'

Fanny gave the hint of a smile. '*And* I detected in your story the influence of your recent dreams about the divided self, of your - *our* - experiences of the power of drugs to alter mind and behaviour. I'm thinking particularly of your recent violent episodes.' Louis took a step towards her. '*My* violent episodes?' he exclaimed so loudly the dog started barking.

Fanny pointed to the hearth where the Japanese vase had shattered. 'Surely you haven't forgotten *that!* But let's not quarrel again. You can read my comments and take them or leave them as you please. My great concern is that the dream, or nightmare, or whatever you choose to call it, has hampered you.'

'*Hampered* me?'

'Yes. Go back to your room and read, if you choose, my reasons for saying so. I'm going into town to get Sam's necessities for Edinburgh.'

Louis paced frantically. Valentine, chancing to look in, saw the entire manuscript slip from his hands and rushed to help him. 'Thankee, lassie, now leave me be,' he said, and when he straightened up he caught his reflection in Henry James' mirror. Certainly, the day was dull and the room unlit. A brighter light might have cheered his impression of the pale, dishevelled creature he saw before him. He tidied his hair with a determined hand then retreated upstairs to his desk.

He searched the text for the reference to Jekyll's 'immoral' behaviour: *From a very early age, however, I became in secret the slave of disgraceful pleasures* . . . He paced the room, then returned to his desk. He needed more time to think about 'in secret'. It could always be amended, if necessary, in the Printer's Copy, and 'disgraceful pleasures' might be changed to 'certain appetites'. He examined the sentence mentioning Jekyll's career of 'cruel, soulless and degrading vice': . . . *as soon as night had fallen and I could shake off my friends, the iron hand of indurate habit plunged me once again into the mire of my vices. I will trouble you with these no further than to say that they were at once criminal in the sight of the law and abhorrent in themselves.*

He paced. Fanny was right. Jekyll's tenor solos - the so-called criminal tendencies that he himself and every other of his male confidants had, of necessity, indulged - would have to be diluted. He rewrote a few paragraphs, wrestling with the unpalatable truth that the society he lived in would not permit him to create the Hyde he truly wanted: Hyde as a sexual pervert and child molester. Yet everyone knew such deviants existed. They appeared daily in the courts of law, yet it would constitute a criminal act to replicate them in fiction. Incarceration at Millbank in his state of health would kill him.

He read and re-read Fanny's comments. 'I feel you have been hampered by the so-called dream. I am uncertain about the powder Dr Jekyll swallows and wonder if the reference to it might be changed; though I don't mean to suggest the reference to some mind-changing drug should be eliminated. After all, you saw that so plainly in the dream.' Further down the page he read: 'You have Jekyll bad all through, and working for the Hyde change only for a disguise, whereas if Jekyll represented Everyman, with a propensity for both good and evil, you would give birth to a great moral tale. Sticking to your dream does not serve you.'

Doesn't serve me?' he muttered, then noticed to his further annoyance that Fanny had crossed out several nouns on the manuscript and made substitutions of her own. The cheek of the woman to tinker with my *words*. He ran his pen through every instance of her interference and wrote in the margin, *Never do this again!*

'I don't like the opening,' Fanny had written. 'The opening is confused.' Louis' fingers drummed on the desk. 'It proposes that Hyde should run over the child, thus showing him as an evil force without humanity.'

Fanny came suddenly into the room and he whirled round in a fury. 'If Hyde were to *rape* the girl would that make him more or less evil?'

She looked horrified. 'You'd be put in Millbank if

you wrote that!'

'Aye, wife, ye see what I'm up against? A dilution of the truth to say the least.'

She fastened her cape at the neck. 'I'm off to town.'

If he had been fit and able, he would have run right away from Skerryvore, from the fat Dutchwoman and her infernal interference. He'd go up to London and stay with Henry James or Henley. With grim determination, he scrunched each page of the draft into balls and aimed them at the miserable coals of the fire. He watched them ignite and illuminate the room. When the flames died down he put a lit taper to the pages that had escaped the fire and stayed until they crackled up and turned to ashes. Then he pulled the new greatcoat out of the wardrobe. He stomped about the garden on his walking stick. The chine was alive with swaying trees and the sooks and claps of the wind. He flayed the bushes so violently leaves flew up like birds; he made to attack the neighbour's cat, innocently prowling in the undergrowth; he banged on the side of the beech trees until the cawing rooks took flight. After that, he needed company and sought out Valentine. 'Get the wheelchair, lassie. I don't mind where we go, so long as I keep on the move.'

Fanny slipped back to Skerryvore carrying Sam's parcels and went straight to her room. Sydney Colvin must know about recent events: *Again Louis is better and possessed by a story that he will try to work at. To stop him seems to annoy him to such a degree that I am letting him alone as the better alternative; but I fear it will be only energy wasted, as all his late work has been. For the last few days he has, however, seemed much clearer in his mind about things, but has been suffering from dreadful nightmares, and headaches at night . . .*

The letter written, she went to peer cautiously into Louis' room. The creaking door wakened him and he sprang out of bed, insubstantial as a wraith in his woollen vest and long johns. He skittered over to the fireplace and pointed at the ashes in the hearth. 'See what you've done?' he wailed. 'Now, *go away*!' Fanny rushed into the room, grabbed Louis' poncho from the foot of the bed and thrust it into his arms. 'Don't catch a chill,' she pleaded then fled.

The door closed softly and, left alone, Louis got into the poncho and broke into tears. He heard a soft pattering of rain on the window and looked out at the darkening afternoon. He felt in his bones a coming storm, and, even as he stood watching, high winds shook the beech trees and rain pelted the glass *in a manner worthy of Caledonia, stern and wild*. He shivered, and when a fit of coughing gripped him, he sought refuge in his bed. No need for the Bedlamite, he muttered, taking the white spittoon in his trembling hands. He coughed up a bright red clot and groaned at its metallic odour before he sank into his pillows. His anxious eyes traced the lineaments of the room and he vowed, *I'll have no more ergotine to unleash my further lunacy.*

He examined the plastered ceiling with its florid

cornice, the Chinese wallpaper with its piercing shoots of bamboo, the fanciful scrap screen. Afternoon in the house. Aggie's day off. Fanny sulking in her room next door. He lay still for some time and spat up no more blood. Valentine will be up with my tea soon, he thought; now there's a cheery notion.

Oh, the comfort of everyday objects, the curtains, the garden and the chine, books piled high beside the armchair, the mantelshelf displaying silver framed images of his nearest and dearest: the parents, Bob and Katherine, Sam and - he lifted the wedding photograph of Fanny off his bedside table. The awful truth is she's right, he thought. What I burned was nothing more than another dud crawler. She *knows* I can do better, *wants* me to do better, *must* do better, go further, delve deeper into the terror. 'Markheim' was far better, so was 'The Body Snatcher'. The effort I burned was a mere nursery rhyme compared to *Crime and Punishment*.

Valentine wakened him from a doze. He asked her to remove the spittoon and kit him up for writing. She fetched a damp cloth to wipe bloodstains from the corners of his mouth. 'It was but a *petit* spasm that's not to be mentioned to Mrs Fanny. Since young Sam will be dining with the Boodles tonight, tell her I'll join her for supper, *ma belle*, and say that on no account is she to disturb me before that.'

In the draft he had burned, he had invented the characters of a narrator, Mr Utterson, and his distant kinsman, Richard Enfield. Although the narrative that now ran in his head had a different structure from the first, he would begin again with these two taking a walk. *Mr Utterson the lawyer was a man of a rugged countenance, that was never lighted by a smile*, he wrote, then surprised the silent room with a laugh. Utterson sounds like the Vandegrifter: *cold, scanty and embarrassed in discourse; backward in sentiment; lean, long dusty, dreary and yet somehow loveable*. Why, apart from the 'lean' and the 'long' here was Fanny again.

Louis smiled. Yes, despite everything, she was loveable.

The first chapter spilled out with Enfield describing to Utterson his glimpse of Hyde: *There is something wrong with his appearance; something displeasing, something downright detestable. I never saw a man I so disliked, and yet I scarce know why. He must be deformed somewhere; he gives a strong feeling of deformity, although I couldn't specify the point . . .* Louis finished the chapter with Enfield saying, *I am ashamed of my long tongue. Let us make a bargain never to refer to this again*, and Utterson replying, *I shake hands on that, Richard.*

With a satisfied sigh, he capped his inkwell, set aside the invalid table and got into his tweed suit. He left off his tie and, in place of brogues, kept to his slippers for comfort's sake.

He found Fanny sitting morosely by the fire, playing a game of solitaire. 'Our drawing room's so beautiful, wife,' he declared, shuffling to her side and perching on the arm of her chair. 'No other room in the world is as lovely as this,' he said, stroking the nape of her neck under its heavy coil of curls. 'You've made it the throne room of a palace where Louis sits like an old Irish beggarman's cast-off bauchle in a pathetic attempt to win the affections of the princess.' When she moved his hand to her lips he whispered in her ear, 'I blush for the figure I cut in such a bower.'

Her mouth curved. 'You certainly don't look like a beggar in that Harris Tweed.'

He went to the drinks cabinet. 'I'm ashamed of myself,' he said, aiming the soda bottle at two nips of whisky. 'You were right and I was foolhardy. I'm keeping the white powder Dr Jekyll takes, as in the burned version, but, in other respects I have begun again on *Strange Case of Dr Jekyll and Mr Hyde*, as the tale is to be called. A novella will serve better than another Christmas crawler.'

Drawn to the desk, he found himself staring down at an unfinished letter in Sam's hand. It was to his mother in Edinburgh: *Louis is doing very well,* he read, *though still very weak etc - writing a most terrible story which he said occurred to him in the night. It is certainly one of the most ghostly and unpleasant stories I have ever heard.*

'Sam keeps a close eye on me these days,' Louis said, handing Fanny her whisky. 'He even reports me to my own mother. Have you seen this letter? Sam keeks into my room when he thinks I'm not looking - like a detective on the trail of a murderer - like the Judge in *Crime and Punishment*.'

Fanny set aside her playing cards. 'It's a phase he's

going through. You know Sam worships you. He misses his own father, yet you mean far more to him than any man on this earth and he needs to feel close to you.'

'Aye, true, it's as if he seeks to bring us closer. Like we were in the old days when he was a boy, but now he's in between a boy and a man.'

'He studies you because he aims to be a writer himself. Besides he goes up to Edinburgh tomorrow.'

Louis sat on the divan. 'I've already written and arranged his pocket money with Charles Baxter. If I'd been as fit and healthy at the age your son is now, I'd be an engineer not a slinger of ink. And, by the way, I saw off BJ when you were out at the shops. There's nothing wrong with me except skyatica.'

Fanny stiffened; the first haemorrhage since Exeter. She questioned Louis closely as to its nature and pleaded with him not to chance his luck. 'Go to bed now, Papa. We'll have supper together in your room and you can continue writing your tale of terror there.'

He finished his whisky and did as bidden.

For several days he kept to his room, alternately writing and napping, his routine unbroken except to say goodbye to Sam. He asked Sam to enlist Thomas Stevenson's help in tracking down a model of the Skerryvore lighthouse. It had been constructed when he had been an apprentice engineer, complete with a 'wee flashing light'.

'Get them to send it down, Sam; it'll be a grand ornament for Skerryvore, Bournemouth. We'll erect it at the gateposts and fix up the light so it flashes cheerily on and off through the long winter nights. Now lad, let's not make a mawkish scene of your departure,' he said, pulling away from an ardent embrace that brought tears to both their eyes. 'Look after yourself, and we'll see you at Christmas.'

Valentine hung up Dr Scott's greatcoat. 'The master and mistress keep to their beds,' she said, leading him to Fanny's room where she was propped up on a mound of tapestry cushions and covered with shawls. 'I'm not ill, only quite weak with insomnia and filled with sadness that my boy Sam has left for Edinburgh,' she said. 'The house is so quiet without him.' Scott took Fanny's pulse. 'I need a change of scene,' she went on. 'London is my destination as soon as my strength returns.' Scott nodded and asked to see her tongue. With practised fingers he exposed the lower rims of her eyelids. 'Nothing organically wrong, but there are signs of anaemia, dear lady, for which I recommend plenty of rest. Continue with stout and iron several times a day. No reason why you can't go to London, if you follow my recommendations.'

'My husband is so brave, Dr Scott. He bears his ills with such courage and magnanimity I'm ashamed to complain myself. The other day he spat up a small clot but by the evening he had recovered. Apart from headaches at night and weakness, he's fairly well. You'll see for yourself, he radiates with the energy of the new story he's writing. I thank God he keeps, if not to his bed, then at least to his room.'

'Out of harm's way, eh? I'd better take a look at him.'

Scott found Louis sitting in his armchair. His long thin hair straggled over the red poncho and his moustache needed a trim. 'I'm a rickety and cloistered specimen, ill prepared for visitors,' he protested with shining eyes. 'But it's always a pleasure to see you.' Scott noted Louis' sallow, shrunken face, the beads of perspiration on his forehead, and laid his hand on his brow, 'Do I detect a fever?'

'Only the fever of writing. My story plays on the notion that all men are imprisoned in their bodies where the struggle between good and evil must be played out. I'm writing about two men in one. A Dr Jekyll takes a powder he has concocted to release a completely separate and monstrous being I'm calling Mr Hyde. The medical advances of our age lead me to think it will not be surprising if some powder might be invented in the future with the power to transform one being into another. Meanwhile as you see, I'm obeying your instructions to rest while my work moves cautiously onwards. I'm like a child filling a sandbag with its little handfuls.'

Scott raised an eyebrow. 'Then is there nothing I can do for you?'

Louis set aside his writing board. 'You can sit with me a bit. I'm at the mercy of Skerryvore's monstrous regiment of women, a prisoner of dry rot. When the prisoner tried to escape he got no further than Exeter where he arrived at death's door and nearly went through it. The message was crystal clear: return to captivity - to Skerryvore - and stay there. The sad fact is illness keeps me in poverty. I'm not fit to turn out enough stories to pay the bills, including yours.'

'My bill's the least of it, Stevenson. My aim is to get you well. Indeed, I'm wondering about inviting a specialist to give another opinion on your condition.'

Louis groaned. 'That'll only confuse the issue and get Mrs Stevenson worked up. She's not alone in fancying me as the consumptive artist, a Keats or a Shelley whose genius feeds off the disease. Women seem to have a taste for Romantic agony, but I must disappoint. I am no consumptive and I'll have no more experts on my case - all they have come up with so far are contradictory diagnoses. No thanks, Scott. I'll be guided by you.' He reached for his tobacco tin and winked at the doctor, 'there's little point in stopping smoking when one's true motive is merely to intensify the pleasure of starting again.'

Scott took the other armchair. 'Bournemouth's not a bad prison for a man with your condition.'

'Between ourselves, what is my condition?'

'The only conditions I can diagnose with certainty are your frequent colds with their severe side effects, catarrh, bronchitis and blood spitting. I suspect you are the *type* of a consumptive. Its manifestations make you ill, yet the disease, if it exists, is unable to get a serious hold on your lungs.'

'Aye, well, that reassures me and, it's true, prison's a good place to write. Why, in prison a man has time on his hands and his mind. And my terrible tale is writing itself, more or less. My mind has reawakened. Some days I get out several thousand words. I only hope the medical references in the story ring true. After all, doctors and their wives will be scrutinizing the book when it comes out.'

'Perhaps, but the intelligent among them will read the story for what it is, a work of the imagination. A novel, not a scientific tract.'

'Still maybe another day you'll take a look at one or two references?'

'The patient doesn't need examining but the manuscript does,' Scott smiled. 'The doctor in your story, I trust I am not the model?'

'There are two doctors, Dr Lanyon and Dr Jekyll. Dr Lanyon has a small part to play, and a trace of you might peek out in that good man. Between ourselves, Jekyll, before he takes his monstrous powder and descends into madness, has something of my friend Henry James about him. His initials are the same, HJ, Henry Jekyll, Henry James.'

Louis gazed beyond the window, lost in thought: *something eminently human beaconed from his eye; something indeed which never found its way into his talk, but which spoke not only in these silent symbols of the after-dinner face, but more often and loudly in the acts of his life.*

The House on the Chine

'I was once called to examine Miss Alice James, and Mr James happened to be present,' Dr Scott was saying. 'It's true, he does have the look of a medical man.'

'I miss Henry James,' Louis said, pulling himself out of his chair. 'A finer friend never existed.' When he stumbled and almost fell, Scott suggested it was time to rest. 'Time to gather your strength for the next thousand words?'

Louis began to weep. 'I've not the strength to stem the tears,' he blurted, and for a few moments Scott held him like a mother with an oversized infant. His patient was so slight, so light, so will-o'-the-wisp, so worn down by illness. 'Both you and your wife are in need of protection from the demands of the outside world,' he said, tucking Louis into bed. 'When I go downstairs, I'll instruct Valentine to hold visitors at bay.'

The following day Louis regained command of *J & H* as he referred to his story, and kept to his bed. Fanny came into the room just as he was writing, *Well, when that masked thing like a monkey jumped from among the chemicals and whipped into the cabinet, it went down my spine like ice, says Utterson.*

'I need a name for Dr Jekyll's butler,' Louis said cheerily. 'He's the very model of our Beaucox. Could I name the butler after him?' Fanny said 'certainly not,' and they considered other names. Dombey wouldn't do, neither would Peterson, Montague or Montrose. Only when Fanny hit upon Poole for the name did Louis declare it fitted like a nut in a shell. He searched the manuscript for an appearance of the butler and inserted the name right away. 'Utterson says, *Your master, Poole, is plainly seized with one of those maladies that both torture and deform the sufferer.*'

'Poole sounds authentic,' Fanny said.

'Poole serves well for the butler's name, and now there's the footman to christen. He has only a brief appearance in the story and might be called Bradshaw after the footman at Boscombe Manor.' Fanny tittered but found no obstacle to Bradshaw.

Every day she took several pages to read in her room and returned them to Louis' desk with her comments. Every day they renewed their pact to be tender with one another. Sometimes they would both get dressed in the late afternoon and sit for an hour or two by the fire, until, one day, Fanny said she felt well. 'I mean to go up to London as soon as my bag is packed.'

'And I mean to send the manuscript to the publisher by the end of the month. It'll be finished by the time you come home. You'll get a last look at it before I post it to Longman.'

'And Valentine?'

Oh, the tedious Vandergrifting model of a nagging hag, thought Louis. 'Valentine shall sleep in my room if I'm ill,' he said, in the manner of a schoolboy reciting a poem to please the teacher.

A Subjective Affection

Fanny had only been gone two days when Louis began to fret about their lack of money and unrest among the servants. He wrote to her in London: *I am all right, but the coins are gone to hell. You must borrow. La Bello has only twice spoken to Valentine since Sunday . . . I drive on with Jekyll, bankruptcy at my heels.* Then he embarked on an inspection tour to confirm his suspicion that Skerryvore was being neglected in Fanny's absence.

For a start, his room resembled the field of action after a battle. Books lay sprawled on the fireside rug; the disordered manuscript pages of *Jekyll and Hyde* concealed the surface of his desk; his shaving towels had seen better days and the bed, heaped with sprawling coverlets, suggested cock-a-hoop couplings. It was all the result of telling Valentine and Agnes not to disturb him. He went cautiously downstairs and found the drawing room fireplace unswept and the furniture in disarray.

Suddenly, he heard the sound of a quarrel in the kitchen and went to stamp it out.

From the safety of the door he said sternly, 'unrest in the kitchen is intolerable to me and Mrs Stevenson will hear about it on her return.' He closed the door then pushed it open on an afterthought, 'and, bye the bye, I'd like Agnes to clean my room and the drawing room tomorrow morning.'

Valentine slipped past him to tidy the coat stand in the hall. 'I'll have lunch in my room at the usual time,' he said kindly. 'You bring it up.'

For a few moments he stayed in the drawing room playing with his fingers on the dusty tabletops. *Jekyll and Hyde* was almost done, and his spirits soared at the prospect of slipping the manuscript into the post box on Middle Road after Fanny's return. Using the cuff of his jacket he dusted off Henry's Venetian mirror and, when he stood back to admire the result, his pale face peering through the dusky glass brought Sargent's painting to mind. Almost three months had gone by, yet the promised painting had never arrived. He hurried upstairs to write to Sargent.

The truth was that Sargent's mind had been elsewhere. He had stayed on at Broadway, struggling heroically with 'Carnation, Lily, Lily, Rose'. Later he would write to Louis that he had seen 'a most paradisiacal sight' at the end of September 'instead of in June when I should have done. Children lighting paper lanterns swung from rose trees and in the middle of flowers, at dusk, when the lanterns just begin to glow. Now my garden is a morass, my rose trees black weeds with flowers tied on from a friend's hat and winter coats protruding under my children's white pinafores . . . With the right lighting and the right season it is a most extraordinary sight and makes one rave with pleasure.'

Unaware of his friend's travail, Louis wrote to Sargent that some treachery must be afoot otherwise he would have had the painting *of the caged animal lecturing about the foreign species in the corner* long before now.

Sargent replied swiftly to reassure Louis that no treachery was afoot. After varnishing and framing the painting, his colourman had taken it six weeks earlier to Mr Colvin's. He thought Louis would like Colvin to see it, and Sargent himself had been curious to know whether he considered the painting 'interesting or obnoxious'. Edwin Abbey, who had also seen it, liked the depiction of Louis, but his remark that the painting was 'paradoxical' made Sargent wonder if he should have 'cut it down to a single figure'. He urged Louis to ask Colvin to send the painting right away, and concluded by saying he wanted to visit Skerryvore again, since his stays at Bournemouth were among his 'pleasantest souvenirs'.

Louis was alone at Skerryvore a few days later, when, alerted by loud knocking on the servants' door, he opened it cautiously and found a delivery man. After he signed for the package, he fetched a sharp knife from the kitchen and slashed open the cardboard container. Carefully, he slipped out the canvas and read on the back 'From your friend, Sargent'.

He propped *Robert Louis Stevenson and his Wife* up on the mantleshelf and stepped back. Nothing had been altered by way of the backdrop of Indian red walls, open door, view into the hall, the position of the chair under the two pictures on the wall, himself pacing, twisting his moustache, and the exotic heap on the chair, cleverly touched in to represent Fanny. Every detail was roughly how he had imagined it. Yet, he thought, it *is* a damn queer painting.

It has a bogey atmosphere that says, look closely, all is not well here. For a start, there's the door between me and Fanny, indicating the vast distances between our personalities. In fact, we are looking *away* from each other, in opposite directions. There's the dark void of the hall and the front door admitting a portentous light. There's myself looking furtive, and there's Fanny, horribly slumped in grandfather's bergère, like a rag doll or even a fallen woman. Is this how Mr and Mrs Stevenson appear to the rest of the world?

Yes, it might have been wiser to leave Fanny out of the portrait after all. Even if it's no surprise that Sargent has seen so deeply into our married life at Skerryvore, it still shocks me. He poured a tot of whisky with a trembling hand. The work as a whole is excellent though; as an artist, Sargent has triumphed over tradition. Yet what the Vandegrifter will have to say about it, I dread to think. Here's a low opinion of my wife, an opinion Sargent picked up, no doubt, from the cads of the Savile Club. He stood glass in hand in front of Henry's mirror.

You've only yourself to blame, he told his reflection. You wanted an honest portrait and invited Fanny into it. His breath left a cloud-like stain on the glass. *Oh, wad some power the giftie gie us*, he sighed, and decided there was nothing for it but to hang the painting next to Henry's mirror as Fanny wished. He must not waste time on further distractions. He still had a hill to climb to get *J & H* onto the publisher's desk by the end of October.

At the toolbox in the silent pantry, rummaging for a hammer and two nails, he almost tripped over the hedgehog's basket. A wee monster, dead to the world under its blanket. Innocent as a sleeping babe by day and a devouring monster at night. He shuddered and rushed away. Distractions such as hedgehogs and paintings must be held at bay. He needed all his brainpower to finish the novella. He banged in the nails and hung the canvas. The result wasn't quite straight but he felt too overwrought to start again, thereby risking Fanny's ire over walls ruined with unsightly holes.

Back in his room he paced and considered how to tie up the loose ends of *J & H*. Two narratives, lately come into the possession of the lawyer, Mr Utterson, would, at last, explain to the reader the mystery of Dr Jekyll's appearances and sudden disappearances. One entitled 'Doctor Lanyon's Narrative' was already written. Now he must tackle the *coup de grace*, 'Henry Jekyll's Full Statement of the Case' - the last chapter, Jekyll's confession, wherein all becomes crystal clear to the reader.

He finished the final draft in the late afternoon, and,

haunted by Sargent's painting, he wrote to an old friend, Will Low. *Sargent was down again and painted a portrait of me walking about in my own velveteen jacket and twisting, as I go, my own moustache; at one corner a glimpse of my wife in an Indian dress and seated in a chair that was once my grandfather's. All this is touched in lovely, with that witty touch of Sargent's; but of course it looks dam queer as a whole. It is, I think, excellent; but is too eccentric to be exhibited.*

October was a good month for letter writing. After the postman delivered a whining letter from his father, Louis dashed off a swift reply: *My dear Father, A lower epistle I certainly never received but I consoled myself by the fact that I have received 'o' them' before now, and that the sun came out again after the cloud. I wish you were in better spirits and in stronger health of mind; but I must say I think there is something in the seasons which acts against the last.* October is a bogey month with its alteration of moods, Louis affirmed, staring beyond the window at scudding clouds and driving rain.

His fears that he and Bob might be growing apart sent him rummaging in his desk. He had used up his vellum, so he wrote to Bob on the reverse of a discarded draft page from *Jekyll and Hyde*.

I went through most of our scenes of battle, and found we had greatly underrated the features, and overrated the distance people could see. You remember the strong heights in front of Cerne Abbas, which you were to hold? I am very hard at work and reasonably fit . . . Dew-Smith has taken a photograph of me which is like you, drunk; very odd, it has your nose instead of mine. Your tabloo is now installed on its red hanging and looks well. At Exeter I read a lot of contemporary 3-volume novels. They struck me as wonderfully steep in the way of tedium and weakness; I thought they could scarcely be worse. It is odd how, in all the arts, downright badness is what the public hankers after.

Through the open door he heard the soft approach of Valentine. 'My story's almost done,' he said, pointing to the manuscript with his pen. 'And I am free to entertain myself. Letter writing's my game until Mrs Stevenson returns to give the story a clean bill of health before the publisher gets it.'

Valentine nodded. 'Shall I bring elevenses?'

He sighed and stretched out his hand. 'Come here, lass, it's been a whiley since we talked. How are you *ma belle*? Your *m'sieur* has been busy these last days with another of his melodramas. I fear I have ignored you.'

Tears pooled Valentine's eyes, '*Nobody* wants me.'

'Tish, tish, lass,' Louis said, getting to his feet. He looked into her eyes. 'You're young enough and comely enough to find a man that loves you even better than I can. Surely that pleases you?'

A smile crept into the watery pools of her eyes.

'No medicine upon earth can enliven a man and a women as love does. We both need comfort, therefore stay in my room tonight? You know you can't come to me often, and when you do it must be our very own secret and no one else's business.'

Fanny returned with a basket she took directly to him without stopping to take off her bonnet. 'I bought him for ten bob at the Crystal Palace Cat Show. Wait till you see him!' She opened the basket and a fluffy, slant-eyed heap of a cat sprang onto Louis' lap. 'He's Persian and will have to be spayed, of course.' Louis smiled into its inquisitive Oriental face and lifted it into the air. 'It weighs a ton, Dutch, but it's love at first sight. Let's call him Gingibber, since his coat's the colour of ginger beer. But what will Bogue make of a feline invader?'

Fanny was cheerful after surviving her stay with Teddy and Anna Henley. While she 'freshened up' before supper, Louis went down to the drawing room, determined to grab the thistle of Sargent's painting. He was sipping a malt whisky in front of his convex mirror when Fanny came in.

'Whatever are you doing? You look so furtive!'

'No painting could be so decorative and so cheerful as a mirror, don't you agree, Dutch?' he dissembled and led her to *Robert Louis Stevenson and his Wife*. 'What d'you make of Sargent's effort? I hung it beside Henry's mirror as you wished.'

'It's not straight, but we can fix that,' Fanny said, her head shifting from side to side to assess the canvas. 'It amazes me that he has caught you to a tee and made me so exotic, so mysterious . . . the whole gives the effect of a treasure box, colourful, enticing and *avant garde!*'

'You *like* it?' Louis waited for a sign, something to indicate her shock that Sargent had depicted the tragicomedy of their life with such acuity. 'I sure do,' she said, stepping into a different vantage point. 'And it looks so well hanging here in our very own salon.'

I can't comprehend her, Louis thought. He retreated, bemused, to roll a cigarette. He had to hold back from saying, but you wanted to be in the damned thing because you felt slighted as an artist, and because everyone wants to portray me and not you. Yet now, when Sargent has displayed you as the mere comma you protested against being, you make no fuss. He thought the better of opening up an honest debate about the painting with his wife. Instead, he pressed her to read the final draft of *Jekyll and Hyde* without delay. The publisher was jumping up and down to get it and they were bankrupt again.

The following day, Fanny said she was still opposed to Dr Jekyll taking a white powder for the transformation into Edward Hyde, but could come up with no satisfactory substitution. With a few minor alterations the manuscript passed her scrutiny and, after he had dropped it into the post box, Louis declared himself ready for fun. For a start, Adelaide Boodle must be sent for. The poor lassie had been waiting weeks for a lesson in writing, and he meant to take up *piano picking* again.

Fanny's return restored order to the house. Louis noticed how the food improved and how everything shone and smelled fresh again after applications of metal polish and furniture wax. He discussed with her the prospect of a trip to America next year, bankrolled by Sargent's friend, Charles Fairchild. It was not, he insisted, an impossible dream. He knew for a fact, he told Fanny, that Fairchild and his wife admired his work. She would like a trip to America, wouldn't she?

'We can't possibly go to America with Mr Tommy trembling at death's door. For all your mother protests that there's nothing wrong with your father but brain fog and hypochondria, he's a very sick man.'

Louis nodded with sorrowful emphasis. 'It'll grieve me sorely when he passes away, though his death'll leave us free to travel. We'll take my mother along on the trip.'

'And Sam?'

'Of course.'

'And Belle and Joe and the children can join us wherever we settle.'

'What about Valentine?' Louis put in.

'She comes, of course, if she wants to.'

Louis finished *Olalla* 'at a gallop' and sent it off to the *Court and Society Review* for publication in its Christmas number.

He took up *Kidnapped* where he had left off. *Aye, man is not truly one, but truly two.* Here was another double portrait in the making: Davie Balfour and Alan Breck, in flight from the Redcoats across the moorlands . . . *the mist unfolding us like as in a gloomy chamber - or, perhaps if the wind blew, falling suddenly apart and showing us the gulf of some dark valley where the streams were crying aloud.*

As he wrote, he recalled himself and Gosse standing on the deck of the *Clansman* many years ago, watching destitute crofters pouring onto the lower decks. *An incident that should have turned any decent thinking man into a socialist.* His thought was tinged with bitterness against himself, and he said as much to Fanny who was in the dining room with the afternoon post.

'I daresay you'll be a socialist when you're fit and well,' she soothed.

He scanned the postmarks. 'Here's a letter from Charles Longman acknowledging receipt of *Jekyll and Hyde*. My hopes are not high for its success, Dutch, but a few coins in the coffer are better than none. I'll reply by return of post. Dear Charles, I'll say, it may interest you to know that the main incident in the story occurred in a nightmare, and that indigestion has its uses. It woke me up, and before I went to sleep again the story was complete.'

Fanny laughed. 'That was the supper of bread and jam I fetched you.'

Over on the Poole Road, Adelaide Boodle was recording her most recent tutorial at Skerryvore: 'R.L.S. welcomed me as usual and took my work but we were not alone for the lesson on description. (I had written a description of a garden.) The *sine qua non*, to all appearances sound asleep, was lying on the divan. With a red silk pillow as her background, she looked so superb that, for a moment, my attention wandered.

Suddenly there was a low (but crescendo) rumble of thunder from R.L.S. "Oh, but this work is disgracefully bad! It could hardly be worse. What induced you to bring me stuff like this?"

My answer was rather wildly given. "At the end of our last lesson you told me to describe a place, and when I said I couldn't do it, you just repeated that I must. I knew I couldn't do it."

"Well, as yet you most certainly can't," came the withering reply. "I never in my life read a worse description, and I hope I never read another half so bad!"

What answer could I make? There was nothing to be said. Weep I would not. Before the lessons began I had told R.L.S. in all good faith that I could bear any amount of criticism without flinching. And here I was almost in tears. So I choked pretty badly instead and strove to make an airy apology without a tremor. But the words died on my tongue.

Mrs Stevenson, like a crouching lioness bereaved of her whelps, sprang to the rescue. All in a moment she reared her glorious head, and, from the divan at the far end of the room, rang out this scorching denunciation, "Louis! You are a brute! I told you your brutal criticism would kill the child - and it *will*."

"No, it won't," I gasped. "I want him to say just whatever he thinks. I don't mind a bit. I will learn to write. *I'm going* to do it or die."

In a moment, all anger gone, R.L.S. was on his knees my trembling hand firmly clasped in his own. "*Of course* you are and I'm *going* to teach you. Fanny is right. I really am a brute. But I did not mean to be so cruel. Oh, but the work is bad you know - very bad, and you must never, never write like that again. It really is intolerable that you should have done it."

When he smiled suddenly into my eyes, what was there to weep about? "I want to know why it is so horribly wrong," I said.

"That's just what I want to explain," he said eagerly. "As a first step in the right direction we will do a sum together. Count the adjectives in that exercise."

I did so.

"Now see how many times that will go into the number of words allowed for the whole description."

The result proved that my modest percentage of adjectives was seventeen and a half. "And mostly weak ones at that," he remarked with a queer little grimace. "You should have used fewer adjectives and many more descriptive verbs. If you want me to see your garden, don't, for pity's sake, talk about 'climbing roses' or 'green, mossy lawns'. Tell me, if you like, that roses twined themselves round the apple trees and fell in showers from the branches. Never dare to tell me about 'green grass'. Tell me how the lawn was flecked with shadows. I know perfectly well that grass is green. So does everybody else in England. What you have to learn is something different from that. Make me *see* what it was that made your garden distinct from a thousand others. And, by the way, while we are about it, remember once and for all that *green* is a word I flatly forbid you to utter in a description more than, perhaps, once in a lifetime."

"And now," broke in the *sine qua non*, "I'll ring for tea."

"Capital idea," said R.L.S. "And Miss Boodle will give me a lesson on the piano with full permission to slap my hands when I go horribly wrong.'"

After an early dinner a hansom arrived to take Fanny and Adelaide into town. Louis settled himself at the drawing room desk and wrote to Henry James: *At last, my wife being at a concert, and a story being done, I am at some liberty to write and give you of my view* . . . He praised *The Princess Casamassima*, conveyed other news, then begged his friend to return to Bournemouth . . . *and the best thing you can do for us and yourself and your work is to get up and do so right away. Yours affectionately* . . .

That should do the trick. Henry will come, he thought, and he realized how happy he was, how satisfied with life. It had been a challenging year, and the best of it was that he had learned how to master Fanny. 'A note for future reference' he wrote in his journal: *I'm almost tempted to hint that it does not much matter whom you marry; that, in fact, marriage is a subjective affection, and once you've made up your mind to go through with it, you can pull it off with anybody.*

Afterword

Robert Louis Stevenson signed the contract for *Strange Case of Dr Jekyll and Mr Hyde* on 3 November 1885, ten days before his thirty-fifth birthday. Henry James visited Skerryvore in mid-November when Margaret and Thomas Stevenson were down from Edinburgh. He wrote to Sydney Colvin that he was appalled by 'the ponderous presence' of Louis' parents who 'sit on him much too long at once . . . I cannot see why *they* don't see how much they take it out of him.'

Strange Case of Dr Jekyll and Mr Hyde was published as a novella in January 1886 and dedicated to Katherine de Mattos with this verse:
It's ill to loose the bands that God decreed to bind;
Still will we be the children of the heather and the wind.
Far away from home, O it's still for you and me
That the broom is blowing bonnie in the north countrie.
He sent a letter with the book: *Dearest Katherine, Here, on a very little book and accompanied with lame verses, I have put your name. Our kindness is now getting well on in years; it must be very nearly of age; and it gets more valuable to me with every time I see you . . .*

The runaway success of *Strange Case of Dr Jekyll and Mr Hyde* and *Kidnapped*, also published in 1886, and the continuing popularity of *Treasure Island*, brought Louis financial independence. When Thomas Stevenson died in May 1887, he travelled to Edinburgh for the funeral but was too ill to attend it. He wrote the inscription for his father's tomb: *By whose devices the great sea lights in every quarter of the world now shine more brightly*. His inheritance made Louis wealthy and freed him to roam once more. Skerryvore was put up for rent and Louis, Fanny, Sam, Margaret Stevenson and Valentine prepared to sail to New York on the SS Ludgate Hill. Henry James had a case of champagne delivered as a seasick remedy. 'They are a romantic lot, and I delight in them,' he wrote to a friend.

After a spell in New York and New England, his love of the sea drew Louis back to California where he hired the splendid schooner, *Casco,* and its skipper. Fanny Stevenson and Katherine de Mattos fell out dramatically after *Scribner's Magazine* published Fanny's short story 'The Nixie' in March 1888. Henley immediately recognized the story as Katherine's original idea, and, when battle lines were drawn, Louis took Fanny's side. The drama dragged on and their relationship deteriorated not only with Henley and Katherine, but also with Bob Stevenson who felt he and his sister had legitimate claim to Thomas Stevenson's estate.

Valentine Roch was dismissed 'under a cloud' from the Stevensons' service in 1889 and settled in California with a Mr Brown. That year Louis dedicated *The Master of Ballantrae* to Sir Percy and Lady Jane Shelley.

Their search for an earthly paradise led the Stevenson party to Samoa in 1891 where they built a bungalow called Vailima. There, for the first time in his life, Louis' health stabilized. He enjoyed the novelty of physical work. '*Nothing* is so interesting as weeding,' he wrote. Yet, for all its exotic attractions, Samoa was a far cry from paradise. Fanny was often ill with a psychotic illness that turned her into 'a violent friend, a brimstone enemy' as Louis wrote to J. M. Barrie in 1893. Until his death he kept up a correspondence with Henry James.

On 3 December 1894, while he was helping Fanny to prepare a salad dressing at Vailima, Robert Louis Stevenson suffered a brain haemorrhage. He was buried with traditional ceremony on the island.

Lloyd Osbourne (formerly 'Sam') married Katherine Durham, an American, in 1896, and brought her to live at Vailima. Their first son, Alan, was born in 1897. That year Margaret Stevenson died in Edinburgh and Fanny and her family moved to San Francisco where she built an impressive home. Lloyd's second son, born in 1900, was christened Louis. In 1914, Fanny died in San Francisco. She was seventy-four. Adelaide Boodle became a missionary and published *R.L.S. and his Sine Qua Non: Flashlights from Skerryvore* in 1926, under a pen name, 'The Gamekeeper'.

'It's all a strange history,' Henry James wrote of the Stevenson saga, 'and histories never end, but go on living in their consequences.'

Acknowledgements

I wish to acknowledge that I have infused the text with words, phrases, sentences and extracts from the writing of Robert Louis Stevenson and his family and friends; I have italicized in the text direct quotations from Stevenson's writing, and incorporated into it extracts from letters held in the archives of The National Library of Scotland, Yale University, Harvard University, Princeton University and Huntington University. Edited extracts from *R.L.S. and his Sine Qua Non* by Adelaide A. Boodle appear in the text.

I have found the following publications extremely useful while working on this book. These include many works of Robert Louis Stevenson and, in particular, the short stories 'Markheim', 'Olalla', 'The Body Snatcher', 'The Story of a Lie', 'Thrawn Janet' and 'The Suicide Club'; the novels, including *Treasure Island, Kidnapped, Prince Otto* and *Strange Case of Dr Jekyll and Mr Hyde*; essays including 'A Chapter on Dreams' and 'The Art of Writing'; travel writing, including *Travels with a Donkey in the Cévennes* and *The Silverado Squatters*; poetry, including *A Child's Garden of Verses;* biographies, and especially *Robert Louis Stevenson: A Biography* by Claire Harman; *The Letters of Robert Louis Stevenson, Vols. 4, 5 and 6,* edited by Bradford A. Booth and Ernest Mehew; *The Letters of Robert Louis Stevenson, Vol. II, 1880-1887,* edited by Sidney Colvin; *The Strange Case of R.L.Stevenson* by Richard Woodhead; *Henry James: A Life* by Leon Edel; *The Violent Friend* by Margaret Mackay; *John Singer Sargent: A Biography* by C. M. Mount; *John Singer Sargent: Complete Paintings: The Early Portraits, Volume I,* by Richard Ormond and Elaine Kilmurray; 'Memoirs of an

Islet' in *Dreams of Elsewhere*, edited by June Skinner Sawyers; *Robert Louis Stevenson and Henry James* by Sydney Colvin; *Leaves of Grass* by Walt Whitman; *Crime and Punishment* by Fyodor Dostoievsky; *Father and Son* by Edmund Gosse; *What Maisie Knew* and *The Princess Casamassima* by Henry James; *Diana of the Crossways* by George Meredith; *Far from the Madding Crowd* and *Return of the Native* by Thomas Hardy; *The Victorians at Home* by Susan Lasdun; *Scottish Victorian Interiors*, edited by Sheila Mackay; *Victorian Style* by J. and M. Miller; *The Bournemouth Gazette, 1885,* and Sydenham's *Guide to Bournemouth, 1884* and *1887*.

I am grateful to the Erraid Community for giving me such a warm welcome to the island; to Bournemouth Libraries for its assistance during my research trip; to the Scottish Section of Edinburgh Central Library, The National Library of Scotland, Moray Libraries, Creative Scotland, Almond Design and Harvard Art Museums. I have many individuals to thank for their contributions to various aspects of this book and, in particular, I'd like to express my gratitude to Fabien Barouch, Lynn Barton, Ariane Burgess, Julita Burgess, Regi Claire, Diane A. Smith, Doreen Taylor, the late Gavin Wallace, John Wragg, Fay Young and the Stranger Than Fiction writers.

Made in the USA
Charleston, SC
08 October 2013